Para Diana —

Un pecado de juventud. Perdona sus faltas — y recibe la amistad de

Mary Ladel

Cornell   septiembre de 1984

THE HISTORICAL PROSE
OF FERNANDO DE HERRERA

MARY GAYLORD RANDEL

THE HISTORICAL PROSE
OF FERNANDO DE HERRERA

TAMESIS BOOKS LIMITED

LONDON

Colección Támesis
SERIE A - MONOGRAFÍAS, XX

© Copyright by Tamesis Books Limited
London, 1971.
SBN: 900411 16 3

Depósito Legal: M. 29.036-1970

Printed in Spain by Talleres Gráficos de EDICIONES CASTILLA, S. A.
Maestro Alonso, 23 - Madrid

for

TAMESIS BOOKS LIMITED
LONDON

For DON

CONTENTS

Preface	xi
Abbreviations	xii
Introduction	1
PART ONE: *Relacion de la guerra de Cipre y suceso de la batalla de Lepanto*	7
I. «Dedicatoria» and «Prefación»	13
II. Herrera and the Imperial Cause	27
1. Friends and Foe	29
2. Herrera and Philip II	44
III. Divine Providence and the Concept of Heroic Virtue	59
1. The Search for Fame	59
2. God in Human History	80
IV. History and Poetry	93
PART TWO: *Tomas Moro*	113
I. The Exemplary Life	115
II. A Recurring Theme: Virtue Embattled	121
1. The Struggle Against Human Weakness	121
2. Virtue and Government	133
III. The Direction of History	159
IV. Herrera and More as Author	173
V. Conclusions: The Meaning of Herrera's Historical Work.	189
A Selected Bibliography	197

PREFACE

The research for the present study was carried out in the libraries of Harvard, Syracuse, Princeton and Cornell Universities, all of which were most generous in facilitating the use of their collections. I also wish to thank Wellesley College, Middlebury College, the Fulbright Commission in Madrid, Spain, the Woodrow Wilson Foundation and Harvard University for their material support of my studies in Spanish Golden Age literature. The especially generous assistance of the Hull Memorial Fund of Cornell University has made possible the present publication.

This study originated in course work on the sixteenth century done at Harvard during the year 1965-1966, specifically in a seminar report devoted to the sonnets of Fernando de Herrera. To Professor Raimundo Lida, leader of that seminar, I owe the initial stimulus for that first project and his continued, invaluable direction and encouragement. He has tirelessly read and reread this manuscript in all the stages of its progress, and to him go my profoundest thanks for innumerable suggestions which have enriched my thinking about this period. I am grateful as well to Professor Stephen Gilman, who graciously agreed to read the penultimate draft and whose perspective inspired important additions. Professor Francisco Márquez Villanueva, presently of Queens College, although he has not seen this essay, shares in the responsibility for my continuing enthusiasm for sixteenth-century Spanish intellectual history.

No account of my indebtedness would be complete without mention of Mrs. Ray Westerfield, who not only provided me with the classical background I have used constantly, but who first introduced me to the joy of this and all learning; and of my parents, whose devotion to my education has been unceasing, and their satisfaction in its progress, deeply gratifying.

Finally, I wish to thank my husband for his insistent and loving encouragement of all my efforts. His patience in listening to my developing thoughts regularly brought about their clarification.

M. G. R.

*Ithaca,
New York.*

ABBREVIATIONS

B.A.E.	*Biblioteca de Autores Españoles.*
B.R.A.E.	*Boletín de la Real Academia Española.*
C.D.I.	*Colección de Documentos Inéditos para la Historia de España.*
H.G.L.H.	*Historia General de las Literaturas Hispánicas.*
M.L.R.	*Modern Language Review.*
N.B.A.E.	*Nueva Biblioteca de Autores Españoles.*
R.F.E.	*Revista de Filología Española.*

INTRODUCTION

When Lope de Vega, in *Guzmán el Bravo,* one of his *Novelas a Marcia Leonarda,* touches upon the subject of the battle of Lepanto, he says, «para esta ocasión pudiera remitirla al divino Herrera, que lo fue tanto en la prosa como en el verso.»[1] This assertion may appear startling to students of the Spanish Golden Age, whose attention in recent years has focused largely on the verse works of the Sevillian. Oreste Macrí, José Manuel Blecua, and A. David Kossoff have, with editions, monographs, and a vocabulary, shed light on many controversial aspects of Herrera the poet. Yet Lope's remarks urge us to consider other, less familiar facets of Herrera's literary personality.

Herrera himself adds force to this challenge. In his reply to the criticism leveled at his annotations to the works of Garcilaso de la Vega by Prete Jacopín, Herrera reaffirms his conviction that imitation of both ancient and modern writers is an essential tool for one who seeks to write distinguished poetry. However, he hastens to say, he has never expressed the belief that through mere imitation of the writings of antiquity one can earn a place among the finest poets. He continues by declaring emphatically: «quanto mas, que nunca [Herrera] a procurado ese nombre, ni ese lugar, porque saue que ni es poeta, ni puede serlo, i quando llegó a leer en esta censura que lo notávades de imbidioso, se rió de bos i os tuvo por ombre de mal juicio i mal ánimo.»[2] This passage is found in the midst of a discussion about the requisite capacities of the student of literature, as Herrera sees them. Herrera may well have been familiar with the solemn decree on poetry in the *Examen de ingenios para las ciencias* of Juan Huarte de San Juan, which had appeared only a few years earlier:

---

[1] Lope de Vega Carpio, *Obras escogidas,* ed. Federico Carlos Sainz de Robles (Madrid, 1964), II, 1378.
[2] Fernando de Herrera, *Controversia sobre sus Anotaciones á las obras de Garcilaso de la Vega* (Seville, 1870), p. 119.

> Todas las artes (dice Cicerón, *Pro Archia Poeta*) están constituidas debajo de principios universales, los cuales aprendidos con estudio y trabajo, en fin se vienen a alcanzar; pero el arte de poesía es en esto tan particular, que si Dios o naturaleza no hacen al hombre poeta, poco aprovecha enseñarle con preceptos y reglas cómo ha de metrificar.[3]

The student of poetry for Herrera, however, need not be a poet himself. Far more important is that he should be equipped with a vast fund of knowledge in poetry of all kinds, and, as well, in all of those disciplines which shed light on the matter of poetry: history real and legendary, philosophy, geography, art, music, even the sciences. In the passage of Herrera at hand, it is clearly with this type of humanist that Herrera wishes to identify himself. His words «ni es poeta, ni puede serlo» eschew a title which he does not find applicable to himself.

Herrera's biographer, the painter Francisco Pacheco, in the *Libro de verdaderos retratos,* published after Herrera's death, lists works which were known to the late writer's contemporaries. Some are lost verse: translations of Claudian, Fracastoro, a tragic poem, *Amores de Lausino y Corona* (Rioja mentions an epic poem on Amadís). Yet the work referred to as his dearest project and life's undertaking is the «Istoria general del Mundo hasta la Edad del Emperador Carlos Quinto, que particularmente tratava las acciones donde concurrieron las armas Españolas, que escrivieron con injuria o invidia los escritores extrangeros.»[4] By the time Pacheco wrote, this work had already been lost. We know that it was in progress when Herrera published his *Anotaciones,* for Francisco de Medina mentions it in his Preface.[5] In 1590, the completed document was presented to Herrera's friends for their approval. Its loss doubtless descends, along with that of the prepared final editions of the poetry, to the «naufragio» which followed the writer's death in 1597, the source of the present tangle of scholarly problems which surround Herrera's career.

From such references as these do we glean what little we know about what must have been Herrera's most extensive work. This, together with his three published prose works, establishes beyond doubt the persistence and seriousness of his vocation as a prose writer and makes it the more

---

[3] Juan Huarte de San Juan, *Examen de ingenios para las ciencias,* ed. Rodrigo Sanz (Madrid, 1930), II, 195-196.
[4] Francisco Pacheco, *Libro de descripción de verdaderos retratos de illustres y memorables varones* (Seville, 1881-1885).
[5] *Obras de Garci Lasso de la Vega con Anotaciones de Fernando de Herrera* (Seville, 1580), pp. 10-11.

INTRODUCTION

surprising that further critical attention has not been given to this facet of his literary personality. The point, naturally, is not to disclaim the evident fact of Herrera's poetic vocation and what it produced, but to use his prose writings to complete our picture of him, allowing each detail a maximum of meaningfulness in the broadest possible context.

While the loss of the *Istoria general,* like that of Herrera's own final edition of his poetry, leaves us with great limitations, still the extant prose works provide at least a secure chronological framework, as well as a kind of variety in subject matter which would not be the case had the *Anotaciones,* for example, been lost and the *Istoria general* survived. As it is, we can see the scope and development of Herrera's prose style and of his ideas in four works: the *Relacion de la guerra de Cipre y suceso de la batalla naval de Lepanto,* published early in 1572, among the first accounts to appear of the successful venture of the Holy League against the Turks; the *Obras de Garci Lasso de la Vega con Anotaciones de Fernando de Herrera,* published in 1580; the *Respuesta al muy Reverendo Padre Prete Jacopín, secretario de las musas,* unpublished until the nineteenth century and unsigned, but long attributed to Herrera and certainly composed in the period immediately following the publication of the annotations; and finally the *Tomas Moro,* published in 1592. There is some discussion over the date of composition of the *Anotaciones,* which had been begun or at least projected by 1571, since Juan de Mal Lara, who died in that year, knew of Herrera's plans to explicate Garcilaso's poetry. Herrera himself was eager that the early commencement of this enterprise be recognized, since El Brocense's *Anotaciones y enmiendas,* published in 1577 and possibly in a still earlier 1574 edition, had preceded his own commentary into print, resulting in numerous accusations of envious rivalry on Herrera's part. What remains certain is that Herrera completed his edition at some time during these nine years, and probably almost entirely at a time after the composition of the *Relacion.*

The publication by Antonio Gallego Morell in 1966 of most of the text of Herrera's *Anotaciones* (regrettably without the Preface of Francisco de Medina and Herrera's life of Garcilaso) makes available the last of the author's extant prose works in a modern edition.[6] We have long possessed accessible editions of the *Relacion de la guerra de Cipre*[7] and

---

[6] Antonio Gallego Morell, ed., *Garcilaso de la Vega y sus comentaristas* (Granada, 1966).
[7] Fernando de Herrera, *Relacion de la guerra de Cipre y suceso de la batalla naval de Lepanto,* in C.D.I., XXI (1852), 244-375.

the reply to Prete Jacopín.[8] Recently the *Tomas Moro* has been given wider circulation (unfortunately still limited in the United States) through Francisco López Estrada's admirable «Edición y estudio».[9] Oreste Macrí's *Fernando de Herrera* expends considerable attention on the poetic theories scattered throughout the *Anotaciones*.[10] Yet López Estrada's essay is alone in recent years in devoting itself to a careful study of Herrera's historical prose. And no one, since Adolphe Coster's *Fernando de Herrera* (1908),[11] has attempted to draw together Herrera's prose and verse — his historical, theoretical, and poetical vision — nor even to seek a continuity within his prose production.

This is made all the more regrettable by the presence of a genuine chronological base for the study of Herrera's prose, particularly valuable in contrast to the maze of hypothetical chronologies and questionable texts in which we must try to make our way as students of the verse. It provides us with some means of tracing the evolution of the writer, in terms both of thought and style, over a period of twenty years of his maturity.

The present study of Herrera's historical writings in the three principal extant prose works — the *Relacion de la guerra de Cipre*, the *Anotaciones*, and the *Tomas Moro* — is offered as a step forward in our understanding of the author's complete personality. I have searched, in the pages that follow, to uncover the underlying unity of Herrera's thought, often obscured in the past by the apparent diversity of the vehicles which the writer has chosen. It is my firm conviction that a common heroic vision unites all of Herrera's work, whether his immediate concern be love or military exploits, the defense of the Spanish language or saintly martyrdom.

At the same time I have tried to formulate some judgments about Herrera's evolution as a writer, although I am still reluctant to make sweeping statements which would be drastically altered by the discovery of the lost *Istoria general*. It is particularly hazardous to attempt drawing any conclusions about stylistic evolution in the prose, when the subjects of the works in question have special requirements which need not depend on the writer's development. Nonetheless, Herrera's evolution may be said to have affected the very choice of subjects in some sense.

---

[8] Herrera, *Controversia*; cf. note 2 above.
[9] Francisco López Estrada, «Edición y estudio del *Tomas Moro* de Fernando de Herrera», *Archivo Hispalense*, XII (1950), 9-56.
[10] Oreste Macrí, *Fernando de Herrera* (Madrid, 1959).
[11] Adolphe Coster, *Fernando de Herrera (el Divino)* (Paris, 1908).

INTRODUCTION

Given Herrera's conscious separation of prose and poetic styles, and indeed the divergencies between these two forms of expression in Herrera's works on Lepanto,[12] we need not look for the last prose work *(Tomas Moro)* to resemble closely the posthumous edition of Herrera's verse. Rather, we must look for subtle shifts in emphasis and concern within a highly unified body of writing. My hope has been to establish the groundwork with which to take a new look at Herrera's evolution as a poet in the near future.

---

[12] Cf. Part I, Chapter IV below.

PART ONE

*Relacion de la guerra de Cipre y suceso
de la batalla naval de Lepanto*

The *Relacion* appears in Seville in 1572, published by one Alonso Picardo, and dedicated to the Duke of Medina Sidonia and Count of Niebla, Don Alonso Pérez de Guzmán el Bueno. Only a brief time had elapsed between the events of October 7, 1571, in the Gulf of Lepanto and the composition of Herrera's historical narrative. Before Herrera's account, as far as we have been able to discover, only briefer pamphlets on the subject circulated in Spain.[1] In his book *La Liga de Lepanto,* Father Serrano mentions two of these: one printed in Rome in 1571, «Relación de la iornada sucedida a los siete del mes de Octubre mil quinientos setenta y vno»,[2] composed by «el maestre de campo don Lope de Figueroa» for Don Juan de Zúñiga, the Spanish ambassador at the papal court; the other issued in Medina del Campo, also in 1571, entitled «Copia y traslado de vna carta venida a la corte de su Magestad a los veynte y tres de Noviembre, en que se cuenta muy en particular la victoria avida de los turcos en la batalla naual, con el repartimiento que se hizo de los baxeles y artilleria, de la armada vencida y otras cosas muy notables».[3] Still a third was reprinted by Fernández Navarrete in *Colección de documentos inéditos para la historia de España.*[4] This last exists in two versions, one longer and one shorter. The shorter was found by Navarrete as a *suelto* in the Biblioteca Nacional at Madrid in 1791, and is a letter written to the Escorial in haste following the battle (the narrative covers the period September 30 to October 10). It omits the tallies of dead and wounded, and the list of booty captured. The longer version, discovered at the Escorial in a codex entitled «Memorias

---

[1] Luciano Serrano, *La Liga de Lepanto* (Madrid, 1918-1919), I, 5-8.
[2] Printed by «Herederos de Antonio Blado, impresores camerales».
[3] Real Academia de la Historia, Madrid.
[4] III, 239. The MS is from the Escorial; the author, one Vicente de Millis.

de Fray Juan de San Jerónimo», includes most of the information from the shorter copy word for word, along with an account of its reception by Philip II, and other more precise information which reached the Escorial subsequently. Both accounts give in substance the same picture of the battle itself as does Herrera's *Relacion,* but in considerably more succinct fashion. Since at least two copies existed, it is possible that there were others as well, and that one such might have found its way to Seville. The minor points of disagreement (for example, Herrera states that the Turkish armada approached the battle in its customary half-moon formation, whereas both copies of the letter to the Escorial report that the Turks did not proceed in their usual order [5]) between the accounts of the letter and Herrera, do not comprise any real obstacle to this possibility, since Herrera speaks in his prologue of having consulted many conflicting sources, and of having had to sort out those which seemed to him most reasonable.

Navarrete does mention, but unfortunately does not reproduce, another account which he unearthed in the Biblioteca de San Isidro el Real of Seville in 1792,[6] and copied personally. It is entitled «Relacion de lo sucedido en la armada de la Santa Liga desde los 30 del mes de septiembre hasta los 24 de octubre de este año (1571) enviada á esta ciudad al muy Ilustre Señor Licenciado Pero López de Mesa, Asistente de Sevilla», and came to be printed doubtless in Seville in 1571.[7] Navarrete claims that it is substantially and almost literally the same as the two he does reproduce. The title indicates that its scope coincides with that of the longer version of the letter to the Escorial, that including the statistics which emerged in the aftermath of the battle. This is the only mention I have encountered of an

---

[5] Fernando de Herrera, *Relacion de la guerra de Cipre y suceso de la batalla naval de Lepanto,* in C.D.I., XXI (1852), 355. The C.D.I. edition is widely available and essentially accurate. For the sake of convenience, all quotations from the *Relacion* will refer the reader to it rather than to the 1572 original. Since some changes in spelling do occur in the later version, however, students of this aspect of Herrera's style should consult the original as well.

[6] «Códice de Misceláneas sin rótulo, número 23».

[7] «Así mismo va aquí la relacion de los turcos muertos y presos, y el número de bajeles que se tomaron al Turco, y artillería, y la particion que de todo esto se hizo conforme á los capítulos de la Liga, y los cristianos que se rescataron, y la gente que de los nuestros faltó, y unas preguntas que declaró Mahomet de Constantinopla, ayo de los hijos de Alí Bajá capitan general de la armada del Turco; el cual Mahomet y los dos hijos de Alí Bajá yerno del turco pasado, fueron presos: con otras particularidades de que se ha tenido relacion.» *C.D.I.,* III, 269.

account published in Seville in 1571, and thus prior to Herrera's history. If Herrera had seen it, as it seems certain he would have, it was only one of his sources, for its statistics differ somewhat and it does not, furthermore, go into the question of the negotiations leading up to the formation of the Holy League, which occupies a large portion of Herrera's work.

Herrera would probably not have seen a work published in 1572 in Barcelona entitled *Primera parte de la Chronica del muy alto y poderoso Principe don Juan de Austria, hijo del Emperador Carlo Quinto. De las jornadas contra el Gran Turco Selimo II. Conmençada en la pérdida del Reyno del Cipro, tratando primero la genealogia de la casa ottomana. Compilada por Hieronimo de Costiol*; nor Ambrosio de Morales' Latin account, now in the library of the Escorial; nor accounts published at around the same time in Italy. Most of the documents which have now been made available to scholars of this episode would not have been accessible to a lower clergyman in a provincial capital. Thus we must accept Herrera's statement to the effect that he compared the word of eyewitnesses with other written accounts which have since disappeared and sorted out the story he finally submitted for publication from an overwhelming mass of conflicting details and figures, and reports of varying credibility. One sentence from the first chapter of the work —«La memoria del cual suceso singularmente dino de ser celebrado en todas las edades, me pareció escrebir con las pocas fuerzas de mi ingenio, ya que ninguno ocupaba este lugar»[8]— leads us to conclude that Herrera did not consider any of the available sources as serious history.

---

[8] Herrera, *Relacion*, p. 262.

CHAPTER ONE

«DEDICATORIA» AND «PREFACION»

Herrera's Dedication to the Duke of Medina Sidonia expresses at once modesty and confidence. The author excuses the audacity («osadía») which he displays in taking for his little book the protection of so illustrious a personage, and in applying his poor wits («lo poco que vale mi ingenio») and artless style («la humildad de mi estilo») to so noble a feat as the victory of Lepanto. He terms the short history «esta pequeña muestra de mi estudio», which has been buried in darkness before its appearance under the Duke's protection. The phrase suggests the humanist's boundless curiosity for all kinds of learning, and the zeal with which he has sought to discover the truth relating to the events which presently concern him.

In the following lines, Herrera discusses the elusive nature of historical truth and the methodology which the chaotic state of information has imposed on him:

> Sola una cosa espero que tendrá valor y será agradecida del tiempo, que he gastado en escrebir esta breve memoria de cosas sucedidas, y es la pureza y modestia (si es lícito decillo así) con que he tratado esta jornada, porque de todas las relaciones que hube de hombres graves y recatados, que se hallaron en aquella batalla naval, seguí con grandísimo cuidado y diligencia lo que me pareció mas razonable, y que mas conformaba con la afirmación de otros, y así procuré templar las pasiones de los que las escribieron por no incurrir en el vicio de muchos ilustres escritores de nuestro tiempo, porque yo me aparté de toda afecion, no queriendo que mi opinion estuviese dudosa en el crédito de los hombres. Y no niego que algunos informados diferentemente sentirán otra cosa; pero yo sé prometer que ninguno tuvo mas copia de relaciones y ninguno inquirió la averiguacion de la verdad con

mas deseo, confiriendo unas cosas con otras y aprobándolas con el parecer de muchos, que intervinieron en aquel hecho, y si esta prevencion no vale con ellos, consideren cuan incierta es la voz de la verdad traida de partes tan remotas y de lenguas tan varias, y que todo no puede estar tan ajustado que venga medido á su gusto y conforme á la pasion de sus ánimos.[1]

This passage lays down the fundamental notions of its author about the nature of history. History must consist, first and foremost, of the truth: it is the mission of the historian to seek to establish what is the truth with uncompromising zeal. Yet, as things are constituted, truth is not always immediately visible. Each man, even though he may have enjoyed the advantages of being an eyewitness to the facts, finds between himself and the truth a soul clouded and perhaps blinded by its passions. Much more serious, then, is the problem which arises when these already suspicious first-hand reports travel long distances, are muddled in translations, suffer time's distortions. The historian faces the delicate task of weighing against each other myriad opinions, seeking that which is most «reasonable». The writer of history must attempt, in so far as is possible, to keep himself from «affection», which seems here to mean prejudice, or any artificial way of using information which does not adjust itself to the demands of truth. Herrera blames some of the «illustrious» writers of his time, who allow their passions to intervene in their interpretations of history. He cautions the reader that truth is not so easily found and does not come tailored to our wishes. Thus, Herrera's passing allusion to his «estudios» takes on further significance: the historian must possess a great store of knowledge, for only from this multiplicity of viewpoints will it be possible to filter out passions and arrive at pure truth. Herrera asserts the value of this method, though he readily admits that, depending on man as it does, it is fallible.

Cristóbal Mosquera de Figueroa (1547-1610) belongs to the circle of humanists which surrounded Herrera in Seville. He must have been an ardent follower to judge from his poetry, which is steeped in Herrerian diction and reflects ideas about poetical syntax which Herrera professed. Something of a chameleon figure, he also composed in the styles of Garcilaso and Fray Luis

---

[1] Fernando de Herrera, *Relacion de la guerra de Cipre y suceso de la batalla naval de Lepanto,* in C.D.I., XXI (1852), 248.

de León. The thoughts put forth in his «Prefacion» to this work (published when he was scarcely twenty-five years of age) probably reflect ideas which he had discussed among members of the circle. We know from Herrera's own writings that these were questions of the liveliest interest to him.

Significantly, the first line of the Preface contains a reference to Aristotle's *Rhetoric,* also dealing with the role of history. Mosquera has gone one step beyond Herrera. While the Dedication exalts the quest of truth for its own sake, the Preface stresses the didactic mission and social value of history. For the student of human nature (Aristotle is thinking of the ruler of a republic), history shows clearly «las costumbres de los hombres y la naturaleza al vivo representada».[2] History, then, brings us as close as possible to reality, one step closer than *mimesis,* that artful reconstruction of life according to the principle of verisimilitude. This places us in the context of the prevalent sixteenth-century concern, stemming from a new familiarity with Aristotelian thought, that literature be «like life» — either by being historical truth, or through imitation, presenting as perfect as possible an «image» or «representation» of reality.

Mosquera here refers to history as «las costumbres de los hombres y la naturaleza al vivo representada». This representation is true, it is actual life enacted before us. Yet to read history is to do more than participate in the everyday business of living, as the following lines suggest. For in history,

> se vee la comun inclinacion de los hombres, y se descubren las costumbres de las naciones bárbaras, y se enseña y purifica el órden y concierto de la vida: qué cosas son pertenecientes para los viejos, para los mancebos, para los nobles, para los viles, para los vencedores, para los vencidos. Fuera desto si se advierte en las diversas formas y estados de repúblicas con qué cosas se suelen aumentar y engrandecer las ciudades, con qué cosas se destruyen y disipan, qué cosas suelen decir bien, qué cosas suelen suceder mal... sola la historia es la que podrá enseñarlo, volviendo al hombre discreto y astuto para poder mostrarse y señalarse en el teatro de la vida humana.[3]

This passage is reminiscent of much advice expended in literary theories on how to imitate life. At any rate the preliminary

---

[2] *Ibid.,* p. 251.
[3] *Ibid.,* pp. 251-252.

problem of coming to understand human life is one and the same. Mosquera's words suggest that real history involves somehow more than simply recording or observing actions and events. What is far more important is what we would call the pattern which emerges from among a large body of events and actions — history's inherently repetitive character. Historical truth, then, constitutes not so much that which any one person has in fact done at a particular point in time, but what has emerged as most seemly for any member of a society on the basis of what similar persons have already done. In his remarks on the proper content of history in *De Oratore*, Cicero lays the principal stress on the historian's duty to analyze the events which he records, to expose the motivations of the actors in an historical drama rather than merely treating of the event itself.[4] Thus history becomes the prime teacher of human conduct, and the ally of morality. In *Orator*, Cicero links the study of history with the attainment of intellectual maturity: «Nescire autem quid ante quam natus sis acciderit, id est semper esse puerum. Quid enim est aetas hominis, nisi ea memoria rerum veterum cum superiorum aetate contexitur?»[5]

History accompanies moral philosophy in the new scholarly curriculum of the Renaissance.[6] We find frequent references in humanistic works to the moral guidance furnished by history.[7] Machiavelli in *Il Principe* declares:

> debbe il principe leggere le istorie, e in quelle considerare le azioni degli uomini eccellenti; vedere come si sono governati nelle guerre; esaminare le cagioni delle vittorie e perdite loro, per potere queste fuggire, e quelle imitare; e, sopra tutto, fare come ha fatto per lo adrieto qualche uomo eccellente che ha preso ad imitare se alcuno innanzi a lui è stato laudato e gloriato, e di quello ha tenuto sempre e' gesti ed azioni appresso di sè: come si dice

---

[4] Cicero, *De Oratore* (New York, 1847), p. 137 (Book II, xv).

[5] Cicero, *Orator*, in *Brutus. Orator*, ed. H. M. Hubbell (Cambridge, Massachusetts, 1930), pp. 394-395.

[6] Myron P. Gilmore, *Humanists and Jurists* (Cambridge, Massachusetts, 1963), pp. 21 ff.

[7] Felix Gilbert, *Machiavelli and Guicciardini: Politics and History in Sixteenth-Century Florence* (Princeton, 1965), p. 216. Among many other examples of Renaissance insistence on the value of history «the master of life» is Jean Bodin's «Preamble on the ease, delight and advantage of historical reading», *Method for the Easy Comprehension of History*, trans. Beatrice Reynolds (New York, 1945), pp. 9-15.

che Alessandro Magno imitava Achille; Cesare, Alessandro; Scipione, Ciro.[8]

And in the *Discorsi sopra la Prima Deca di Tito Livio,* Machiavelli seeks a systematic interpretation of Roman history which will have a practical utility for his own era.[9] Erasmus in the *Institvtio principis Christiani* is among the few who doubt the utility of historical studies for a prince, who might be misled by the example of tyrants. In its place Erasmus recommends philosophical studies from the ancients and from Scripture.[10] But in any case, these studies, like those of history for Cicero and his Renaissance disciples, belong to the same search for imitable models of conduct.

These remarks lead us back to Herrera's words in the Dedication. Historical truth for both writers seems to imply a middle ground. For Mosquera, it is the «común inclinacion» of men, that which is «perteneciente». Herrera says much the same thing when he warns that «todo no puede estar tan ajustado que venga medido á su gusto y conforme á la pasion de sus ánimos». He seems to imply throughout that not only is it impossible that everything accord with an individual's inclinations, but that it is necessarily in the nature of historical truth not to coincide with any passions, since they inevitably breed distortions. For this reason Herrera flees «toda afecion», and considers that the lasting value of his work is embodied in its «pureza y modestia».

Herrera emphasizes the elusive nature of truth, and the chaos which confronts him who seeks it. But he does suggest that this search and the struggle against one's passions will be rewarded ultimately. Mosquera particularly reflects the conviction that history reveals a fundamental order and harmony in life («el orden y concierto de la vida»), to which one may then seek to conform himself. The notion that «all the world's a stage» («el teatro de la vida»), much repeated throughout the Middle Ages and in the Renaissance, comes to have its significance reinforced and amplified in the context of these ideas about

---

[8] Niccolò Machiavelli, *Il Principe,* in *Tutte le opere storiche e letterarie,* ed. Guido Mazzoni and Mario Casella (Florence, 1929), p. 30.
[9] Gilmore, p. 27.
[10] Erasmus, *Institvtio principis Christiani saluberrimis referta praeceptis* (Basel, 1518).

truth and order. The theater of life embodies universal principles: that is, it is arranged harmoniously, we might say like a work of art, in which each part has its proper place and function. Thus by studying the nature of his part, a man can contribute to the harmonious order of the whole by acquitting himself more perfectly, more artistically, in his role.

Having gone to considerable lengths to explain the special usefulness of history, Mosquera declares that this is not necessary:

> Bien entiendo que no será necesario captar benevolencia al lector ántes que lea este libro, como los oradores tienen de costumbre, porque demás de que en ellos es importante esta parte, los que escriben historia no tienen necesidad de favorecerse con este remedio, sino que el lector preste atencion y disposicion en sí para ser enseñado.[11]

The confidence that learning is of itself a source of pleasure has far-reaching importance for the literature of the sixteenth and seventeenth centuries. It is used here as the *raison d'être* of historical writing, but it similarly constitutes the underpinnings of justification for didactic literature of all kinds. And, of special importance in Herrera's case, as we shall have occasion to observe, it is one of the ideas used in support of a poetry whose understanding requires an intellectual effort, which it is claimed yields up satisfaction and delight to the reader. The enjoyment derives, for the dispassionate reader of history, Mosquera tells us, from the «virtud y abundancia de vario mantenimiento» which he will find therein, namely.

> cierta y verdadera relacion de cosas pasadas y acontecidas con loor y con vituperio, donde se proponen ante los ojos los estados de las cosas, los consejos en los negocios arduos, la administracion, los fines, los hechos de señalados varones con verdadera descripcion de geografía, crónica y genealogía, que son las partes de mayor calidad en la historia.[12]

Herrera's humanistic background again comes to mind. Part of the delight of history appears to spring from its affinity to the miscellanies of the time: history is interesting because it is

---

[11] Herrera, *Relacion*, p. 254.
[12] *Ibid.*, p. 255.

crammed full of useful information. Information, we remember, is the mainstay of Herrera's ideal literary scholar, just as it has made interesting the poetry itself.[13]

According to Mosquera, the virtuous man will of his own accord be moved by history, which he sums up as «una viva pintura con que nuestros ánimos se incitan y se mueven con los señalados ejemplos á las grandes empresas y hazañas dignas de inmortal memoria».[14] History is capable of moving or inspiring us because of something inherent in man, for

> los ánimos en ningun lugar pueden estar reposados mientras tuvieren el suelo por morada, ántes encendidos en llamas de deseo aspirarán á cosas mas altas, procurando mejorarse, todos aquellos que quisieren engrandecerse y fueren inclinados á gloria y fama.[15]

Mosquera's view of the desire for fame recalls Sallust's description of the thirst for glory as an almost biological self-preservation instinct common to good and evil alike.[16]

History's effectiveness appears only as a function of this thirst for fame in which all men partake. In the pages to follow, Herrera portrays his heroes as bound up by the demands of their immortal honor to make their conduct exemplary. Mosquera does feel obliged to qualify slightly this optimistic view of human nature, by allowing for the possibility of a few «mal inclinados». For these, he asserts, history, without adopting the persuasive arts of oratory, «tendrá poder... para que espantados con el miedo de la perpetua infamia se aparten y huyan de los vicios».[17] The suspicion that such people may actually exist intrudes only as a fleeting shadow of doubt, however, for in the final lines of the Preface, Mosquera returns to the subject of man's positive

---

[13] One finds the presence of information as a justification for types of literature in the most varied of situations. The best known perhaps is the passage in *Don Quijote* where Cervantes has the Canon discourse at length on the advantages which extend to the writer of the epic in prose, the novel, the principal advantage being that the poet is at liberty to display his mastery over any one or all of an endless variety of subjects. See also Jean Bodin's confidence in the «delight» which the information drawn from history affords. *Method*, pp. 9-15.
[14] Herrera, *Relacion*, p. 255.
[15] *Ibid.*, p. 252.
[16] María Rosa Lida de Malkiel, *La idea de la fama* (Mexico, 1952), pp. 33-35.
[17] Herrera, *Relacion*, p. 255; cf. Jean Bodin, p. 9.

desire for immortality, which is rooted deep in the very fibre of his being:

> considerando que ninguna cosa hay que así sea estimada de todos como el ardiente deseo de la fama y el loor, tanto que... ninguno hay dotado de tanta humanidad, ni tan aspero y inhumano, tan señalado en honra, ni tan escuro y desconocido, tan adornado de virtud, ni tan abatido con vicios, que no desée con infinita codicia llegar á la alteza de la gloriosa fama, y de tal suerte lo traen todos estampado en el alma, que ni con fuerza de razon, ni con ley, miedo ni costumbre, seria posible privarles deste deseo, el cual tienen por derecho de herencia adquirido de nuestra madre naturaleza. [18]

Here, the search for immortality appears as a common denominator uniting men of many different moral make-ups. The words «infinita codicia» seem to teeter between the connotation of lofty aspiration and that of greed. Mosquera has evidently arrived at a more complex vision. All men do not share the pure enthusiasm «encendidos en llamas de deseo». But all, for whatever reason, because they are human, and because there is always room for men to improve themselves, seek to place themselves nearer to an ideal of heroic achievement, for which they will gain the favor of posterity. This applies not only to the military hero, but to the writer as well, since

> los que escriben historias navegan á vista de los que están por venir, considerando que los presentes son ramos y flores que no se debe confiar en ellos tanto en cuanto es razon que se estime el juicio que con perpetuidad le dará el tiempo con la antigüedad. [19]

As for those figures of classical antiquity whom we now venerate, enduring fame for men of Herrera's day will be due not to the judgment of one's contemporaries as much as to the verdict of time.

History, then, is a literature which will of itself seize the imagination of men, and incite them to action. The historian's role is to seek the truth by revealing in events the orderly pattern of human life. But the historian's fairness must not be interpreted as prohibition or reluctance to pass judgment on the

---

[18] Herrera, *Relacion*, p. 257.
[19] *Ibid.*, pp. 257-258.

deeds he is recording. His may only be the opinion of one man, of less weight ultimately than the judgment of posterity; yet history is a «cierta y verdadera relacion de cosas pasadas y acontecidas *con loor y con vituperio*».[20] One of the responsibilities of the historian is to make clear who has done nobly and who has failed to measure up. The complete picture, its resplendent heroism with shadowy patches of pettiness and vice, will without rhetorical suasion speak to the twin impulses to seek fame and to shun infamy with which every man is endowed. It is important to take into account the positions of the Preface's author on the questions of human aspiration to virtue and intervention by the historian before undertaking an examination of Herrera's *Relacion*.

Mosquera de Figueroa touches on other questions of the theory of historiography. For one of these, the virtue of brevity, he summons classical figures such as Herodotus, Sallust, Tacitus and Thucydides to lend support with their authority. Mosquera's remarks are intended as a justification for the publication of so brief an account by a highly serious author. The question of brevity, however, is offered in the context of a theoretical consideration of the differences between poetry and prose:

> porque si su intento fuera dilatarse y hacer largos discursos podia el autor hacerlo en verso heróico, tan grave y numeroso que viniera á igualar su estilo con la grandeza del sugeto; pero él quiso tomar esta empresa y escribilla en oracion desatada, por huir de las ficciones de la poesía, porque como el fin della sea delectacion, el fin de la historia es la pura verdad. Y para el ornato del verso por fuerza habia de haber partes que con sus fabulosas digresiones quitarian á la verdad aquellas fuerzas, que en la historia son tan necesarias y le dan tanta calidad.[21]

He mentions two genres which are equipped to handle heroic material: heroic verse and history, in both of which Herrera worked. The «Cancion en alabanza de la Divina Magestad por la vitoria del señor Don Juan», a Biblical Pindaric hymn, appears appended to the *Relacion de la guerra de Cipre,* affording a contrast in styles of which (Mosquera's Preface assures us) Herrera

---

[20] *Ibid.,* p. 259. Italics mine.
[21] *Ibid.,* pp. 255-256.

was abundantly conscious. He never produced a narrative epic in the tradition of Vergil's *Aeneid* and its multitudinous imitators. We shall take up the poet's preference for the hymnic style in Chapter IV. Mosquera's comments give us a valuable hint as to the reason for this prejudice.

Is the qualitative distinction made here between historical prose and poetry an assertion of the greater value of prose? The expression «huir de las ficciones de la poesía» might seem to suggest this possibility. Certainly, the connotation of «untrue» is tied to the word «ficcion».[22] Grahame Castor has painted an illuminating picture of changing medieval and Renaissance attitudes to all fictitious literature, and of the defense of poetry.[23] Castor quotes C. S. Lewis, who suggests that «The defence of poetry... is a defence not of poetry as against prose but of fiction as against fact.... What is in question is not man's right to sing but his right to feign, to make things up.»[24]

In the latter part of the sixteenth century, imaginative literature which was comprised of «ficciones» or «fábulas» came under fire in Spain and elsewhere. One has only to think of the case of the romances of chivalry, which, although they depicted an essentially praiseworthy ideal of heroic virtue, were still rigorously denounced for their fantastic content by learned men: among them Luis Vives, Malón de Chaide and Cervantes. Poetry itself, if not as frequently as had been the case at the end of the previous century, at least periodically was placed on trial.[25] And the ultimate defense of poetry (and fiction) was to depend on repudiating its unreality. With the help of Aristotle poetry was linked to truth:

> In Aristotle was to be found a full-scale metaphysical justification of poetry as an «imitation of reality» which portrayed not the actual but the possible, not *le vrai* but *le vraisemblable*. We

---

[22] Plato appears to bear some of the responsibility for the bad reputation of poetry. In the *Phaedo*, Socrates explains why it is that he put Aesop's fables into verse while in prison. Having been commended in a dream to compose something, he decided to write verses to a god. But, he says, «After the god, I considered that a poet must compose fiction if he was to be a poet, not true tales, and I was no fiction-monger, and therefore I took the fictions that I found to hand and knew, namely Aesop's.» *Great Dialogues of Plato* (New York, 1956), p. 464.
[23] Grahame Castor, *Pléiade Poetics* (Cambridge, England, 1964), pp. 10-11 and 114 ff.
[24] *Ibid.*, p. 10.
[25] Cf. Castor.

> may question whether Aristotle's doctrine of imitation was fully understood by sixteenth-century theorists, but its great merit from their point of view was that it treated the arts as a unique kind of human activity, which was not to be judged in the light of criteria borrowed from other kinds of human activity. Thus poets could now hope to establish for themselves some independent position, which did not condemn them to the alternative of being historians on the one hand, or liars on the other. [26]

Finally, and perhaps ironically, Plato's own notion of the *furor poetae* came to the rescue, giving the poet the stature of a prophet, an interpreter of ideal beauty beyond the ken of mere mortals. [27] Herrera praises poetry in the *Anotaciones* using both of these concepts.

While it is not altogether apparent from this passage whether Mosquera is placing poetry in a morally inferior position with respect to history, he has evidently come a long way towards granting respectability to poetry. Poetry is no longer forced into a didactic role in order to be recognized. Of Horace's formula for poetry —*dulce et utile*— only the *dulce* remains a necessity for their verse. Its aim is not truth, but rather enjoyment, which is achieved by embellishing the verse with «fabulosas digresiones». But poetry turns out to have at least one actual advantage over prose in heroic matters, that dignity of style particularly suitable for such lofty subjects. Prose history retains intact its claim on truth, but poetry is not stripped of all respectability in the process. The relevance of these passages to Herrera's own thinking should become clear in subsequent chapters.

Another of many questions raised in this Preface and interesting for its bearing on Herrera's literary personality is that of the primacy of military virtue and the military vocation. Mosquera dwells at some length on this point, showing how civilizations throughout history have bestowed their highest honors for military distinctions, thus making bravery and the arts of war the shortest road to immortal fame. The Christian, and especially the Spanish, victory at Lepanto provides an example of the way in which men will outdo themselves when immortal glory is their promised reward.

---

[26] *Ibid.*, p. 11.
[27] Marcelino Menéndez y Pelayo, *Historia de las ideas estéticas* (Madrid, 1946-1947), II, 7 ff.

We must take these words into consideration when attempting to evaluate Herrera's own statements about vocation. There are several poems, some written to friends of Herrera who participated in military campaigns like Lepanto, which contrast the military vocation with that of the artist, an enamored poet at that. The lover, unable to free himself from the demands of servitude to a woman, thinks of military prowess and bemoans his weakness, but nevertheless still does not clearly find the soldier's lot a happier one.[28] Herrera never, as far as I have been able to discern, professes to a military calling. More of his poems dwell on the conflict between heroic and erotic subjects in his writing. His calling is essentially a literary one. With the Pindaric notion of the poet as immortalizer of heroic deeds, Herrera combines the Propertian idea of the poet who perpetuates the memory of his beloved in verse.[29] We are definitely not in the presence, as with a Cervantes, of a man who has discovered the world unfit for heroism. This situation is more nearly exactly opposite: any circumstance demands heroism. Herrera would make a heroism also out of literary creation and out of love.[30] One of the laudatory poems which precede this work, two octaves by D. Félix de Avellaneda, suggests this:

> A vos, Fernando, debe nuestra España
> este nombre inmortal de su vitoria,
> pues no ha sido menor que su hazaña,
> la vida que le dais con la memoria.[31]

Mosquera announces, too, the patriotic quality of Herrera's history. The Spanish forces have achieved this, the most glorious of all naval victories to date, «dando claridad á la patria donde se criaron, pero con justos inmortales títulos glorificaron el nombre español».[32] Herrera will likewise immortalize his country for posterity with his historical narrative. A warning against rhetorical flattery, however, is issued: «Los historiadores guardan el órden de lo sucedido y usan de materia preparada, y los

---

[28] Cf. sonnets VII and XVIII in José Manuel Blecua, *Rimas inéditas* (Madrid, 1948), two among numerous examples.
[29] María Rosa Lida de Malkiel, *La idea de la fama*.
[30] Oreste Macrí, *Fernando de Herrera* (Madrid, 1959).
[31] Herrera, *Relacion*, p. 260.
[32] *Ibid.*, p. 254.

oradores sobre falsos fundamentos y con razones aparentes aunque galanas y hermosas, muchas cosas fingen y tuercen á su gusto.»[33] The connection between poet and orator —both feigners and distorters of a sort— is hinted at, a common one in the sixteenth century.

Mosquera's comments repeatedly echo Lucian's *The Way to Write History*. Lucian's own instructions for the historian warn him of the perils inherent in avoiding a balanced report of the truth: «History with fancy is like poetry without wings.»[34] Poetic phraseology, excessive description, the «rhetorician's arsenal»[35] — all these are grouped together as comprising similar temptations. Mosquera underlines his desire to separate orator and historian with an anecdote about Alexander the Great and Aristobulus borrowed intact from Lucian:[36] the work of an historian who falsifies events, even in his ruler's favor, deserves to be tossed away, and its writer with it. The historian may heap praise upon his heroes and reproaches on his villains, but only where justly deserved. Herrera's work is offered as a model in this respect: «procede [Herrera] con tanta verdad y moderacion, que antes se podrá decir que disimula muchas cosas, que no que es demasiado en escribirlas particularmente».[37] Herrera has written a chronicle of Spanish deeds, with praise and censure but also with truth and moderation. Thus Mosquera concludes:

> Y seria justa razon que no perdiese el hilo de pasar con esta empresa mas adelante, celebrando la honra y valor de España, que con tanta magnificencia de estilo comenzo en el principio de su florida edad, celebrando ahora juntamente el valor destos animosos españoles, cuyas imágines son adoradas y temidas en toda Asia, Africa y parte de Europa y América, donde se hará mencion de tantas coronas murales, cívicas, triunfales y navales, colocándolas en el cielo, pues su dignidad y grandeza no puede tener morada en la estrecheza de la tierra.[38]

Does this sentence give us grounds to connect the *Relacion* with the lost *Istoria general*? Certainly the description Pacheco gives

---

[33] *Ibid.*, p. 256.
[34] Lucian of Samosata, *The Way to Write History*, in *The Works of Lucian*, trans. H. W. and F. G. Fowler (Oxford, 1905), II, 113.
[35] *Ibid.*, II, 130.
[36] *Ibid.*, II, 115.
[37] Herrera, *Relacion*, pp. 256-257.
[38] *Ibid.*, p. 257.

has much similarity to this one. But Pacheco does say that the *Istoria* reaches just up to the age of Charles V. This may or may not be accurate, since there could have arisen a certain amount of confusion over the contents of the work by the time Pacheco put together his book of portraits.[39] Do Mosquera's words suggest that Herrera had embarked on his larger project at an earlier age («su florida edad»), or that he was at that time in the very beginning stages? Would he then have written the latest episode first? Had the *Relación* had any connection with something on a related subject which he had plans to publish, Herrera himself would likely have sought an occasion to create interest in the forthcoming work. Perhaps Mosquera is using his Preface as a means to urge Herrera on in this task. In any case, it seems unlikely that the *Relacion* was ever intended to become part of the *Istoria general* in quite the form it took as a separate account.

---

[39] Coster believed that the *Relacion* was separate from the *Istoria*, thinking that the former work would have been expanded before being incorporated into the latter. It is hard to imagine how a still longer account of one episode would have fit into a work of that scope.

CHAPTER TWO

HERRERA AND THE IMPERIAL CAUSE

The battle of Lepanto, the victorious climax of the Cyprian episode, occupies only a small part of Herrera's *Relacion*. The struggle for possession of Cyprus between the Venetians and the Turks, the most obvious cause of the encounter between Islam and the Holy League at Lepanto, is treated at some length. Herrera begins with a summary of the import of this entire chapter in Mediterranean history as it appeared to the observer of 1571-1572: at last the ambition of the Turk to dominate the Christian world had been broken, and never again would he cause Europeans to cower before his might. He asserts that, in the same manner as the ancient historians, he is entitled to claim that this battle is the most spectacular and significant to have been fought to date.

Such introductory statements were standard practice among Renaissance disciples of antiquity. Indeed a survey of the importance of one's cause takes on the character of a prescript.[1] Nor is it surprising that this should be the case, for historians like Herrera and his Italian counterparts who view history in terms of its didactic value must naturally feel driven to establish the importance of those models of conduct which they offer their readers.[2] The vigor of this principle among Renaissance historians is attested to as well in the need felt by those who recorded less than glorious exploits to explain the absence of the sort of

---

[1] Thucydides, *The Peloponnesian War* (New York, 1959), p. 13; *The Way to Write History*, in *The Works of Lucian of Samosata*, trans. H. W. and F. G. Fowler (Oxford, 1905), II, 132-133; Felix Gilbert, *Machiavelli and Guicciardini* (Princeton, 1965), p. 210.
[2] Gilbert, p. 217.

statement in question. The Italian Rucellai, in his account of the French invasion of Italy, excuses himself by saying that «he is unhappy that he has to report not about glorious and virtuous deeds, but about stupidities, weaknesses and crimes». [3] Likewise among Spanish historians, Don Diego Hurtado de Mendoza makes an apology (perhaps with ironic intentions) for the subject matter of his *Guerra de Granada*:

> Bien sé que algunas cosas de las que escribiere parescerán livianas y menudas para historia, comparadas a las grandes que de España se hallan escritas: ...libre y estendido campo, y ancha salida para los escriptores. Yo escogí camino estrecho, y aunque trabajoso, estéril y sin gloria; pero provechoso y de fruto para los que adelante vinieren. [4]

Hurtado de Mendoza thus finds his ultimate justification in the same didactic framework alluded to by Mosquera de Figueroa in the Preface to Herrera's *Relación*: even the most evil deeds can serve, in a negative sense, as examples.

Herrera then plunges right in to supply a thorough background to the episode, dealing with Cyprus itself, the events which led to its falling into Venetian hands, the state of Turkish power and the Turkish succession, the Turks's challenge to the Venetians, the siege of Cyprus, the first joint efforts to rescue Cyprus and their ultimate failure, the arduous and lengthy deliberations which eventually resulted in the formation of the League, the exact composition of the allied forces in great detail, and finally the momentous naval battle and issue thereof.

The title of the account indicates its bipartite character. Fully half of the chapters deal with the preliminaries, the other half pertaining specifically to the naval victory. In the first half, Herrera uses the events leading up to Lepanto to describe the state of disunity which plagued Christendom prior to the League's formation. This half records the drama of the reunification of the Christian powers; the second part, the drama of the preparation of men's souls for victory.

It is the careful consideration of significant related events —particularly those chapters which evoke the complex diplo-

---

[3] *Ibid.*, p. 212.
[4] Diego Hurtado de Mendoza, *Comentario de la Guerra de Granada*, ed. Gómez Moreno (Madrid, 1948), p. 1.

matic flirtation among Venice, Spain, and the Vatican, and the intricate web of motives which intruded at every turn— that gives the *Relación* its air of modernity. Father Luciano Serrano gives Herrera first credit among the early chroniclers of Lepanto for having seen so well the human factors involved, and thus pointing the way (though in the flush of his optimism he did not actually suggest this possibility) to the dissolution of the League, especially the Venetian compromise with the Turks.[5]

1. Friends and Foe

For an account which puts the religious question in such bold relief, Herrera's work begins in quite a low key. Indeed, the introductory passage seems to evaluate the situation in purely political terms:

> Florecia en las armas el imperio de los otomanos, espantoso á todos los Príncipes por la grandeza de sus ejércitos y gloria de la disciplina militar, y por la abundancia maravillosa de sus tesoros, en que habia por largo curso de años extendido los términos de su potencia por todo aquel espacio, que hay de tierras entre el Euxino y Archipiélago, Mediterráneo y Egito con los senos de Arabia y Persia, cuando confederados contra él la iglesia romana y los venecianos con el Rey Filipo de España le quebrantaron en una sangrienta y memorable batalla todos los brazos de su poder, y rompieron los intentos con que aspiraba al dominio de la tierra toda.[6]

The Turks are not labeled as «infidels» nor is any reference made to the role of divine providence in the victory of the League. The only words which even hint that there is any more than a territorial struggle in the balance are «la iglesia romana». Otherwise the question is described as a Turkish attempt at national aggrandizement which poses a threat to all other monarchs, and which is frustrated by an alliance of Western Mediterranean powers. In the first chapter of the *Relacion*,

---

[5] Luciano Serrano, *La Liga de Lepanto* (Madrid, 1918-1919). For a different discussion of Spain's idea of her destiny, related to the entire chapter, see Otis H. Green, «Self-realization», in *Spain and the Western Tradition* (Madison, 1965), III, 1-172.
[6] Fernando de Herrera, *Relacion de la guerra de Cipre*, in *C.D.I.*, XXI (Madrid, 1852), 261-262.

there are only two fleeting references to the religious question. Prince Suleiman, father of the current ruler, is referred to as «perpetuo enemigo de la religion cristiana», and Herrera alludes to the traditional arrogance and disdain of the Turks toward Christian forces. He then proceeds to paint a picture of Cyprus, the prize immediately at stake, including an extremely straightforward explanation of the origin of Venetian rule on that island.

The Turks emerge in this sketch as a haughty race, with limitless aspirations of territorial conquest, as long as no obstacle is placed in their paths. The secret of their success, an exaggerated self-confidence which remains intact only insomuch as it goes unchallenged, has been reinforced historically by a combination of unwillingness and inability on the part of the Christian powers to check its moves. Annexing Cyprus is for Selim mere child's play, hardly to be considered daring:

> que lo hallava muy fácil por ser dentro en su tierra, y no ser las fuerzas de los venecianos poderosos contra él,... porque para la grandeza de aquel imperio, ¿qué resistencia podia hacer una gente á quien de dia en dia los Príncipes otomanos habian estrechado en los últimos fines del mar Adriático, quitandole el señorío de las islas y la libertad de la navegacion todas las veces que les agradaba? ¿Y quién no sabia que estaba en mano de Selin, de la suerte que sus antecesores, concedelle la paz, despues de haberse hecho señor de Cipre? [7]

Buoyed up with the conviction that success is already his, Selim allows no scruples to deter his «libre y ambicioso deseo».[8] The

---

[7] *Ibid.*, p. 266.
[8] *Ibid.*, p. 267. For other sixteenth- and seventeenth-century views of the Turks, see Herrero García, *Ideas de los españoles del siglo XVII,* 2nd ed. (Madrid, 1966), pp. 527-548. These portraits commonly coincide with Herrera's in indicating the perfidy, arrogance, ambition, lasciviousness and greed of the Turkish people. For other European viewpoints, see Marcel Bataillon, «El doctor Laguna», in *Erasmo y España,* 2nd ed. (Mexico, 1966); and Clarence D. Rouillard, *The Turk in French History, Thought and Literature 1520-1660* (Paris, 1938). French portraits contrast starkly with those of most Spanish authors in stressing Turkish moderation, discipline, piety (albeit misguided) and the «aristocracy of virtue» which they maintain. As with the *Viaje de Turquía,* French travel literature represents an incipient self-criticism. Sir Thomas Sherley's *Discours of the Turkes,* ed. E. Denison Ross (London, 1936), written in 1607, repeats the Spanish portrayal: the Turks are «unciuile & vicious» (p. 2). Luigi Bassano's *Costumi et i modi particolari della vita de' Turchi* (facsimile of the Rome 1545 edition, Monaco di Baviera, 1963) is typical of much of the European literature concerning Turkey in that its author professes both admiration and dismay in the face of different customs. One series of exceptions to the usual Spanish view of the Turks belongs to the history of the

actions of his father and grandfather have proved the Turks capable of terrible cruelty, not only in dealing with enemies but also in suppressing rivals of their own race and religion. The Turkish ruler does essentially as he pleases in international affairs, and concerns himself with no justification other than the power of a well-trained army and his whim. Herrera's opening sentence acknowledges the superiority of Ottoman military discipline, an unusual concession in a day when the Spanish armies were often held up as the perfect models of training and skill. [9]

Doctor Andrés Laguna had some years before ventured a rather blunt challenge to the accepted veneration of Spanish military might. In the *Viaje de Turquía*, following, as Marcel Bataillon has shown, earlier Italian accounts and not any personal experience of the situation, [10] Pedro de Urdemalas discourses at length about the highly skilled Turkish soldiers, better organized than the Spanish, with markedly satirical intent. [11] Outside of Spain, both Machiavelli and Brantôme find room in their works to praise the valor of Spanish troops. [12] In the final chapter of *Il Principe*, Machiavelli expresses a particular admiration for the tenacity and fearlessness of the Spanish infantry in hand-to-hand combat, and at the same time deplores the state of Italian armies. [13] Nevertheless, Machiavelli is not inclined to build up myths of human infallibility in any form, and finds that Spaniards

---

conquest of Rhodes by Suleiman in 1522. Spaniards had access to this history from several sources: the translation by Cristóbal de Arcos entitled *La muy lamentable conquista y cruenta batalla de Rodas* (Seville, 1526) of Giacomo Fontano's *De bello Rhodio*; Vasco Díaz Tanco de Frexenal, *Libro intitulado Palinodia* (Orense, 1547), a compendium of many accounts of the Turkish empire, principally that of Paolo Giovio; and finally Lope de Vega's *comedia*, *La pérdida honrosa y caballerosa de San Juan* (*Obras*, ed. Menéndez y Pelayo, Madrid, 1901, Vol. XII). Lope's portrait of Suleiman the Magnificent follows the Fontano account quite faithfully (Menéndez y Pelayo, Introduction, p. xliii) in portraying the Grand Turk as a chivalresque figure who treats his defeated enemy with unaccustomed magnanimity and good faith, and who even sheds a tear at the sight of the old Grand Master being evicted from his home (p. 63). Lope stresses that this constitutes a departure from the norm by showing Suleiman chastising his own «canalla turca» (p. 55) for unseemly behavior. This other view informs *La Santa Liga*, a curiously named work, for nearly two full acts are devoted to portraying Selim as a victim of his own effeminacy and lasciviousness (*Obras*, Vol. XII).

[9] Don Diego Hurtado de Mendoza, in the *Guerra de Granada*, is even more critical of Spanish army discipline in suppressing the Moorish uprising.

[10] Bataillon, p. 669 ff.

[11] *Viaje de Turquía*, ed. M. Serrano y Sanz, in *Autobiografías y memorias*, N.B.A.E., Vol. II (Madrid, 1905), pp. 118-132.

[12] Felipe Picatoste, *Los españoles en Italia* (Madrid, 1887), II, 42-45.

[13] Machiavelli, *Il Principe*, in *Tutte le opere storiche e letterarie*, ed. Guido Mazzoni and Mario Casella (Florence, 1929), p. 51.

do have their weaknesses, in this case their cavalry. That the individual valor of Spanish infantrymen was acknowledged in Europe seems clear,[14] but it is equally evident that due to Spain's position in Italy as foreign ruler this respect was tempered with distaste for Spanish arrogance.[15] In any case, Herrera's intention here is certainly not satirical or even deprecatory. Rather it constitutes part of the author's literary technique. By giving the enemy this sort of advantage, real or imagined, the *Relación* allows Philip's forces a dramatic revindication. Furthermore, Herrera must leave himself room to make his main assertion: military power alone is an insufficient arm. Arms are only rights «con que los poderosos hallan por suya toda la justicia».[16]

The Turks are condemned for having broken a solemn pact made with the Venetians over the control of the Mediterranean territories of both parties. This pact (Herrera does not elaborate on it) represented already a considerable moral defeat for the Republic of Venice, since its provisions drained vast sums in tributes from the lifeblood of the mercantile state. The peace and «amistad» which Venice enjoyed with the Turks point to compromise and humiliation on her part. Yet the historian's judgment is that the Turkish monarch has sinned against the integrity of a solemn oath. The Venetians' unpreparedness to meet the new threat came about because

> no creian que Selin sin alguna causa quisiese así romper malvadamente la paz, que tan poco habia que confirmó por solene juramento; mas pues él olvidado de la amistad que tenian queria con no harta codicia deshacer todos los vínculos de la fe, que es la mayor de todas las cosas humanas, y sin quien ninguna razon puede haber del comercio y trato.[17]

The Venetians, whom the pact made rulers of Cyprus, having kept good faith in their agreement with Selim, confide in divine favor of God «vengador de los injustos deseos».[18]

Events prove for Herrera that not only the word of the Turks, but also their courage can be easily deflated. The occasion first arises with the siege of a Turkish fortification on the Alba-

---

[14] Picatoste, II, 49.
[15] Herrero García, pp. 78 ff.
[16] Herrera, *Relacion,* p. 265.
[17] *Ibid.,* p. 272.
[18] *Ibid.,* pp. 272-273.

nian coast. The Venetians enlist the aid of the terrorized inhabitants and march against the normally impregnable stronghold. The Turks, seeing this alliance lined up to challenge their control, «turbados de súbito miedo»,[19] allow the balance to be tipped against them for no reason other than fear, Herrera asserts. Another case, where their cowardice does not have such utterly disastrous consequences, is the siege of Famagusta, where the Venetians are making their last stand for the possession of Cyprus. The Venetians, faced with overwhelmingly superior Turkish troops, still manage by their determined opposition to disconcert their enemies and relinquish their last fortress only for a very heavy price in Turkish lives. The Turks, having overcome their fear thanks to their superior numbers and ammunition, take victory no more gracefully than impending defeat, and with great treachery and cruelty the Turkish commander,

> trabando unas palabras de otras, se quejó al Bragandino que habia muerto en el tiempo de las treguas algunos turcos, y tomando aquella ocasión no verdadera, con ánimo sangriento y bárbaro delante de sí los hizo pasar á todos por el hierro, que en un punto por extraña crueldad fueron hechos pedazos, y haciendo cortar las orejas al Bragandino, despues de ejercitar en él todo lo que la ira y soberbia del vencedor quiso, con inhumana y ferocísima rabia á cabo de doce días lo mandó desollar vivo, que con generosa constancia lo afrentaba por la fe quebrantada.[20]

This bloodthirsty, avenging passion of a fierce, inhuman, barbarous enemy marks the other face of a false courage which will be punctured once again at Lepanto when the proud Turks learn that they are due to be matched against Spanish valor.

Herrera's characterization of the common enemy is thus spelled out in very human terms of courage and fear, of prowess and pride, of cruelty and limitless greed. He does not even choose to dignify the Turks with persisting devotion to some ideal, however mistaken it might be. He ventures only a passing reference to «los torpes y nefandos ritos del abominable Mahoma» compared to the «verdadera religión de Cristo»,[21] used as an explanation of the Albanians' willingness to rise up against their seemingly all-powerful oppressors. The «torpes y nefandos

[19] *Ibid.*, p. 279.
[20] *Ibid.*, p. 305.
[21] *Ibid.*, p. 281.

ritos» do not even qualify as religion. They are a cult to which only inhuman barbarians could subscribe.

Only when the sketching of the true villain has been accomplished, does the religious question, in which the Turks have only negative standing, emerge with clear contours. Christianity claims for itself not only the right to repulse the traitor, so deemed according to the dictates of human justice, but also its own exclusive right to the support of divine providence. Pope Pius V takes it upon himself to unite the strengths of the Christian powers to repel the enemy:

> como padre de la república cristiana, y celoso de la honra divina, conociendo que á él solo tocaba el cuidado y vigilancia del bien comun de la cristiandad,... juzgando por la mayor importancia dello, juntar en confederacion con su autoridad y amonestaciones la potencia maravillosa y grandes fuerzas del Rey Católico y las suyas y de los venecianos en un vínculo de firmísima concordia, con que le parecia que eran poderosos para allanar la soberbia de aquel grande Príncipe. [22]

The Pope recognizes that in this menace divine honor is at stake. The expression «allanar la soberbia» placed deliberately in this context assumes the full force of its Old Testament resonance. God will avenge all unjust desires.

Yet the picture Herrera paints of the state in which Christendom finds itself is not at all a happy one:

> Verdaderamente quien considerára en aquella sazon el estado lloroso de la cristiandad, escondida en los postreros términos de Europa, y desnuda de aquella grandeza y resplandor antiguo, con que levantó la cabeza gloriosa entre todas las religiones, no hallára quien pudiera poner freno al libre y ambicioso deseo de Selin, pues de una parte las herejías y de otra las discordias intestinas la tenian casi toda opresa. [23]

France, first of all, once «el solo refugio de la iglesia romana y cabeza de nuestra religión», [24] is currently torn by internal struggles with the «hugonotos, que así se llamaban los luteranos», [25] who seem to have the upper hand, unjustly inflict persecutions

---

[22] *Ibid.*, p. 278.
[23] *Ibid.*, p. 267.
[24] *Ibid.*, p. 267.
[25] *Ibid.*, p. 267.

on the true believers, «derribando con infame y impía memoria de su maldad los templos dedicados al culto divino».[26] In the *Querela pacis* (translated into Spanish by Diego López de Cortegana and published in 1520), Erasmus envisions a Europe torn with dissension, in which «Sola Francia ceu flos illibatus Christiani ditionis», and all others, including Spain, are defiled with heresies.[27]

France in Herrera's vision becomes a new Israel who has erred in her ways and must suffer in consequence the destruction of the temple. The vivid echoes of Biblical diction underline a fundamental assumption governing Herrera's interpretation of events. He goes on to say that, although it seemed, after a major Catholic victory, that the forces of the heretics had been scattered sufficiently to take away the threat of their rising again to power,

> habia crecido el mal tan extendidamente, que no por eso se remedió algo el daño que habia padecido la mísera Francia, porque casi no se hallaba quien quisiese alzar los ojos al cielo y conocer su ceguedad y perdicion, sufriendo afrentosamente que se alentase el mal en lo íntimo de su pecho.[28]

The French, like the Israelites before them, have allowed themselves to be consumed with corruption, unable to see their own blindness and perdition.[29] In Herrera's cosmic view, Providence operates on the side of the just, who are first of all Christians. Christianity is contrasted with barbarity, inhumanity, turpitude familiar from Herrera's portrait of the Turkish nation. But the fact of professed or nominal membership in the Christian fold is not enough to assure the automatic continuance of divine favor, without the collaboration of the upright conduct of each individual, his «costumbres». France continues to suffer the Lutheran menace not because her armies are incapable of crushing this enemy, but because all Frenchmen cannot purge their hearts of this scourge.

---

[26] *Ibid.*, p. 268.
[27] Desiderius Erasmus, *Querela pacis vndique gentium ejectae profligataeque* (Lugduni Batavorum, 1641), p. 41; Bataillon, p. 80 ff.
[28] Herrera, *Relacion,* p. 268.
[29] Cf. Sonnet III, 31, of the Pacheco edition (Seville, 1619):
  Mas, ¡ô mesquina! en impio error porfias,
    i enciendes fiera el fuego en tus entrañas,
    i corres a tu muerte ya sin miedo.

Erasmus years before blamed the internal strife of Europe on men's corrupt passions. Refuting the notion that God commanded his people to wage war, Erasmus pointed out that those wars mentioned in the Old Testament were fought by the Israelites with infidel foreigners. Rome's wars, too, were designed to subdue the barbarians. No idealism, however, informs the wars of his time:

> id [war] Christianis gerendum adversus vitia, quibus nunca vitiis convenit, cum hominibus bellum est..... Christianos, si praetextibus detractis rem vere aestimas, transversos rapit ambitio, agit ira pessimus consultor, pertrahit habendi nunquam satiata cupiditas. Atque his [the Jews] fere cum exteris erat. Christianis cum Turcis foedus est, inter ipsos bellum. [30]

Throughout the *Querela,* Peace bewails man's inhumanity to man, the unchristianness of Christianity: «Quoniam ore praedicabitis eis Christum pacis auctorem, ipsi perpetuis dissidiis inter vos tumultuantes?» [31] The hypocrite is worse than a declared pagan: «Malo Turcam ingenuum quam fucatum Christianum.» [32] Peace pleads, «Si cupimus Turcas ad Christi religionem adducere, prius ipsi simus Christiani.» [33] For Alfonso de Valdés, even the Pope cannot call himself a Christian, despite all the authority invested in his person, without conforming himself to Christ's will: «para que nos quedasse acá en la tierra quien muy de veras representasse la vida y sanctas costumbres de Jesu Cristo nuestro Redemptor: porque los humanos coraçones mas aina se atraen con obras que con palabras». [34] So go the words which Latancio draws from the Arcidiano. Juan de Mariana will go so far as to insist that a nation has the moral right to destroy its monarch if he has sinned against God's laws. [35]

Herrera's universe operates on a rigid system of punishment and reward. Under this scheme, it is understood not only that

---

[30] Erasmus, *Querela*, p. 38.
[31] *Ibid.*, p. 70.
[32] Erasmus, *Dulce bellum inexpertis* (Brussels, 1953), pp. 90-91.
[33] Erasmus, *Querela*, p. 70.
[34] Alfonso de Valdés, *Diálogo de las cosas ocurridas en Roma*, ed. José F. Montesinos (Madrid, 1956), p. 16; and Bataillon, p. 368.
[35] *Del Rey y de la institución real*, in *Obras del Padre Juan de Mariana*, B.A.E., Vol. XXXI, pp. 479-483. Cf. also R. Lida, «Sobre Quevedo y su voluntad de leyenda», *Filología*, VIII, No. 3 (1962), 273-306.

the wicked will be castigated and the virtuous find their reward, but also that he to whom punishment is meted out must necessarily have sinned in some way in order to have merited such treatment by a God who in his omniscience is the pure embodiment of justice. Similarly, Erasmus imputes the strength of the Turks to God's punishment for Christian disunity; and Herrera's hero, Sir Thomas More, in his *Dialogue of Comfort against Tribulation,* does likewise:

> Howbeit, if the princes of Christendom everywhere about would, where as need was, have set to their hands in time, the Turk had never taken any one place of all those places. But partly dissension fallen among ourself, partly that no man careth what harm other folk feel, but each part suffereth other to shift for itself; the Turk is in few years wonderfully increased, and Christendom on the other side very sore decayed. And all this worketh our wickedness, with which God is not content.[36]

Valdés' Latancio demonstrates:

> como todo lo que ha acaecido [i.e., in the sack of Rome] ha seido por manifiesto juizio de Dios, para castigar aquella ciudad, donde con grande inominia de la religion cristiana, reinavan todos los vicios que la malicia de los hombres podia inventar, y con aquel castigo despertar el pueblo cristiano, para que, remediados los males que padece, abramos los ojos e vivamos como cristianos, pues tanto nos preciamos deste nombre.[37]

For this reason, Herrera will depict Don Juan de Austria exhorting his men as they set sail on the way to their encounter with the Turks to keep their personal conduct above reproach. If they debase themselves, they will forfeit God's support and thus the victory.

It is this notion which affords an explanation for the victories of a thoroughly base enemy, such as the Moslem nations personify. Herrera surveys a series of Christian and Spanish defeats at the hand of the Turk and is quick to give his reason for the seeming neglect on God's part. If God has abandoned the Christian cause, it is because he wants to punish his people and put them in mind of their sins. If Christians truly possess moral integrity,

---

[36] Thomas More, *Selections from his English Works,* ed. P. S. and H. M. Allen (Oxford, 1924), p. 118; cf. Erasmus, *Querela,* pp. 70-71.
[37] Alfonso de Valdés, p. 14.

they cannot fail. We are reminded of Herrera's interpretation of the disaster of Alcázarquivir in 1578, which is cast very much along the same lines.[38] Herrera, unlike most recorders of the catastrophe, concentrates his attention on the cowardice evinced by the Portuguese troops, the «vano error del vulgo temeroso» of the famous elegy «Voz de dolor i canto de gemido». This poem too is filled with Biblical overtones: Portugal, indeed all of Christendom, becomes the new Israel bewailing its apostasy from God's way. God never turns his back on his own without good cause.

In the passage which concerns us here, Germany, England, Hungary and Transylvania have all fallen into the ways of ruin and are in no position to come to the rescue of Christianity. The German states, which so learnedly repudiated the Lutheran heresy, are divided and intimidated by Ottoman power. The Emperor Maximilian, the only one willing to risk the wrath of so dangerous an enemy, has not strength enough to oppose them alone. Thus an ignominious truce exists, a scant source of protection. In England, following the death of the devout Queen Mary, Queen Elizabeth has usurped for herself «con sacrílega maldad» the title «Cabeza de la iglesia de Inglaterra»: «porque como de una mortal pestilencia acometidos los mas de los hombres perdieron la fe y negaron las antiguas y divinas tradiciones con que Dios sustenta su iglesia.»[39] The only possible defender of the cause is Philip of Spain, whose own house Herrera pictures as far more in order:

> Príncipe mucho mayor y de mas riqueza y opinion que todos los que la cristiandad ha tenido de muchos años á esta parte, porque florecia su imperio en nobleza de milicia y en número de gente belicosa, y en fertilidad de tierras y fortaleza de lugares, y que tenia en su mano la paz y la guerra de todos.[40]

Yet even Philip is plagued with «discordias», two very pressing ones being the Flemish campaign and the Moorish uprisings in Granada. Thus the confidence of Selim is hardly surprising, for he knows, Herrera affirms,

---

[38] Canción I, *Poesías*, ed. V. García de Diego (Madrid, 1962), p. 45 ff.
[39] Herrera, *Relacion*, p. 269.
[40] *Ibid.*, p. 270.

que las ligas otras vezes hechas por los Príncipes cristianos no habian tenido tanta fuerza que llegasen al fin pretendido, ántes deshechas al principio sin conseguir algun efeto dejaban de sí una memoria afrentosa, porque preferian sus pasiones á las causas de Cristo, consintiendo por sus discordias que la cristiandad padeciese y creciese el imperio de los turcos. [41]

The passage evokes Erasmus once again and Peace's complaint against the wars which divide Christians:

At pudet meminisse quam pudendis, quam frivolis de causis Christiani Principes orbem ad arma concitent. Hic obsoletum ac putrem aliquem titulum aut reperit aut commentus est. Quasivero ita magni referat quis regnum administret, modo publicis commodis recte consolatur. Ille causatur omissum nescio quid in foedere centum capitum. Hic illi privatim insensus est ob sponsam interceptam, aut scomma liberius dictum. [42]

In his continued echoes of the *Querela pacis,* Alfonso de Valdés rails against the Pope, cardinals and bishops for causing France and Spain to break their peace, when they ought to be exhorting all nations to avoid war. But duty has taken second place to vanity, «Y agora, por no perder ellos un poquillo de su reputacion, ponen toda la cristiandad en armas.» [43] Vives laments European divisiveness in *De Europae Dissidiis*; [44] the epistles of John Colet, Erasmus' English tutor, protest against the suffering of the masses at the hands of warring monarchs; [45] and closer to Spain, Doctor Andrés Laguna delivers a discourse on «Europe, torturer of herself» whose title indicates its affinity with other attacks on war among Christians. [46]

For Erasmus, More and Herrera, the petty quarrels which persist with the Christian nations have as their direct result the increase of Turkish power. God disciplines his own in this way for continuing to prefer their passions to the Christian cause.

---

[41] *Ibid.,* p. 270.
[42] Erasmus, *Querela,* p. 39; Bataillon, p. 80 ff.
[43] Alfonso de Valdés, pp. 22-23 ff.
[44] Bataillon, «Sur l'humanisme du Docteur Laguna», *Romance Philology,* XVII (1963-1964), 207-234.
[45] Robert P. Adams, «Erasmus' Ideas of his Role as a Social Critic c. 1480-1500», *Renaissance News,* XI, No. 1 (1958), 11-16; and *The Better Part of Valor: More, Erasmus, Colet and Vives on humanism, war and peace 1496-1535* (University of Washington, 1962).
[46] Bataillon, *Erasmo y España,* p. 677; and «Sur l'humanisme».

In Herrera's view, Christians will have first to achieve self-control within their own ranks, dominating their passions and mending their selfish ways, if they are to defeat this peril. Erasmus on the other hand cherishes the more idealistic notion that true Christians might be able to win the Turks over by the simple example of their goodness.

Herrera's attitude vis-à-vis the Venetians appears somewhat ambiguous, as exemplified in the following passage from Chapter IV:

> pero aquel sapientísimo ayuntamiento de aquella República escogido de hombres graves en consejo y de severo juicio, y constantes en la adversidad de la fortuna, que no velaban en otra cosa sino en defender su libertad y acrecentar sus estados, con igual ánimo se dispusieron á la proteccion y defensa de aquel reino, juzgando por afrenta grandísima rendirse á las amenazas de Selin, que con infidelidad de tirano les quebrantaba la fe y la paz que ellos le guardaban inviolablemente.[47]

Here the Venetians receive the highest sort of praise: their conduct represents exactly the opposite end of the spectrum from the «infidelidad de tirano» shown them by Selim. Deliberate men of sober judgment, constant in the adversity of fortune, they meet threats to their liberty with equanimity and courage. Yet Herrera hints too at the territorial acquisitiveness of the Venetians when he says that they are watchful both for their liberty and for the aggrandizement of their estates.

Spanish authors of the sixteenth and seventeenth centuries reiterate this vacilating portrait of the Venetian Republic. To most, Venice's principal characteristic is prudence, «una prudencia tal vez rayana en falsía, en doblez, y de objetivos muy positivistas».[48] The admiration which Cervantes evinces through the eyes of Tomás Rodaja in *El Licenciado Vidriera* is overshadowed by judgments such as those of Gracián, Vélez de Guevara, Salas Barbadillo, and the most scathing of all, Quevedo's remark in *La hora* that «Venecia es el mismo Pilatos».[49] In a manuscript of the Biblioteca Nacional of Madrid, cited by Herrero García, *Relación de la Serenisima República de Venecia y*

---

[47] Herrera, *Relacion*, pp. 273-274.
[48] Herrero García, p. 372.
[49] *Ibid.*, p. 374.

de sus Estados, its author pays Venetian circumspection a somewhat dubious compliment: «Tienen los señores venecianos, al presente, paz con todos los príncipes del mundo, y por ser ellos de su naturaleza tímidos, desean la quietud y aborrecen la guerra.» [50]

The Venetians came into power on Cyprus in the first place through means of which Herrera seems even more directly critical. The last king of Cyprus, an illegitimate son of the previous ruler, and thus having only a dubious right to the monarchy, [51] marries the daughter of a Venetian gentleman. When the daughter, widowed, remains as sole ruler, great upheavals ensue; the Venetians seize upon this opportunity to gain control of the island:

> reduciendo la isla á la obediencia de los venecianos, por ser, como ellos decian, justos herederos de su hija la Reina Catalina...; pero el justo derecho que ellos tenian era el de las armas, con que los poderosos hallan por suya toda la justicia. [52]

The Venetians are described here in very much the same way that Herrera speaks of the Turks. The Cypriots themselves abhor Venetian domination, «ó por sentirse opresos con rigor de justicia y eceso de los derechos impuestos, ó por la antigua enemistad que tenían á los que se hicieron señores de su tierra», [53] and many, thinking that the Turks could very well be more liberal masters, readily give their allegiance to the new invader.

More recent accounts tend to justify Herrera's censure of the Venetians. At least they clearly place their taking over of Cyprus in the realm of the *raison d'état*. Herrera may or may not have been aware of the existence of a more legitimate heir to the throne than Caterina Cornaro, wife of Jacques II, the bastard son of the last legitimate Lusignan ruler. Charlotte, the legitimate daughter of the same King Jean and Queen Helena, enjoyed the support of the Cypriot nobility, which Caterina's regime was at constant pains to subdue. Indeed, the match of Caterina Cornaro with Jacques represented a victory for the Venetians in a Mediterranean power play involving the Mamelukes

---

[50] Herrero García, p. 373.
[51] Herrera says, «si es lícito á quien escribe decir llanamente la verdad, yo entiendo que con poco justo derecho entró en la posesión dél». *Relacion,* p. 265.
[52] *Ibid.,* p. 265.
[53] *Ibid.,* p. 276.

of Egypt, Naples and thus Spain. Modern historians have portrayed Caterina as the helpless victim of her compatriots, who gradually forced her to give up her power and retire to Venice, where she was compensated with the rule of Asola. The Venetians gave the Cypriots no motive for loyalty to their rule by imposing Venetian-style government on the recalcitrant aristocracy. As Herrera theorized, the Cypriots probably did not at all regret changing hands. [54]

Thus the Venetians appear variously as unjust usurpers, as oppressive rulers, as models of diplomatic integrity, as sage political thinkers and steadfast defenders, or finally as indecisive, careless and compromising. Herrera is quick to underline the valor of many Venetians in the defense of Famagusta, with a fervor nearly equal to that of French and Venetian accounts, but he also clearly lays the blame for the series of delays which obstructed the pacting of the League to the indecisiveness of Venice. Venetian steadfastness in attempting to keep peace with the Turks appears now as good faith, now as almost cowardly reluctance to incur the wrath of a menacingly powerful enemy. In the councils of war among the Christian powers, the Venetians are pictured as being excessively cautious, all too willing to put off an expedition against the Turks another season because of inadequate supplies.

Naturally Venetian histories and those written in countries more friendly to her can be expected to impute these delays to Spain rather than to Venice, as we shall see in more detail. However, in all fairness to Herrera, it must be acknowledged that he shows nothing like the ruthlessness in exposing Venetian motives as he might have done, or even as Venetian historians like Paolo Paruta did, writing from a more fully informed vantage point. In the Parte Seconda of his *Historia vinetiana,* Paruta describes the Venetians' hesitation on the eve of the signing of the «perpetual league» with Pope Pius V and the Spaniards. They are doubtful about confirming the alliance, he says, desiring particularly to keep the door open for a private peace with the Turks, with whom they must ultimately come to terms if their economy is to survive. [55] They still have not determined which

---

[54] Horatio F. Brown, *Venetian Studies* (London, 1887), pp. 291-333.
[55] Paolo Paruta, *Historia vinetiana, Parte Seconda* (Venice, 1605), pp. 139-140.

will offer them «maggior sicurtà, & che si sarà da Nostro Signor Dio inspirata per conservatione della Republica nostra».[56] The Frenchman Thomas de Fougasses and his English translator W. Shute echo Paruta's remarks.[57] Furthermore, it appears that Venice in fact had refused Spain's help in the form of an alliance before the question of Cyprus' rescue came up, primarily for selfish reasons.[58] The Mediterranean interests of Spain and Venice had hitherto appeared quite distinct to each of the parties concerned. Philip II was preoccupied with his claims to territory in North Africa and the Moorish threat to Spain's coastline, while Venice's prime concern was that of keeping her trade routes in the Eastern Mediterranean open, by means of conciliation with the Moslems, if necessary. Neither wished to chance diluting his strength in risky encounters which did not bear directly on his own safety. History's judgment with respect to Venice is that she sought Spain's aid not out of any «crusading ardor» but out of opportunism.[59] Not even the Pope could have cherished any illusion as to her objectives.

This picture of the Venetians reminds us of Herrera's conception of Italian people in general. In the *Anotaciones* to Garcilaso, he characterizes Italian poetry as

> mui florida, abundosa, blanda i compuesta; pero libre, laciva, desmayada, i demasiadamente enternecida i muelle i llena de afetación. admite todos los vocablos, carece de consonantes en la terminacion; lo cual, aunque entre ellos se tenga por singular virtud i suavidad, es conocida falta de espiritu i fuerça... pero la nuestra es grave, religiosa, onesta, alta, manifica, suave, tierna, afetuosissima, i llena de sentimientos, i tan copiosa i abundante; que ninguna otra puede gloriarse desta riqueza i fertilidad mas justamente. no sufre, ni permite vocablos estraños i baxos, ni regalos lacivos. es mas recatada i osservante.[60]

Italy herself is «laciva», «regalada», and thus quite far from the intense seriousness of purpose which Herrera takes to be typical of Spaniards. Even Naples, which in actuality was as

---

[56] *Ibid.*, p. 139.
[57] Thomas de Fougasses, *The Generall Historie of the Magnificent State of Venice,* trans. W. Shute (London, 1612)) pp. 398-399.
[58] Roger Bigelow Merriman, *The Rise of the Spanish Empire* (New York, 1934), IV, 124.
[59] Merriman, p. 126; Luciano Serrano, I, 41-46.
[60] *Obras de Garci Lasso de la Vega con Anotaciones de Fernando de Herrera* (Seville, 1580), p. 74; ed. Gallego Morell (Granada, 1966), p. 288.

much a Spanish city as an Italian one throughout the period, still has the reputation of «lugar de ociosos» for Herrera at least.[61] In the *Relacion,* Cyprus too partakes of some of this Mediterranean flavor. Because the island suffers a dangerously severe heat in summer,

> los hombres que hacen aquí su habitación son delicados y de mucho regalo, que no pueden sufrir alguna fatiga, ni durar en los trabajos, ántes ocupados y entregados todos al deleite y ocio, viven de todo punto olvidados de los ejercicios militares, porque las mujeres son extremadamente lascivas desde sus primeros habitadores; y de aquella fama nació la fábula de ser consagrada á Venus.[62]

Cyprus is hardly endowed with the necessary fortitude to repel the Turks.

2. Herrera and Philip II

Only the aid of Spain will suffice to save the day. At the moment of greatest indecision in the negotiations concerning the League, a dispatch arrives from Philip II:

> vino un correo del Rey Católico que traia comision para que su Santidad hiciese y prometiese todo lo que quisiese, que como hijo obediente de la Santa iglesia con su antiguo estudio del comun bien de la religion cristiana lo cumpliria todo y obedeceria.[63]

The Catholic King —so called by Herrera in testimony of his exemplary position among other Christian monarchs— gives the Pope unlimited assurances. He will supply whatever is required of him for the divine cause. In doing this, Philip consciously subordinates his own passions to the demands Christ makes of him, which other Christian rulers have thus far failed to do:

> porque aunque el Rey tenia justo enojo de los venecianos por haber negado el socorro de Malta, queriendo en caso donde pen-

---

[61] *Anotaciones,* p. 363 ff.
[62] Herrera, *Relacion,* pp. 263-264. On the sixteenth century's creation and destruction of ethnic myths, see Georges Cirot, *Les Histoires générales d'Espagne entre Alphonse X et Philippe II, 1284-1556* (Paris, 1904). For the phenomenon in Quevedo, see R. Lida, «Sobre Quevedo y su voluntad de leyenda», pp. 273-306.
[63] Herrera, *Relacion,* p. 289.

dia la salud de la Cristiandad no romper la paz á un enemigo
bárbaro que amenazaba la universal ruina lo cual volvió en mayor gloria suya, pues sin ellos le hizo alzar el cerco, no quiso
faltar al servicio de Dios, juzgando aquella causa por suya pro-
pia, porque considerando que la divina Providencia lo habia en-
riquecido en tanta grandeza de imperio entre todos los Príncipes
cristianos, entendia que era para que hubiese quien sirviese á
la iglesia de Cristo, y defendiese y sustentase la fe católica. [64]

Herrera allows a political sense for Philip's action as well
as a religious one. Everyone, he says, should understand that
«el mayor cuidado de los turcos era acercarse al poniente para
meter el pie en España, y hacerse señores de lo que restaba». [65]
Furthermore, the Turks had in recent years dealt Spain a series
of humiliating blows in the struggle for control of Northern
Africa. Philip II inherited from his father a rapidly deteriorat-
ing situation in the Mediterranean. Venetian co-operation in
an earlier league with Spain had come to an end owing to such
fiascos as the battle of Prevesa («la vergonzosa retirada de la
Prevesa» [66]) and squabbles over Castelnuovo which resulted in
its unsuccessful defense. The burden of the Prevesa defeat, in
which, having Barbarossa's inferior forces penned up inside the
gulf, Doria for whatever reason decided not to attack and, be-
calmed, was unable even to make his escape without the loss of
several ships, had fallen heavily on the Spanish admiral. [67] Herrera felt the deep scars of this embarrassment on Spanish honor,
but staunchly defends Doria, «capitán de gran nombre, y de tanto
valor y prudencia», [68] blaming instead the friction between Venetians and Spaniards, and specifically the Venetian distrust of
Spanish collaboration and the «malicia de los capitanes». [69] Thus
our historian manages to cast Doria in the role of a brave captain
afflicted with less ardent subordinates. Herrera does not find
it necessary to spell out the subsequent losses sustained by the
imperial forces in North Africa at Algiers, Tripoli, Bugia, Tenes,
Dellys and Vélez de la Gomera in the remaining years of
Charles V's rule, which left Spain with less strength than she had

[64] *Ibid.*, p. 289.
[65] *Ibid.*, p. 292.
[66] *Ibid.*, p. 332.
[67] Merriman, III, 326-327.
[68] Herrera, *Relacion*, p. 332.
[69] *Ibid.*, p. 337.

enjoyed at the end of Ferdinand's reign. Instead he jumps to Philip's first severe Mediterranean setback, the defeat of Gerba (Gelves) in 1560, where an ill-informed Spanish fleet, headed by the Viceroy of Sicily, Juan de la Cerda, Duke of Medinaceli, with the elder Doria's grandson, Gian Andrea, and Don Álvaro de Sande, Spanish commander at Naples, while seeking the Turkish foe, was taken unawares by him at Gerba. The Viceroy and Doria managed to escape, leaving Don Álvaro and six thousand men (Herrera says five) to defend the castle. While Philip procrastinated about sending aid to Gerba, the Turks were not so hesitant; and Gerba, with Don Álvaro, was captured. Sande, according to the judgment of modern historians, failed to seize any opportunities he may have had to strike his assailants.[70] Herrera describes these thousands of «fortisimos soldados» as overwhelmed by the unexpected «fortaleza y obediencia y orden militar que los turcos mostraban en las jornadas de tierra», but fully impressed by the peril to which their timidity would expose all of Christendom.[71] Later, while lambasting «la poca prudencia con que se tentó aquella empresa»,[72] he conjures up once again the miraculous recovery of Spanish valor in the face of overwhelming odds and the great amazement of the Turks, «espantados de tan grande valor, cuanta era la fortaleza y tolerancia de los españoles».[73]

For Herrera, Philip II, though never a direct combattant, takes on the familiar pose of the spirited warrior, undaunted by even the greatest of odds. Herrera never points, as do twentieth-century historians, to the crippling delays which the Prudent King forced on his captains, often making their defeat nearly a foregone conclusion.[74] Rather he remarks of the monarch's attitude in the wake of disaster at Gerba: «mas no por eso habia desmayado el Rey Filipo, aunque le sucedio tambien el infortunio de su armada en la tempestad del puerto de la Herradura.»[75] He refers to the seemingly needless tragedy in which twenty-five out of twenty-eight Spanish ships and vast numbers of men, including one of Spain's best admirals, Don Juan de Mendoza,

---

[70] Merriman, IV, 101 ff.
[71] Herrera, *Relacion,* pp. 333-334.
[72] *Ibid.,* p. 337.
[73] *Ibid.,* p. 338.
[74] Merriman, IV, 101 ff.
[75] Herrera, *Relacion,* p. 338.

were dashed against the Spanish coast where they had sought refuge in a storm. Instead of giving way under the weight of this series of catastrophes, Herrera tells us, Philip ordered his forces to take the Peñón de Vélez as well as to go to the aid of Malta. In neither case does he give us the slightest indication of the false starts involved in these situations.[76] It now appears that Philip's indecisiveness very nearly caused Malta's fall, despite the repeated urgent appeals of Don García de Toledo, who in the end saved the day. In his account of the succor of Malta, far from complete, Herrera does concentrate his praise on the person of Don García and his «singular osadía».[77]

These defeats and narrow scrapes of Christendom in years past rightly inflame Christian monarchs to vengeance rather than cow them into defensive postures. Yet to seek to thwart the Turks precisely by entering into an alliance with Venice, who stood to gain the most in any event, and who had not come to Spain's aid in her hour of need, meant setting aside a personal grievance, seeing one's own actions in their total significance.

Herrera sees Philip's action in Messianic terms, as dedicating him to a new and glorious crusade:

> ¿Y cual podia ser mas glorioso título y honra mas estimada, que poniendo aparte las pasiones proprias, seguir la causa de Cristo, y por su defensa oponer las armas á los que lo perseguian? Con esto se hicieron esclarecidos y admirables los antiguos Reyes cristianos; esto fué lo que les dió nombre de justos y piadosos, de católicos y cristianísimos. Por esto habian muchos Príncipes poderosos desamparando su tierra, su casa y sus proprios contentos, y en regiones muy apartadas de las suyas, entre el rigor del frio y del calor, sufriendo mucha hambre y trabajos, con las armas en las manos peleando con infieles gentes y bárbaras, habian defendido la honra de Jesucristo, que no olvidado de su piedad los favoreció siempre en todo y les dió victorias maravillosas en la tierra y gloria en el cielo.[78]

Herrera thus casts the present in a literary mold, based on the now legendary conflicts of the past. He makes as much as possible of the fact that the Christian prince who takes up arms for Christianity performs a selfless deed, denying himself the

---

[76] Merriman, IV, 117 ff.
[77] Herrera, *Relacion,* p. 338.
[78] *Ibid.,* pp. 291-292.

comforts of the good life which he has been given in order to defend the «honra» of Jesus. It is important for him to remove the enterprise of the League from the realm of individual political ambition. In the case of Philip II and the Pope, he achieves this to a greater extent than with Venice, which seems to obey a pendular motion from good to evil, from self-interest to noble motivation.

In actual fact, Spain shared deeply in the blame for delay in forming a league. Philip II, it must be said, was set about with troubles when Pius V first sent out the alarm, much more so than Herrera, with his concern for preserving the integrity of Spain's reputation, is willing to admit. The situation in the Netherlands, the Moorish revolt and the turbulence which surrounded the life and death of Prince Carlos were only the beginning of his troubles. By the latter two circumstances, Spain's prestige had suffered considerable damage.[79] If Philip found himself able in 1569 to respond favorably to the Pope's appeal, he could do so because his own affairs for the moment showed at least a semblance of order, and because he was eager to restore the damage done to his reputation. However, although he sent word to Zúñiga, his ambassador in Rome, that «En lo que toca a la liga con venecianos, será bien que[s] estéis prevenidos para dezir a S. S. quando halgo os preguntare sobre ello, lo que se os scrivió a XII de octubre, de lo mucho que yo holgaria dello aviendo de ser para tan buen effecto y servicio de N. Senor»,[80] he appears to have been in no hurry to fit out an expedition for Venice's benefit, especially when it seemed more and more obvious that Venice wished merely for a temporary arrangement.[81] Thus Philip did probably do much to delay the preparations for the departure of the fleet in 1570, when Venice might actually have been able to regain Cyprus, and finally placed so many conditions on Doria's departure that his general's hands were virtually tied.

Both Paruta and Fougasses find much to criticize in Philip's

---

[79] Merriman, IV, 127.
[80] Luciano Serrano, *Correspondencia diplomática entre España y la Santa Sede* (Madrid, 1914), III, 50. Cf. also *Correspondencia privada de Felipe II con su secretario Mateo Vázquez, 1567-1591*, ed. Carlos Riba García (Madrid, 1959), Vol. I.
[81] Merriman, IV, 128.

dilatory tactics: «the Kings Councell made sundry difficulties»[82] such as insisting on a Spanish commander-in-chief for the enterprise, while allowing for the very real and reasonable possibility that the Venetians might be using Philip's name to improve their position for an early settlement with the Turks.[83] According to Paruta, only the insistence of Luis de Torres, the Pope's envoy to Philip, managed to obtain orders which would permit Doria and his fleet to sail for Sicily and release Spanish grain stores to feed the hungry troops already aboard Venetian and Papal ships.[84] Philip's unbridled magnanimity as Herrera saw it was in fact responsible for delaying departure of the fleet until the favorable season for navigation had nearly ended. His letters to Zúñiga indicate that Philip's eagerness to ascribe his actions to selfless motives matched Herrera's, but it seems fair to say that reasons of state and of God were not always in harmony.

Spanish intervention in the conflict in 1571 is decisive in a very literal way. Philip II, obedient servant of Christ and the Pope, furnished from his royal coffers at least one-half of the material support for the enterprise and in fact more, since he also helped the Pope bring his actual strength up to the one-sixth which had been part of the terms of the agreement. Herrera's facts about Philip's share in the financial burden of the League are corroborated by every account I have seen, including Paruta and Fougasses, and the modern historians. What Herrera neglects to mention, whether out of loyalty or ignorance, is that Philip withheld final approval on the condition that Pius V give him certain clerical benefices, and that he insisted that both Admiral and Vice-Admiral of the fleet be Spaniards, delays which elicited Venetian suspicion of the Spaniards' «idle excuses» and «excessive demands».[85] The French historian accuses Spanish distrust of the Venetians, «which suspicion still increasing did much coole the treaty of the league, which was begunne with such earnest heate».[86] Historians who lean toward the side of Venice inevitably blame a sixteenth-century bureaucratic tangle,

---

[82] Fougasses, p. 382.
[83] Ibid., p. 382.
[84] Paruta, pp. 27-28.
[85] Fougasses, p. 395.
[86] Ibid., p. 395.

«la lenta ed esasperante macchina burocratica spagnuola»,[87] for the late departure of Don Juan and his fleet. Fougasses portrays the Venetians as eager to set sail from Sicily in pursuit of the Turkish armada, while the Spaniards insist on waiting for Don Juan, thereby inflicting an unreasonable delay on the entire enterprise.[88] Paruta describes the Venetians' unhappiness over the fact that Philip seemed perfectly willing to allow still another summer to elapse without taking decisive action.[89] His sense of mission appears to have been far stronger on the occasion of the Invincible Armada, if we follow Mattingly's conclusions.[90] There, too, however, Philip managed to delay the proceedings by his unrealistic underestimates of the military strength demanded for the venture. Mattingly pictures the Prudent King urging on the much more circumspect Duke of Medina Sidonia against the latter's better judgment.

Yet Herrera everywhere insists that Philip's financial backing of the League is of far less importance ultimately than the spirit of determination and valor brought by the Spanish commander and his men which proved decisive in making the desired League a fact, and in tipping the balance in the Christians' favor in the hour of battle. Philip II and Don Juan de Austria, who, Herrera is quick to point out, are sons of the Emperor Charles V, emerge as the most illustrious champions of a national and religious cause pictured in terms inherited from the imperial days. This ideal, «la ilusión de una cristiandad dirigida moralmente bajo la vigilancia de las armas»,[91] attaches itself particularly to the person of the Emperor in Cervantes as well, far overshadowing Philip II. Maravall remarks that the author of Don Quijote could not fail to be more attracted to the king who challenged his opponent (Francis I) to a duel in hopes of settling the differences between them.[92] But in Herrera, though Philip is

---

[87] *Corrispondenza di Leonardo Donà (1570-1573)*, ed. Mario Bruneti and Eligio Vitale, introd. by Fernand Braudel (Venice-Rome, 1963), p. xxvi.
[88] Fougasses, p. 407.
[89] Paruta, p. 121; P. Daru, *Histoire de la République de Venise* (Paris, 1821), IV, 160-161.
[90] Garrett Mattingly, *The Defeat of the Spanish Armada* (New York, 1965).
[91] José Antonio Maravall, *El humanismo de las armas en Don Quijote*, prologue by Don Ramón Menéndez Pidal (Madrid, 1948), p. 229.
[92] *Ibid.*, p. 231 ff. See also Américo Castro, *Hacia Cervantes* (Madrid, 1960), p. 338, note 1, on Cervantes' antipathy toward Philip II. For another of Herrera's contemporaries who had scant liking for the Emperor's son, see Francisco

not emperor, he presides as the strong arm of the Church over an effort which will culminate in gathering all of Europe and the Mediterranean world into the camp of Christ.

What, if any, is the relation of Herrera to the defenders of Charles V and his role in the international scene? We might consider the works of Alfonso de Valdés as an example. The *Diálogo de Latancio y el Arcidiano,* or *Diálogo de las cosas ocurridas en Roma,* is published following a highly controversial event, the sack of Rome in 1527 by the imperial troops, which resulted in a volley of criticism being leveled at the Spanish monarch, primarily from ecclesiastical quarters both within Spain and without [93]. Valdés finds himself in a difficult spot. He must explain away Charles's role in the distasteful event, if possible, or find a justification for what has occurred. One such explanation might have sufficed, but he prefers to work with both questions at once, perhaps a little inconsistently at that. First of all, Charles, who is performing a divine mission in his European campaigns, can do no wrong. [94] Valdés asserts that the sack of Rome was not ordered by the Emperor and did not carry his approval. It was due rather to the impetuous, even bellicose nature of the troops, who simply became carried away by a thirst for violence and plunder. Charles does not in any way partake in this unattractive picture. Valdés, then, pursuing the matter of a justification for the atrocities committed, claims that God chose to make Charles V an instrument of divine will without the latter's knowledge in order to punish the leaders of the Roman Church for having neglected their sacred trust and fallen into an abject state of mortal sin. [95] Valdés seeks to remove from the tainted sphere of political maneuver a rather sordid episode and elevate it to a position of importance as part of a transcendental scheme. In this case the enemy is both external and internal: politically Rome resisted Spain's advances, but she still belonged inside the fold of the faith. Valdés places his emphasis on the latter aspect. This follower of Erasmus concentrates on the need for reform within the Church now debased with corruption.

Márquez Villanueva, *Don Luis Zapata o el sentido de una fuente cervantina* (Badajoz, 1966), p. 32 ff.
[93] Alfonso de Valdés; Bataillon, *Erasmo y España,* pp. 368-386.
[94] Valdés, pp. 17-18.
[95] *Ibid.,* p. 14 ff.

Herrera's protagonists are not divine missionaries for the reform of orthodoxy. In the days following the Councils of Trent, Erasmus had fallen nearly to the level of a heretic.[96] It had become unfashionable and unwise to mention his name, and ideas such as those of Valdés were voiced only in the most carefully disguised fashion. If there was an enemy within, it was most certainly not in the person of the Roman Church. The so-called «luteranos» of Seville, the most vocal critics of the clerical establishment in the generation after Valdés, were systematically eliminated by the Inquisition in the 1550's for daring to suggest the importance of faith and private prayer, and for deploring the lack of knowledge of the Scriptures among their fellow clergymen.[97] Imaginative literature which echoed, however circumspectly, these themes was officially purged and continued its life underground. Herrera was doubtless exposed to this struggle within the Spanish Church. Doctor Constantino Ponce de la Fuente,[98] and Doctor Egidio[99] as well were connected with the Cathedral in Seville at a time which would correspond to Herrera's most formative years. Both were extremely popular and widely heard preachers. Furthermore, their denunciation was staged publicly in order to bring maximum infamy upon them. Herrera's writings are filled with denunciations of heresy, of traitors to the Divine Cause, but he does not mention any Spanish or Sevillian instances, for whatever reason.

We should not look for mention of Erasmists by Herrera were it not for several connections which suggest themselves among Herrera's acquaintances and literary sources. One of these is the already mentioned work of Alfonso de Valdés, a possible source (whose substance, to be sure, was greatly recast) for Herrera's Messianic concept of the Spanish monarchy, and particularly for the Old Testament Biblical language he employs constantly to describe the ruler as God's instrument to castigate the proud, to break the oppressor's yoke and destroy his ambitions.

---

[96] Bataillon, *Erasmo y España*, Chapter XIII, «El Erasmismo condenado», p. 699 ff.
[97] *Ibid.*, p. 515 ff.
[98] Bataillon, *Erasmo y España*, p. 522 ff.; Constantino Ponce de la Fuente, *Suma de doctrina cristiana*, ed. Luis de Usoz, *Reformistas Antiguos Españoles*, Vol. XIX (Madrid, 1863).
[99] Bataillon, *Erasmo y España*, p. 524 ff.

To be sure, divine punishment and reward form the basis for more than one interpretation of history in sixteenth- and seventeenth-century Spain.[100] This view informs Pero Mexía's evaluation of the Comunero uprising in the *Historia del Emperador Carlos Quinto*:

> Dos años y medio habia, y aun no cabales, que el Emperador habia venido á estos reinos, y gobernádolos por su persona y presencia, y los tenia en mucha tranquilidad, paz y justicia, cuando el demonio, sembrador de mañas, comenzó á alterar los pensamientos de algunos pueblos y gentes, de tal manera, que se levantaron después tempestades, alborotos y sediciones. como digo, fué obra del demonio; el cual, pesándole de los buenos sucesos deste rey, y de la paz y justicia que en Castilla habia, se dió tan buena maña *(permitiéndolo Dios por nuestros pecados, y por ventura para castigo del mismo pueblo, y para prueba de la paciencia y clemencia del Emperador, y otros fines que él sabe)*, que en lugar de quietud y tranquilidad, puso desasosiego y temor.[101]

Divine justice governs the sucess and ultimate failure of Catalan and Aragonese arms in Greece in Francisco de Moncada's account of the *Expedición de los catalanes y aragoneses contra turcos y griegos*. Diego Hurtado de Mendoza, in the *Guerra de Granada*, admits a divine arbiter of that conflict; yet Spanish Christian virtue seems to him so little in evidence, that the outcome remains in doubt until the last. In general, this interpretation plays a much humbler role in these other histories than in Herrera's *Relación*, where it is present not only as a fundamental assumption behind the events described, but also in the extremely conspicuous Old Testament diction. Only Juan Rufo, who borrows heavily from Herrera, gives such thoroughgoing emphasis to this view.

Another factor is Herrera's close association with the Sevillian humanist Juan de Mal Lara, who, being older than Herrera by a decade, and occupying an extremely distinguished position among the intellectuals of the city, would have encouraged and perhaps at times guided Herrera's studies and literary efforts

---

[100] For the history of this concept in fifteenth-century Spanish works, see Américo Castro, *Aspectos del vivir hispánico* (Santiago, Chile, 1949). One striking example of Messianic interpretation of history in this period is the Bachiller Palma's *Divina Retribución sobre la caída de España en tiempo del noble rey Don Juan el primero* (Madrid, 1879).

[101] Pero Mexía, *Historia del Emperador Carlos V*, ed. Juan de Mata Carriazo, in *Colección de Crónicas Españolas* (Madrid, 1945), p. 367. My italics.

until his death just before the battle of Lepanto. We know that Mal Lara did his share of writing to the glory of the Spanish monarchy, for example by his account of the «Recebimiento que hizo la ciudad de Sevilla al Rey D. Phelipe II» (1570).[102] This amounts mainly to a description of the elaborate pageantry Seville had prepared to greet the monarch. The *Philosophia vulgar,* published in 1568, is actually of more interest to us here. Américo Castro and Francisco Sánchez Escribano have pointed up the Erasmist echoes in this work. Sánchez Escribano's study[103] shows how citations of Erasmus by name were eliminated from the text by the Inquisitorial censors, and subsequently restored surreptitiously by Mal Lara himself. The themes of the good life as portrayed by Erasmus are everywhere present. Surely so faithful a disciple as Mal Lara appears to have been would at least have mentioned his name among friends and discussed his ideas if he were so bold as to offer a manuscript containing overt mention of him for publication in 1568.

Perhaps it was Mal Lara who introduced Herrera to the *Poetices Libri Septem* of Julius Caesar Scaliger, the French literary theorist and critic. The last book of this treatise on the art of poetry is filled with references to Erasmus («magnum fuit Erasmi nomen»), the extent of his learning and the skillfulness of his style. Although Herrera followed Scaliger quite closely in the *Anotaciones* to Garcilaso's work, not one of these concrete references passed into his own commentary.[104]

The lack of any concrete mention only means that the paths of influence, if indeed they exist, can be perceived more vaguely. Perhaps they are only indirect ones. Herrera's heavy use of Biblical diction does suggest a connection with Alfonso de Valdés. Another aspect of his thought which could tie him to the Valdés brothers is his emphasis on individual «costumbres». God sides with the just, not merely with those who have a nominal claim to his support. Herrera emphasizes Don Juan's exhortation to his men to look to their moral conduct in order that the expedition retain divine favor.[105] The Turks perish at

---

[102] Published by the Sociedad de Bibliófilos Andaluces, 1878.
[103] Sánchez Escribano, «Algunos aspectos de la elaboración de la *Philosophia vulgar*», *RFE,* XXII (1935), 274-284.
[104] Julius Caesar Scaliger, *Poetices Libri Septem,* facsimile of the Lyon 1561 edition (Stuttgart, 1964), p. 364.
[105] As does Cervantes in *La Numancia.* In the first *jornada* (ll. 40 ff.), he

Lepanto not only because they are infidels, but because they are motivated by greed. Finally, as we shall have occasion to see again, Philip II and Don Juan de Austria emerge not only as the right arm of the Lord, but as models of the perfect Christian prince.

The cast of characters has changed from 1527 to 1571. In 1571, Rome and Spain find themselves political allies: theirs is a common enemy. Herrera states that the Turks's ultimate aim is to extend their influence to the westernmost end of the Mediterranean and Spain. In 1527, Rome had fallen into sin, and what might otherwise have been merely a petty squabble of a purely political character, had to be justified as God's punishment for his wayward flock. The enemy is within, and the plea, one for reform for its own sake. Herrera too urges the reform of Christian peoples, but in order to win God's help in repelling the Moslems. The cosmic view is essentially the same: God will avenge the just and castigate the proud. To be a nominal Christian is not sufficient; one must live an upright life.

Thus there seems to be some reason to believe that Herrera had been influenced by the thinking of the Spanish Erasmists. But the religious question is necessarily posed in different terms. Catholicism as a form of worship and as a doctrine is not challenged. Rome once again stands for pure orthodoxy. Herrera is not at all interested in reforming the fibre of Roman practice. Alfonso de Valdés, like his brother Juan, was interested in purifying the underlying faith and in eliminating what he considered to be superficial trappings and an unnecessary, vain show of false piety. To their opponents in the ecclesiastical establishment, the Valdés brothers and other kindred spirits were flirting dangerously with Protestant heresies. After the Council of Trent, the lines of orthodox faith have been much more clearly drawn. Luther and the Protestants —English and Dutch— have been denounced as heretics, and the Roman Church has raised its own banners of reform. In comparing Valdés to Herrera, we see that reformer and wayward sinner have exactly changed places. Valdés' reforms were directed from the periphery to the center. Herrera sees the core of faith, Rome, solid and intact. The di-

shows Escipión urging his men to put aside vice before they seek a military victory. *Comedias y entremeses,* ed. Schevill and Bonilla, V, 106.

rection of reform becomes centrifugal. The church hierarchy, once looked on as the scourge of the faith, now sees the same seeds of destruction being planted by the erstwhile reformers. Spain alone evinces hardly a shadow of internal restlessness. She has drawn herself together, and presents to the world a united front, the determination of one at peace with herself. Herrera does not seem to share Mal Lara's concern, still very Erasmian in 1568, for the integrity of the Church herself. He sees countless Catholics going astray, but there are no Spaniards among them; and their waywardness is always depicted as a pestilence, an evil spell cast by Protestants and Lutherans, not a pestilence which is born within, even though it may send down very deep roots. Furthermore, as we shall have occasion to consider later, the ideals of virtue which Herrera sees as being threatened have a curiously secular character.

Optimism and pessimism about human nature keep close company in Herrera's thoughts. There are essentially two kinds of men, human and inhuman, Christians and barbarians. Of the latter, not much can be expected, and the attitude to be adopted toward them is fundamentally one of distrust.[106] But what of the other group? These are human, which always seems to imply potentially virtuous. Herrera expresses deep dismay over his own historical moment: Christians have fallen into the way of sinners. Christian nations are torn with dissension. Under the fatal spell of widely extended heresies which Herrera places together under the single term «luteranismo», Christians everywhere have allowed themselves to grow forgetful of the one true religion and to ignore its plight. Philip II, Don Juan de Austria and the Spanish soldiers represent the heights to which man can rise when he places himself in harmony with divine will. Furthermore, men are capable of being moved in this direction by exhortation and example. Don Juan's conduct, and that of his captains, in particular Don Álvaro de Bazán, Marquis of Santa Cruz, inspire and transform spirits of lesser strength. Herrera, who is followed in this by Mariana, places great emphasis in his narrative, too, on the untiring efforts of the Pontiff,

---

[106] An exception to this rule is found in the case of Alí Bajá, commander-in-chief of the Turkish forces. On the occasion of his death, Herrera states that «Fue su muerte llorada de los esclavos cristianos, de quien era muy amado por el buen tratamiento y humanidad que usaba con ellos.» *Relacion*, p. 363.

seeking in his greater wisdom to weld the differing wills of his flock into the firmness of one single purpose. Herrera pictures the company of the just beseeching God with prayers and tears that He might fire the hearts of Christians with the desire for victory. Finally, after much fasting and penitence on the part of the Roman clergy, God grants «por la industria y solicitud de aquel ministro suyo» [107] that the serenity of peace should dawn among such darkness and confusion: «esclareció un sereno dia entre aquella confusion y tinieblas». [108]

Modern accounts tend to give the Pope a lion's share of the credit for the eventual accomodation of Venetian and Spanish interests. That more than prayers and tears were involved in these arrangements should be evident by now. One historian shows the Pope as utterly unwilling to be swayed by either Spanish or Venetian reasons of state, but sufficiently persevering to end their stalemate. [109] Only the contemporary Venetian and French accounts attempt to take away the Pontiff's glory. After piously presenting the resolve of the Venetian Senate to place their cause in the hands of the «padre commune» [110] of all Christianity, Paruta takes Pius V to task for delaying the League with his credulity:

> era il Pontefice di facile impressione, essendo da quelli, che immoderatamente per loro particolari interessi fauoriuano la causa de gli Spagnuoli, diversamente persuaso, ò adheriua, ò non si opponeua gagliardamente con la sua auttorità à quelle cose, che tuttauia si vedeuano potere, ò indebolire la lega, ò ritardarne la conclusione. [111]

If the Pope did lean in the direction of Spain, he had obvious financial reasons for doing so. No doubt his decisions were reinforced by the insistent presence in Rome of Cardinal Granvelle and Zúñiga, who ultimately managed to enlist Philip's full participation in the 1571 expedition. [112] Following Lepanto the Pope appears to have been almost alone in his interest to preserve the League intact.

---

[107] *Ibid.*, p. 292.
[108] *Ibid.*, p. 292.
[109] John Lynch, *Spain under the Hapsburgs* (New York, 1964), I, 226.
[110] Paruta, p. 25.
[111] *Ibid.*, p. 122; Fougasses, pp. 398-399.
[112] Henri Hauser, *La prépondérance espagnole 1559-1660* (Paris, 1948), p. 89.

CHAPTER THREE

DIVINE PROVIDENCE AND THE CONCEPT OF HEROIC VIRTUE

1. The Search for Fame

Mosquera de Figueroa's Preface, as we have seen, situates the *Relacion* in the context of a notion of heroic virtue widely held during the Renaissance. This concept emerges as perhaps the central concern of Herrera's narrative, holding at least equal sway with the religious struggle at issue. Herrera's verse, too, envisions his political and military heroes reaching upward with their noble deeds to an immortal realm of light. This realm is described in terms identical to those which portray the gleaming regions of Beauty and Love in the erotic poems, and may quite probably be one and the same to Herrera. The dead heroes of Spain have their apotheosis as they are converted into the pure, undying light of Virtue. In a sonnet of the 1582 edition, which for inexplicable reasons was not kept in the Pacheco edition, Herrera finds in the irrevocable passing of time reason to shun worldly beauty and fame and to take refuge in the only permanent value — Virtue:

> Ya el rigor importuno i grave ielo
> desnuda los esmaltes i belleza
> de la pintada tierra, i con tristeza
> s'ofende en niebla oscura el claro cielo.
>   Mas, Pacheco, este mesmo órrido suelo
> reverdece, i pomposo su riqueza
> muestra, i del blanco mármol la dureza
> desata de Favonio el tibio buelo.

> Pero el dulce color i hermosura
> de nuestra umana vida cuando huye
> no torna, ¡ô mortal suerte!, ¡ô breve gloria!
>   Mas sola la virtud nos assegura;
> qu'el tiempo avaro, aunqu'esta flor destruye,
> contra ella nunca osó intentar vitoria.[1]

Time's tragic flight impels man to find his salvation within the eternal light of Beauty or Virtue. All of the soul's striving will be to deserve to attain this goal:

> Mas el valor, el noble entendimiento,
> el espirtu, el intento generoso
> aciende a la region de luz serena.[2]

Mosquera, in talking about why men enjoy reading history, asserts that it is because they are uplifted by the mention of glorious exploits and spurred on to seek immortality for themselves in similar ways. Men not naturally wooed by the prospects of eternal fame —being unusually base souls— tend nonetheless instinctively to shun action which would immortalize them in infamy. In the *Relación*, «all the world's a stage», and the audience is eternity. Each actor in this temporal drama has confidence that his actions will achieve a resonance beyond the span of his lifetime. He is conscious of the immanence and imminence of divine and human judgment of his conduct. This appears to hold true as much for the infidel as for the Christian. The man of valor acts out of a positive impulse toward virtue and thence toward glory; the coward tries to shield his deeds from everlasting notoriety.

The perfect hero remains steadfast and above any form of fear at all times, keeping his sights exclusively on the furtherance of a noble cause, which will automatically heap fame on him. Yet simple confidence in the felicitous outcome of one's enterprise cannot be said to be a necessary or even desirable asset. The Turks, for example, have an inflated false courage, or rather confidence in their own invincibility. This they possess by virtue of having intimidated their less powerful enemies. The arrogance of their brute strength alone creates the illusion of valor

---

[1] Herrera, *Poesías*, ed. Vicente García de Diego (Madrid, 1914), sonnet 65.
[2] Herrera, *Versos*, ed. Pacheco (Seville, 1619), Bk. II, sonnet 64.

which often descends to outright cruelty. Furthermore, the minute their superiority is challenged, they fall into confusion and dismay, as when they discover the Albanians conspired against them with the Venetians, or as when they find that their intelligence has been faulty just before the battle of Lepanto is to be joined. Not only have they underestimated the forces of the League by almost a third, but they are also unexpectedly facing Spaniards as one-half of their enemy.

Venetian, French and Spanish accounts indicate that there was faulty intelligence on both sides of the conflict. The Venetian accounts (Paruta) do not make any mention of Turkish fright when Turks find themselves pitted against Spaniards. Paruta explains in his *Historia della guerra di Cipro* that Turkish forces easily seized Cyprus, «Essendo molto maggiore la perizia e la virtù de' suoi soldati, nell'espugnare le fortezze, che non era l'arte e l'industria de' christiani nel fabbricarle o nel diffenderle, come s'avea per tante esperienze potuto conoscere.» [3] Whether this is in fact intended to embrace all Christians, or merely Venetians, is not clear; but the Turks appear to warrant admiration in any case. Herrera attributes the eventual rallying of the Turks, in the first instance, to realization of their own cowardice and of the shame this could shed on them. In the second, it is a question of the aforementioned «obstinada furia y desesperada bestialidad». To fight vigorously for fear of shame does not count in Herrera's scheme of things. This type of fighting still must be reckoned with, of course, since it makes for an often formidable enemy; but it does not constitute true heroism.

Heroism in Herrera's account often seems to be the opposite of prudence as well, especially the sort of cautiousness which shuns a battle because it does not feel adequately prepared in material terms. While Herrera does not condemn such an attitude, he shows it in a light which can only be considered disparaging. We see this, I think, in the episode of 1570 which immediately precedes the final negotiations of the League. Spanish forces under Don Álvaro de Bazán, the Marquis of Santa Cruz, and Doria have already joined the Venetian and Italian fleet in the Mediterranean with the idea of helping them to

---

[3] Paolo Paruta, *Historia vinetiana, Parte Seconda* (Venice, 1605); quoted in P. Daru, *Histoire de la République de Venise* (Paris, 1821), IV, 147.

combat the Turkish menace. A council of war is held, and the consensus is that they return to Venetian strongholds, according to Herrera, «contra el parecer de D. Álvaro de Bazan, que decia que pasasen adelante y peleasen».[4] The crushing blow to the enterprise comes when news reaches the fleet concerning the defeat and massacre of the defenders of Nicosia. This disaster fills the Venetians especially with terror of their enemy who had now actually entrenched himself in the territory of Venice.

> Considerando esto los venecianos, y la grande fuerza del enemigo, y la comodidad que tenia para reformarse, y con cuanta desigualdad de gente lo iban á buscar, *tomaron por expediente* volverse y proveer á las cosas de Candía, y enviar algun socorro á Famagosta.[5]

Don Álvaro de Bazán thinks not in terms of an equal match, in terms of expediency. Venetian timidity has unfortunate consequences:

> Con esta resolucion dieron todos la vuelta, engañando las esperanzas que muchos tenian del infelice suceso y de la vitoria de tan grande armada, lo cual quebrantó grandemente los ánimos de los hombres, que por los principios juzgaban ya el fin de aquella empresa y esperaban mayores daños, temiendo de aquella la última ruina, y con un dolor general, que hizo desmayar los ánimos de todos, se dolia aquella esclarecida Republica enseñada a varias mudanzas por la altivez y confianza que le naceria á Selin de haber tomado á Nicosia sin que osasen socorrella los venecianos, teniendo en su favor las galeras de Italia, y con igual sentimiento de todos gemia aquella grande perdida.[6]

Dread of a far more powerful enemy is a normal reaction among the rank and file of fighting men. Yet a fine commander will not permit this emotion to take over the minds of his men. Herrera observes here that in avoiding the object of their fear, the Venetians do not find peace. Defeated and fleeing another encounter, their spirit is broken, and they are oppressed by the knowledge that they have fed the raging beast of their opponents' self-confidence. Furthermore, rumor spreads the possibility that there is discord among the Papal and Venetian admirals, and

---

[4] Herrera, *Relacion de la guerra de Cipre*, in C.D.I., XXI (Madrid, 1852), 287.
[5] *Ibid.*, p. 288. Italics mine.
[6] *Ibid.*, p. 288.

even that Venice has decided once again to seal her own defeat in an agreement with the Turks. Expediency simply does not constitute a justifiable motive in a heroic world.[7]

The Venetian version of this episode reads quite differently. Paruta dwells in somewhat greater detail on the war councils. Two divergent plans emerge, according to his account. One proposed that the Christian armada should seek to harrass the Turks, thus drawing them away from Cyprus, to which the Christians could then have free access.[8] The other advised against undertaking so risky a venture late in the season. The Marquis of Santa Cruz's views do not hold the same interest for the Venetian historian as for Herrera. One could argue that Herrera's view of Don Álvaro de Bazán's character was already well formed before he conceived of writing the *Relacion,* since it had been converted many times into poetry. Be that as it may, Paruta has an entirely different set of heroes for the war of Cyprus. General Zane, a Venetian, is one of these. In the war councils he urges a bold attack on Cyprus, supported by General Veniero.[9] At the news of the loss of Nicosia, Paruta points an accusing finger at Gian Andrea Doria, who, he says, declares that he only has permission to bring aid to Nicosia and carries Philip's authorization for no other expedition.[10] This determination, Paruta claims, merely serves to reinforce the will of the «ardentissimo» Veniero.[11] Nonetheless Doria and Spain ultimately undo the expedition by their abrupt departure. The judgment of modern historians has inclined to blame Doria,

---

[7] It is regrettable from many standpoints that Herrera's evaluation, if there was one, of the defeat of the Armada is not extant. For one thing, it would be enlightening to have his judgment of the Duke of Medina Sidonia, commander of La Gran Armada. Here is a figure who, though certainly not out of mere expediency, judged his forces to be insufficient for the job to be accomplished, and judged himself inadequate to guide such an enterprise. His pleas to Philip II to be relieved of his responsibility and to gain delays for the Armada's departure were constantly refused by the man who bore the title «el Prudente». When the Armada met defeat, much of the blame was cast on the Duke, and he was accused of lack of valor and lack of confidence. From all that can be ascertained about his performance in the hour of battle, it appears that he fought steadfastly and with great valor, against odds of whose extent he was only too aware. Yet his initial caution was interpreted as disastrous by his contemporaries. It remained for the twentieth century to vindicate his extraordinary abilities. Cf. Garrett Mattingly, *The Defeat of the Spanish Armada* (New York, 1965).

[8] Paruta, pp. 139-140.
[9] *Ibid.,* p. 97.
[10] *Ibid.,* p. 99.
[11] *Ibid.,* p. 100.

although Father Navarrete has urged that all the responsibility should not be laid upon him.[12] For, despite his delaying tactics and small regard for the Venetians (which was apparently mutual), the Venetians' fleet was highly unprepared for an encounter at such a moment; and Doria could be considered wise for having avoided it.

In Herrera's narrative, Don Álvaro's role in this episode foreshadows the dynamic presence of Don Juan de Austria in the encounter at Lepanto. For Philip II, once again the only factor which carries any weight is his duty. He does not think about the odds which he faces, and he puts aside his own personal grievance with the Venetians.[13] The Turkish threat is a question of honor — divine honor, to be sure, as well as human, but honor which exacts the same requirements as secular, human honor. The proper reaction on learning of defeat is one of renewed determinations and a desire for revenge. With Herrera, it seems to be a requirement of true courage that the odds be overwhelmingly against one. Otherwise, one's courage might be suspected of being reinforced by the confidence that one has almost no chance of losing. This is true of all instances of real heroism in the *Relacion*.

The episode of Famagusta's defense is a case in point. The Venetian defenders of this Cyprian city-fortress hold out against insuperable odds for nearly a year. Herrera praises their determination in the face of death in terms which recall eulogies of Numancia's heroic residents, who suffered incredible privations rather than surrender to the Romans.[14] Herrera has special praise for Astor Baglione, leader of the Venetian band on Cyprus:

> jamás cesó de hacer reparos á este diseño de los turcos Astor Ballon, que siempre procuró perturbar y prevenir el intento dellos con todo el ingenio y arte que se podia requerir, porque su prudencia y valor era tan grande, y el amor que le tenian los soldados dispuestos á no dejallo, que cuando mas confiaban los turcos ganar la ciudad, hallaban mas difícil y peligrosa la esperanza.[15]

---

[12] Luis Fernández y Fernández de Retama, *España en tiempo de Felipe II*, in *Historia de España*, ed. Ramón Menéndez Pidal, Vol. XIX (Madrid, 1959), II, 75.
[13] Herrera, *Relacion*, pp. 289, 291-292; cf. pp. 44-45 above.
[14] Cf. J. A. Pérez-Rioja, «Numancia en la poesía», *Celtiberia* (Soria, 1954), IV, 69-103.
[15] Herrera, *Relacion*, p. 300.

Prudence and valor here are treated as complementary concepts. «Prudencia» seems to be associated with the «ingenio y arte» of which the Venetian captain availed himself to thwart the Turkish efforts. It is the classical virtue of «providentia», balanced judgment and equanimity in the moment of crisis, not a quality which would lead one to shy away from an encounter of doubtful outcome.

Herrera stresses the fact that the Venetians' bravery at Famagusta can almost be said to be due to the overwhelming odds they face:

> estaban ya reducidas todas las cosas en tanto extremo, que todo les faltaba sino la esperanza y el valor de los capitanes, y el ardor de los soldados, que animados de Ballon se mostraban tan valerosos y sin temor que eran forzados los turcos á celebrar y estimar en mucho la fortaleza de aquellos hombres determinados á sufrir todos los trabajos y fortunas de un cerco tan largo, y admirarse del valor de Astor Ballon, que dispuesto á morir en defensa de aquella ciudad, excedió las grandes esperanzas que todos tenian de su prudencia, constancia y valor. [16]

Hope and courage are the pure essence of heroic virtue and, to be seen in their most exalted form, must go unbuttressed by any material guarantees of victory. Even the Turks are made to appear more valiant after the odds have turned against them at last in the battle of Lepanto. So much so, in fact, that Don Juan counsels his generals to ease their prey towards land, for, as he says, on the high seas «la desesperación saca fuerzas». [17]

The long history of Turkish victories over Christians in the Mediterranean enables Herrera to show the heroism of Don Juan de Austria in a similar light. [18] He has elaborately set the stage for the battle of Lepanto by showing the physical superiority of the Moslems and all the psychological advantages they have gained by so thoroughly intimidating their enemies into a meek defensive posture. Don Juan does not succeed in bringing the Christian forces up to an equal level with those of the Turks, although his courage and enthusiasm do have the effect of rallying more such support to the League. But his heroic spirit has a far more important influence on the minds of his men.

---

[16] Herrera, *Relacion*, p. 303.
[17] *Ibid.*, p. 360.
[18] Cf. p. 45 above.

While the first half of the *Relación* in a sense belongs to the Turks who repeatedly overwhelm their enemies and put Christianity on the defensive, the last half belongs to the cause of the True Religion and in particular to Don Juan de Austria. Don Juan's arrival marks the midpoint of the narrative, the beginning of Chapter XV (there are twenty-eight chapters in all). He will thus right the balance between the Mediterranean powers in terms of the little book's structure as in actual fact.

Don Juan's status as hero and defender of the faith rests on solid foundations before his intervention in the Eastern Mediterranean. He comes fresh from putting down the revolt of the Alpujarras. Don Juan represents his brother King Philip II. Herrera most frequently measures them both not against ancient models, but rather against the exalted figure of their father, Charles V. After the naval battle has turned in the Christians' favor, Herrera remarks, «y pareció cosa maravillosa que así como á Solimano solo el Emperador Carlo Quinto pudo hacer huir afrentosamente, así al hijo Selin su hijo D. Juan pudiese vencer solo».[19] In so far as they inherit physically the stamp of Empire, they also stand for European religious unity in the face of growing discord.

Don Juan's will prevails in the councils of war at Messina. In response to the fears of more timid souls, Don Juan voices the ideals for which he and Philip stand:

> la voluntad del Rey su hermano era favorecer á la cristiandad contra la ruina que amenazaba Selin, y que para aquel efeto no convenian palabras, sino tales obras que le diesen á entender que en la religión de Cristo habia ánimos verdaderamente piadosos y que por la causa de Dios estaban prontos á sufrir todos los trabajos y peligros, y que aun no estaba acabado aquel antiguo valor de los cristianos.[20]

The brother of the Rey Católico emerges as a perfect Christian prince, bent on using his works in defense of the faith. His first order to the assemblage of troops urges the same moral standards for all:

> mandando primero á todos los que tenian gobierno en la dicha armada que procurasen que toda la gente viviese con mucha re-

---

[19] Herrera, *Relacion*, p. 370.
[20] *Ibid.*, p. 311.

> ligion, y paz y quietud para tener propicio á Dios en aquella jus-
> ta y santa empresa, porque muchas veces se ha visto por la poca
> piedad y disensiones de los soldados y por la codicia y maldad
> de los capitanes perderse empresa justísima contra los infieles,
> porque se ofendia la Magestad Divina de la torpe vida y falta
> de religion de los que seguian su causa. [21]

Not only do we find a moral and religious imperative imposed for its own sake, but as a precondition for the favor of a God who rigorously judges and castigates even his own.

What does this indicate about the underlying view of history? Herrera repeatedly asserts that it is man who must defend the faith on earth. That is to say, God no longer, as in truly mythical history, steps in to rescue his chosen favorites. Yet God retains a modified sort of omniscience and power. He rewards and punishes in a highly reasonable fashion. Herrera's scheme holds no place for the truly just and righteous who fail to obtain their goals. If they do not prevail, they must necessarily have done some kind of wrong, or at least some among their numbers must have erred. For the historian with this outlook, establishing the moral perfection of his protagonist becomes a prime concern.

Herrera depicts Don Juan's noble spirit as interested not in reinforcing his own self-confidence with minor victories, but in settling major issues. «Conforme á la voluntad que tenia», [22] Don Juan declines to let any of the armada's capacities be funneled off into enterprises of lesser consequence. He agrees with others of his generals:

> no les parecia á su juicio que se empleasen tantas fuerzas jun-
> tas de cristianos en empresas tan flacas y de tan poca importan-
> cia, las cuales aunque les sucediesen prósperamente, no eran para
> traelles aquella honra que podian alcanzar de seguir á la armada
> enemiga. [23]

Don Juan and the more illustrious of his captains share a drive for glory and honor which will be satisfied by no mean feats.

This will to glory meets the cry of rashness from among the ranks of the fearful, particularly the black sheep Venetians. The

---

[21] *Ibid.*, pp. 322-323.
[22] *Ibid.*, p. 330.
[23] *Ibid.*, p. 330.

latter insist again that it would be «mejor y mas puesto en razon» [24] simply to guard the fort until winter could make further harrassment by the Turks impossible. This kind of prudence does not deserve the name; it simply conceals cowardice. Don Juan's determination furthermore does not rule out caution. The very size of the enterprise makes it essential that there be at least a reasonable chance of success. Don Juan, however, presses reason into the service of courage. He assures the forces of the League that, with such a large army assembled under such great leaders and in the service of God, «no se intentaria cosa alguna incierta, sino con mucho conocimiento de las fuerzas del enemigo y cierta confianza de la vitoria». [25] Prudence may ally itself only with an aggressive posture in the true hero.

Confidence both in one's own capacities and in one's cause are preconditions of victory and constitute a kind of reason as well. Don Juan first wages battle against ignorance and fear. For those who continue to be intimidated by the recent record of Turkish victories, Don Juan asserts that they do not therefore automatically hold sway over the future: conditions change. He adds that the Christians are responsible for the rise of Turkish power, «por sola ignorancia». [26] Lack of knowledge in this case is tantamount to moral turpitude: timorous passivity, lack of wisdom in risking truly overwhelming odds (as in the case of the defeat of Gelves), and the petty stupidity of those who have used the Turks to tip the political balance within their own countries and later find themselves trapped. The armada of the Turks «con solo el nombre espantaba á la cristiandad». [27] Herrera's indignation characteristically vents itself in a long series of interrogatives which recount Don Juan's exposure of the Turkish myth. The hero must concern himself only with real obstacles:

> porque el buen suceso, no pendia de la mucha gente sino del valor y noticia de la guerra, y mayormente de la divina voluntad, que nunca desamparó las causas justas, ni apartó su favor de los

---

[24] *Ibid.*, p. 334.
[25] *Ibid.*, p. 340.
[26] *Ibid.*, p. 335.
[27] *Ibid.*, p. 332. In this passage, Herrera appears to echo Doctor Andrés Laguna in the *Viaje de Turquía*, where Pedro de Urdemalas declares that the ungrounded fear of the Christians «les da a ellos [the Turks] ánimo y victorias». In *Autobiografías y Memorias*, N.B.A.E., ed. M. Serrano y Sanz (Madrid, 1905), II, 120.

que la seguian con verdadera piedad; mas que la vitoria de los turcos no era dificil por su grandeza y imposibilidad, sino porque no la osaban emprender y intentar los cristianos, porque los hechos osados y gloriosos, aunque los deseaban muchos, los acometian pocos. [28]

Don Juan, with knowledge and confidence on his side, can make his enemies victims of fear. In fact, the fearlessness of the Spaniards has accomplished this in the past. By introducing the Maltese campaign as an example, Herrera again suggests that the Venetians are the culprits, that is, those who have allowed themselves to be put on the run. He also prepares, before the battle, the basis for a dramatic turn in the combat itself. When the Turks find that they are fighting against Spaniards, they lose their determination utterly. Herrera here as elsewhere stresses in exaggerated fashion —to judge from the absence of these details in other accounts— the power of the Spanish soldiers' reputation. Once again, Herrera seems to make this notion serve a literary purpose, that of portraying the Turks as antiheroes.

For Don Juan, the urgent imperative of action rests on his gentleman's honor. How long, he cries, must one wait to feel an affront? Must one wait until his very home is threatened to take up arms? [29] What kinds of war may one reasonably wage without incurring accusations of greed, acquisitiveness and cruelty? Herrera replies for his hero, in terms that recall the dilemmas of our own age: «Nunca mereció alabanza la guerra solamente defensiva. Aquella era digna de toda gloria que impedia al enemigo la libertad de hacer el daño que quisiese y lo forzaba á temer siempre el suceso.» [30]

Herrera's ideas on war have Old Testament and classical sources. For the Old Testament writers, Yahweh is a warrior god who urges his chosen people to holy war against their pagan

---

[28] Herrera, *Relacion*, p. 335. A number of *refranes* found in the 1568 edition of the *Philosophia vulgar* of Juan de Mal Lara coincide strikingly with the themes of heroic virtue expounded in the *Relacion*: «Del mal que hombre teme, desse muere»; «El hombre metido en afrenta haze por treynta»; «Al hombre osado, la fortuna le da la mano.» On the one hand, their presence in a collection of popular maxims could argue their banality. Yet the fact that Mal Lara should give these ideas repeated attention suggests that they make up a framework for interpreting human conduct and historical events which Herrera perhaps got from Mal Lara, or at least shared with him.
[29] Herrera, *Relacion*, p. 339.
[30] *Ibid.*, pp. 339-340.

enemies. All wars of the chosen people are just, so long as they keep moral right on their side. But the ancient Greeks and Romans justified war as the gateway to peace. «It is as a result of war that peace is most firmly established, but there is not the same security in the mere avoidance of war for the sake of ease and quiet», said Thucydides,[31] who was echoed by many after him. The ancients offer two other reasons for war: «vengeance upon an enemy and aggressor»[32] or the desire to reform the conduct of one's foe.[33] Cicero and Sallust repeat the refrain: «The wise make war for the sake of peace, and endure toil in the hope of leisure.»[34] Christian theologians were increasingly concerned to find a justification for the atrocities of war within a creed of love. St. Augustine insisted that war must be designed to maintain peace. St. Thomas Aquinas held that the enemy must have some tangible guilt and that a war must somehow embody a good intention, presumably reforming zeal.[35] The continuing search for justifications of war in the sixteenth century took place primarily in Spain, where Francisco de Vitoria and Suárez built a more developed theory of just war, based on the principles of natural law, and embodying the concerns of St. Augustine and St. Thomas Aquinas that war be waged by a nation either in self-defense or to avenge a great wrong done by its enemies.[36] Herrera never betrays a shadow of a doubt over the legitimacy of armed conflict for a Christian fighting against an infidel. Although the war on which he focuses his attention can be seen as a defensive war, generally admitted by Catholic theologians, Herrera's answer evidently implies a more radical posture.

Despite his almost certain familiarity with the *Querela pacis,*

---

[31] Augustine Fitzgerald, *Peace and War in Antiquity* (London, 1931), p. 5; quotes Thucydides, Bk. I, 124, ii. One of Thucydides' imitators was Vegetius, who urges in the Prologue to Bk. III of *De Re Militari* that he who would enjoy peace should prepare himself for war.

[32] Fitzgerald, p. 11; quotes Thucydides, Bk. VII, 68, i-ii.

[33] *Ibid.,* p. 15; quotes Polybius, *Historia,* V, 11(3)-12(3).

[34] *Ibid.,* p. 49; quotes Sallust, «Oratio I ad C Caesarem», 40.

[35] Saint Augustine, *De Civitate Dei,* ed. J. E. C. Welldon (London and New York, 1924), II, 420-424 (Lib. XIX, Cap. xii); Saint Thomas Aquinas, *Summa Theologica* (New York, 1964), XXXV: 2a2ae, 40.

[36] Francisco de Vitoria, *De Indiis et De Ivre Belli Relectiones,* ed. Ernest Nys (Washington, 1917); Francisco Suárez, «Diputatio XIII de Bello», in Luciano Pereña Vicente, *Teoría de la guerra en Francisco Suárez* (Madrid, 1954), II; Bernice Hamilton, *Political Thought in Sixteenth-Century Spain. A Study of the Political Ideas of Vitoria, De Soto, Suárez and Molina* (Oxford, 1963).

Herrera appears not to have espoused its fullest meaning. By depicting wars among Christians, which after all were closest at hand, Erasmus condemned not only these wars, but all war. War is inhuman, far worse than beastly, and wholly unchristian.[37] The literature of a whole circle of Northern Europeans, including John Colet and Herrera's own Thomas More, was dedicated to fighting the scourge of war.[38] Herrera, perhaps in youthful exuberance over military glory, did not yet share their concern. (It is true as well that Erasmus would not rule out altogether an attack on the Turks, but he insisted that it must be done as a last resort and in the hopes of effecting their eventual conversion.[39])

Herrera's ideal is to maintain a position of strength such that none dare threaten it. Don Juan's sensitivity to the demands of heroism deems any need to cower a stain upon his honor. When the contagion of the Spanish spirit —

> tan buenos y dispuestos estaban los ánimos de toda España para cualquiera grande empresa, como cuando siguieron las invencibles banderas del Emperador Carlo Quinto, que no le faltaba al valor de muchos, que no tenian alguna opinion y nombre, otra cosa que la ocasion de señalarse [40]

—has won over the remaining troops, the advantage is virtually with the League.

Herrera insists on Don Juan's decisiveness and boldness. It would appear that he consulted a source which reported or transmitted directly an account of Marco Antonio Quirino («el proveedor»), in which the latter claimed that the commander's decision to seek out the Turks «in their own house» was merely his acceptance of something which Quirino had been proposing all along. Herrera finds Quirino's need to have exclusive claim on such an honor a foolish attempt to deceive «la universal fama»: «¡Tan dulce es el nombre de la gloria y el deseo de la inmortalidad de la memoria en las cosas humanas!»[41] Having painted

---

[37] Erasmus, *Querela pacis* (Lugduni Batavorum, 1641), pp. 11-13.
[38] Cf. Robert P. Adams, *The Better Part of Valor: More, Erasmus, Colet and Vives on Humanism, War and Peace* (University of Washington, 1962).
[39] Erasmus, *Dulce Bellum Inexpertis* (Brussels, 1953), pp. 92-93.
[40] Herrera, *Relacion*, p. 340.
[41] *Ibid.*, p. 344.

daring initiative as Don Juan's principal trait, he is unable to see this decision as originating in anyone else:

> que solo se debe al valor de D. Juan de Austria por general confesion de todos, porque el ánimo imitador de las hazañas de su padre y con dichosa y considerada determinación, comparando las fuerzas de ambas partes, se dispuso á la batalla y movió á su parecer á muchos. [42]

Don Juan's disposition to do battle rises to the level of passion and charisma.

At one point, when the general has decided to sail all night in search of the approaching Turkish force, against unfavorable winds, Herrera even feels the need to say that Don Juan acts «por inspiracion divina mas que por alguna razon de la diciplina de mar». [43] But the presence of the enemy leaves open only one course of action to him. When the Turkish fleet sails into full view, Don Juan is asked whether he will fight that day. He answers, «¿Veis la armada enemiga tan cerca y decis eso?» [44] And although the Italians and even Veniero make fearful objections, «él respondió generosamente que no era aquel tiempo de consejo, sino de pelear». [45] Finally the commander cruises among his assembled ships in a light craft, exhorting them to valor for their cause, which produces a great cry portending victory, as the soldiers are inflamed with a desire to meet the enemy. (Many accounts dwell on Don Juan's decision when he finds himself outnumbered in vessels. While concurring with the Spanish sources in their praise of Don Juan's boldness, Paruta implies that Don Juan's older Spanish advisers were even at the last moment counseling retreat. [46]) The cry of victory, which

---

[42] *Ibid.*, p. 344.
[43] *Ibid.*, p. 344.
[44] *Ibid.*, p. 348. This is one of the few occasions in which Herrera describes his hero as attaining heights of nobility reached by the ancients: «con alegre muestra de confianza imitó aquella grandeza de ánimo de Alejandro en la pasada de Asia.»
[45] *Ibid.*, p. 349. Herrera does not only stress Don Juan's own enthusiasm, but he chooses on occasion to diminish that of the men who surround him, particularly the Venetians. Of Veniero he says: «el general Veniero que tanto lo [the battle] habia deseado, conforme á lo que dicen muchos, pareció que no mostró aquella viveza y ardor que solia, dudando el suceso por la grande potencia del Turco.»
[46] Paruta, p. 212. Cf. *Historia de España*, in *Obras del Padre Juan de Mariana, B.A.E.*, Vols. XXX-XXXI (Madrid, 1854); Baltasar Porreño, *Historia de Don Juan de Austria*, ed. Antonio Rodríguez Villa (Madrid, 1899). Lope de Vega seizes

comes before the battle has been joined, signals a psychological or spiritual triumph. It is principally this triumph which interests Herrera throughout the remainder of the *Relacion,* which comprises only three of the twenty-eight chapters. These chapters largely concern the way in which the Turkish and Christian soldiers meet danger and death, and a numerical accounting of the casualties involved.

As we might expect, Paruta's version (with that of Fougasses) offers a very different view. Don Juan falls far short of Herrera's picture of the youth as Emperor reincarnate. Herrera does not even mention an episode that is belabored by Paruta and Fougasses both. According to these authors, an incident arose involving Veniero and one of his subordinates, whom Veniero hanged for misconduct, without consulting his commander-in-chief. Don Juan's youthful pride offended, he quarreled severely with Veniero over this question of authority. Paruta comments that this friction was handled by the Provveditore Barbarigo «con singolare destrezza & prudenza», and that the Provveditore subsequently served as go-between for Veniero and Don Juan.[47] The Venetian historian could hardly be expected to take more kindly to the suggestion of error on the part of his «ardentissimo» hero Veniero, than Herrera had at Quirino's usurping some of Don Juan's glory.

Not only does Paruta venture to criticize Don Juan's quickness to take offense, but he shows him as vacillating long between the excessive caution of his Spanish advisers and the Italians' eagerness for battle:

> Era dall'un canto desiderio grande di combattere, speranza non poca di vittoria, dall'altro per gli incerti, & sospetti consigli con liquali si vedeva procedere gli spagnuoli, molto dubbio del partito, che s'havesse à prendere, molto timore di buon successo.[48]

Barbarigo and Marcantonio Colonna finally succeed in convincing Don Juan that he should seek out the Turk. Once again

---

on Don Juan as the embodiment of the purest heroic impulse in several comedias collected by Menéndez y Pelayo in his volume *Crónicas y leyendas dramáticas de España,* in *Obras de Lope de Vega,* Vol. XII (Madrid, 1901). Among these are *La Santa Liga, Los españoles en Flandes,* and *Don Juan de Austria en Flandes.* In this last play, Don Juan is pictured as a frustrated active hero in an essentially administrative situation.

[47] Paruta, pp. 205-206.
[48] *Ibid.,* p. 206.

modern historians have been considerably more generous with Don Juan. Merriman allows Don Juan full credit for the decision, with the following remark: «It was a daring decision: one which the Emperor at the height of his power had never been able to bring himself to make, and one which the sages of the time universally condemned as utterly contrary to the dictates of common sense.» [49] The last phrase phrase refers to the dicta of such heroes as the Gran Capitán. In fairness to the Venetians, it is known that Philip consistently sought to restrain any imprudent fervor on the part of his half-brother. In a letter of instructions which Philip addressed to Don Juan when he was made General de la Mar in 1568, the Prudent King counseled the youth not always to expect victory, «estando cierto en que más contentamiento me dará el veros rendido por prudente que victorioso por temerario y desesperado». [50] Furthermore Philip did not endear himself to his half-brother in plaguing him with counselors like Don Luis de Requesens. To some, it appears that Don Juan's thirst for action was tempered by firm orders that he should not expose the fleet unless the victory seemed virtually certain. [51] In addition, the frequent squabbles among his advisers caused delays the Venetians were quick to criticize.

Another historian, Daru, approaching the conflict from the Venetian side, admits that Don Juan was, among the Spaniards at any rate, a fortunate commander for the Venetians, in that he was able to overcome the «circumspection» of his countrymen, which had been a great distress to the Republic. [52] Fougasses praises Don Juan for his moral integrity and insistence on maintaining this same morality among the fighting men. [53] He speaks

---

[49] Roger Bigelow Merriman, *The Rise of the Spanish Empire* (New York, 1934), IV, 134.

[50] Manuel Fernández Álvarez, *Política mundial de Carlos V y Felipe II* (Madrid, 1966), I, 217.

[51] John Lynch, *Spain under the Hapsburgs* (New York, 1964), I, 228. Cf. *C.D.I.*, III, 187-191, 194. This notion is corroborated by D. Diego Hurtado de Mendoza in the *Guerra de Granada*, as he describes Don Juan's difficult position in that campaign. The affable youth found himself with his «libertad tan atada que ni de cosa grande ni pequeña podía disponer sin comunicación y parescer de los consejeros y mandado del rey». *Comentario de la Guerra de Granada,* ed. M. Gómez Moreno (Madrid, 1948), p. 89. The normally critical Mendoza praises Don Juan particularly for the zeal with which he sought to eliminate the corrupt «excesos» of his men.

[52] Daru, IV, 161.

[53] Fougasses, *The Generall Historie of the Magnificent State of Venice,* trans. W. Shute (London, 1612), p. 422.

of «this noble, temperate captaine», who carefully rations the wine so that his soldiers will not fall prey to the debauchery of certain «northerly nations».[54] And following the humanist prescripts for the writing of history, Fougasses includes an oration delivered before the battle, in which Don Juan «by breefe, but effectuall speech, breathed courage into his men».[55]

Yet for Paruta and Fougasses, the unfortunate Barbarico and Veniero have the greatest stature. They, like Herrera, dwell on Barbarico's heroism as he meets death.[56] In Paruta, Veniero's exhortatory speech completely overshadows Don Juan's both in length and ardor.[57] But Paruta does relate two details found in Herrera's narrative, which hint at some sort of connection between the sources of the two, or at Paruta's familiarity with the *Relacion*. These are the anecdotes which picture Don Juan as the Turkish fleet comes into view, answering a question as to whether he will fight, «à i quali egli subito con animo prudente, & generoso rispondesse: tale essere lo stato delle cose presenti, che haveva bisogno d'ardire, non di consiglio»,[58] and sailing about among the fleet in a small frigate urging his men on to victory.[59] (Paruta also duplicates Herrera's description, in the thick of the battle, of the fighting on the royal flagship, where men strove with special zeal to impress their generals with their prowess.[60]) Fougasses is especially lavish in his praise of Veniero. He and Paruta pay more attention than Herrera could have in 1572 to the further ventures of the League. Paruta is sufficiently generous to picture Don Juan eager to capitalize on the victory at Lepanto and gather «maggior fruto» from the affair.[61] But both record unhappily that Veniero's enemies take advantage of the lateness of the season to persuade Don Juan to return to Sicily rather than go on to liberate Greece and ultimately chase the Turks back to Constantinople.[62] For these writers, Veniero becomes the audacious and ardent defier of more common prudence which Don Juan is to Herrera. For

[54] *Ibid.*, p. 421.
[55] *Ibid.*, pp. 429-430.
[56] *Ibid.*, pp. 441-442; Paruta, p. 218.
[57] Paruta, p. 212.
[58] *Ibid.*, p. 212.
[59] *Ibid.*, p. 212.
[60] *Ibid.*, p. 216; Herrera, *Relacion*, p. 359.
[61] Paruta, p. 228.
[62] *Ibid.*, p. 228; Fougasses, pp. 445-446.

Fougasses, he is «indefatigable in doing nobly, ...whose actiue, vntired spirit, neither the yeeres winter, nor his owne, could benumbe, was excited, not deterred by his [Don Juan's] departure, so far from being retrograde in his course of victory that he determined to goe a step farther». [63]   Daru, too, blames Don Juan's excessive prudence and a youthful desire to reap his earned praise, for the failure to make more of this triumph. [64]

Herrera appears at times to be quite taken with the boldness and characteristic fearlessness of the Turkish infidels. In the actual battle, however, this fearlessness rests simply on ignorance of both the size and the spirit of the enemy. Like the Christians, they are wrong to accept the verdict of the past. They spend the night preceding the battle reveling in what resembles a victory celebration before the fact. Herrera chooses to stress their moral laxity as an omen of their subsequent fate. Furthermore, he relates that the corsair scouts, whose job it was to reconnoiter the Christian position and strength, failed to report accurately. The Turks then found even greater cause to accept their victory as a foregone conclusion. Herrera emphasizes their error in calculation in the interest of undercutting the bravery for which they are famed. Truly heroic bravery does not feed itself on the knowledge of its adversary's certain inferiority. The Turks are in this way made out to be something of bullies who take sadistic pleasure in gobbling up such foolish souls as care to present themselves. Don Juan's idea of heroic virtue, as has been seen, is quite the contrary: a mighty fleet cannot waste its time in petty enterprises. The only meaningful superiority in combat is that of skill and determination, plus the moral uprightness which guarantees divine favor.

Having set the stage in this fashion, Herrera can make the encounter of the two fleets a dramatic one:

> Ya la armada de los turcos venia tendiéndose en el mar con grande lozanía y contento de todos ellos en general, estimando en poco á sus enemigos y riéndose de la ceguedad dellos que les llevaba la presa hasta sus mesmas casas, *porque* al principio no podian descubrir todo el número de sus galeras, cubriendo una montaña casi la tercia parte dellas; *mas* despues que poco á poco se descubrieron, acostándose todas, admirados de su determina-

[63] *Ibid.*, pp. 446-447.
[64] Daru, IV, 183-184.

> cion y multitud, quedaron algun tanto suspensos, y entre los hombres principales dellos y que por el uso de la guerra conocian el valor de sus contrarios, despues que entendieron que las galeras del Rey Filipo, que ellos suelen llamar Ponentinas, se hallaban en aquel lugar, se temió y dicen que Ochiali dijo al Bajá que mirase bien lo que se debia hacer.[65]

The Turks have not prepared a strategy for battle against equals in strength. The Bajá, however, gives orders not to turn back, since «haciendo el contrario [se] ponia en condicion de perder la cabeza».[66] The imperative of fighting represents not so much an inner drive such as that which impels Don Juan to the combat, but rather an external requirement enforced by fear of physical punishment.

Henceforth, although the Turks fight with valor, their bravery has been punctured. They continue to be described as «admirados», especially as they discover they are fighting against Spaniards, whom they have already learned to fear. In the encounter of the flagships of the two fleets, «jamás se ha visto que los turcos embistiesen con tanto ánimo y osadía como esta vez; pero recibiólos D. Juan con tanta furia de artillería y una rociada de arcabucería les derribó la presunción y braveza».[67] Initially they display tremendous daring, but they are easily overwhelmed. In addition, the Turks are infidels and may be expected to fight as such. In the thick of the battle they emit their barbarous war cries to shake the courage of their enemies.[68]

The Christians owe much of their valor and confidence to the exhortations of their leaders. The desire for vengeance further impassions them, not only for Turkish crimes against humanity, but for their sacrilegious treatment of holy temples and images. Herrera treats this urge with ambiguity. En route to the Gulf of Lepanto, the fleet passes the village of Corfú, which has just been sacked by the infidels:

> Estaba el burgo de la miserable Corfú arruinado y quemadas las casas y templos, y sacados los ojos á las imágenes de los santos y particularmente á las de la santísima Vírgen, la fiereza del cual

---

[65] Herrera, *Relacion*, pp. 351-352. My italics.
[66] *Ibid.*, p. 352.
[67] *Ibid.*, p. 357.
[68] *Ibid.*, p. 358.

espectáculo movió maravillosamente los ánimos de todos y encendió en ardiente deseo de venganza.[69]

On the other hand, during the actual battle, the Venetians lose a valiant captain, Barbarico, who incites them to valor as he falls dead:

> Los venecianos con el dolor de su muerte y rabia de venganza peleaban animados de la ventaja que tenian los turcos, que daban al través, porque muchas veces el dolor de la afrenta y el deseo de la venganza aun á los soldados viles enciende en valor.[70]

The Italians, other than the Venetians, throughout the account merit less attention than any others of the League's participants, although Herrera praises the «sabiduría y la prudencia y el ingenio de los italianos»[71] and staunchly defends those Italians who are allied with or controlled by Spain — Doria, the Duke of Savoy and others included in the lengthy enumerations of the battle order.[72] While the Pope emerges as champion of European unity, Herrera allows us glimpses of the French and Spanish power politics that paralyze the once-glorious peninsula.[73] Yet Lepanto allows the Italians their revindication along with Spain and Venice. Under the command of Colonna, «en aquella ocasion mostraron todos que aun no era muerto aquel antiguo valor de los ánimos italianos, porque muchos con deseos de vengar las injurias comunes en aquellos fieros enemigos de la religion cristiana ecedieron todas las esperanzas que se tenian de su fortaleza».[74]

The inspiration, however, most frequently ascribed to the combattants of the League is that of man's innate desire for glory and immortal fame which the preliminary remarks to the *Relacion* emphasized:

> Como se debia esperar en la junta de tan grandes y poderosas armadas, á los unos y á los otros encendia las fuerzas la codicia de la gloria y alabanza; los unos y los otros estimaban por último grado de honra, peleando en la presencia de sus generales,

---

[69] *Ibid.*, p. 329.
[70] *Ibid.*, pp. 360-361.
[71] *Ibid.*, p. 337.
[72] *Ibid.*, pp. 322-323.
[73] *Ibid.*, pp. 297, 308-309.
[74] *Ibid.*, p. 365.

mostrar cual fuese mas aventajado en fortaleza y conocimiento de la naval disciplina.[75]

In this passage it is recognition in terms of human criteria of skill and valor which the fighting men seek. Their superiors, through this recognition, will open the door to immortal renown among the generations of men. Don Juan himself appears preoccupied with the human judgments that his demeanor will produce. After disposing of the Turkish flagship, he sets out to aid those of the right wing, «pero jamás quiso ayudar alguna que no tuviese encontrados enemigos, porque no se dijese que su Real algunas veces se halló con ventaja, y rindiendo á una seguia luego las que huian».[76] Don Juan's audacious determination to seek out for himself the worst possible odds, in order to put his valor in bold relief, has a dual psychological effect. On the one hand, the Turks fairly swoon away, losing their former spirit. On the other, the Christians ride the rising tide of their enthusiasm until victory is in fact won. The heroic spirit, then, «ánimo», becomes a powerful weapon to conquer men, to inflame their valor and to reap their unending praise.

The instinct to heroism emerges in Herrera's account as the most immediate determining force for man's conduct. The drive for recognition and glory can turn an inferior army into a victorious one. With artillery booming about them, and swords and arrows flying, the men,

> acometiéndose con tanto ímpetu, que sin temor de la muerte, cada uno procuraba aventajarse, porque el que se via atrás se juzgaba por mas flaco y de menos valor que el otro, y todos revolvian en su ánimo la grandeza de aquella vitoria, de que pendia la opinion y el imperio de la tierra y la honra de su religion.[77]

---

[75] *Ibid.*, p. 359. Similar motivation is ascribed to the French and Spanish soldiers alike by Pero Mexía in his account of the battle of Pavia:

> en la parte francessa, allende de la ventaja que tenia en el número de la jente, esforçauase mucho con la presencia del rrey y con la nobleza de Franzia, que con él estaua. A los españoles y a los de su parte, esto mismo les ponía espuelas, considerando la onrra que ganarían venciendo a un rrey tan poderoso. Animáuales tanbien el nombre del Emperador, y su buena fortuna, ... determinados de antes morir que perder la rreputación y onrra ganada en las vitorias passadas.

Historia del Emperador Carlos V, ed. Juan de Mata Carriazo, in *Colección de Crónicas Españolas* (Madrid, 1945), p. 383.

[76] Herrera, *Relacion*, p. 368.
[77] *Ibid.*, p. 362.

In the struggle to merit «opinion», respect among men, the Church herself is bound up. Herrera depicts the Church as participating in the chivalresque honor code. She is no more or less, in human terms, than the determination of her sons to keep vigil over her honor. In Herrera's account, we recall, the Church finds herself in her current straits because Christian men have been too cowardly to defend her. The new venture will restore the Church to her pristine purity, «limpiando las manchas de las pasadas discordias».[78]

2. God in Human History

War is a human pursuit, and Herrera sees its workings in terms of human emotions — fear and bravery, shame and the search for lasting fame. Yet presiding over the entire scene, and framing it, are the convictions of the Christian. Man governs himself, or appears to govern himself within his own sphere, but all the while he operates beneath the hand, and in the interest, of divine providence. Human valor can tip the balance of victory by moving men's souls and because, in Herrera's Old Testament scheme of things, unimpeachable moral conduct cannot fail to win divine favor. The Christians move toward victory at Lepanto, «confiados en su valor proprio y en la divina piedad á quien seguian, igualando con la grandeza del ánimo á la multitud enemiga».[79] The drama of the combat proceeds on two levels, the one inevitably bound up with the other in a fixed relationship. Herrera does not know the anguish of Job. If the Christian cause on earth fails, it is traceable to human shortcomings, for God is just. According to this scheme, Herrera's interpretation of historical events becomes wholly predictable.[80]

---

[78] *Ibid.*, p. 291.
[79] *Ibid.*, p. 359.
[80] One possible exception is found in the sonnet that commemorates the defeat at Castelnuovo:

> Mostrò virtud su precio, i la ventura
>   negò el sucesso, i diò a la Muerte entrada:
>   que rehuyò dudosa i admirada
>   d'el eroico valor la suerte oscura.

Versos, sonnet I, 84.

Herrera writes exemplary history. That is to say, any situation is conceived of as verifying a general theory of human conduct, that of heroic virtue, and a general theory of divine providence. He treats the information which falls into his hands in very much the same way that a scientist approaches a chaos of data. He formulates the theory which, he feels, best explains the phenomenon under consideration. The nature of this theory may depend as much on his expectations of reality as on his experience of it: that is, it is largely an *a priori* formulation. Once in possession of this explanatory theory, he then proceeds to give most credence to the evidence which corroborates his view, until, of course, the evidence becomes wholly negative in character. But in the meantime, the points which do not fall along the «curve» of Herrera's formulation will be dropped from the picture. Bits of information which are not verisimilar in the context of the general picture will be laid aside. Herrera, not an eyewitness to the event he has chosen to recount, must weigh conflicting evidence not against what he himself did or did not see, but against an archetype of the situation, what might once again be called verisimilitude. He even goes so far as to claim that the archetypical view is closer to Truth than any individual's first-hand account could hope to be: «consideren... que todo no puede estar tan ajustado que venga medido á su gusto y conforme á la pasion de sus ánimos.»[81] One man's ability to observe events will necessarily be hampered by his passions. Truth is inevitably a universal. Mosquera's Preface directly reflects this concern.

What is striking about Herrera's *Relacion* is the extent to which it concentrates on the human sphere. Lepanto manifests God's design for man on earth, but in an immediate sense, man affects the course of history, and precisely through his mastery of the inner self. The inner man becomes the true protagonist in history; moral perfection, the lever by which Destiny is manipulated. Herrera's heroes display tremendous will power, utter fearlessness, unswerving determination against great odds. Yet they are anything but Stoic heroes. Herrera energetically condemns Stoic philosophy in an entry to the *Anotaciones* to Garcilaso. His reasons for doing so are clear: the Stoics would

---

[81] Herrera, *Relacion*, p. 248.

deny human emotions the right to express themselves.[82] The poetry of Herrera presents Reason battling and rarely winning against morbid passion for sway within man's soul. Passions, however, do not have exclusively negative connotations. The impassioned pursuit of glory, impassioned defense of religion and king and personal honor, are the highest forms of human activity. Fear and hesitancy in such pursuits indicate almost negative being.

In *The Idea of History,* R. G. Collingwood says:

> Man, for the Renaissance historians, was not man as depicted by ancient philosophy, controlling his actions and creating his destiny by the work of the *intellect,* but man as depicted by Christian thought, a creature of passion and impulse. History thus became the history of human passions, regarded as necessary manifestations of human nature.[83]

The Italian humanist historians sought to define the role of man in history and to explore the limits of his power. As in the Middle Ages, they wrote of events on earth, «placed in relation to a permanent order of values that men ought to recognize and follow. But whereas in the Middle Ages history served to show the power of God, the humanist concept according to which history taught man to strive for virtue and to avoid vice emphasized the power which man could exert».[84] Machiavelli advised the systematic analysis of the past so that its lessons might gain still greater utility.[85] Such writers as Guicciardini gradually came to be impressed with the power of Fortune, whose abrupt and frequent changes could alter situations beyond

---

[82] *Obras de Garci Lasso de la Vega con Anotaciones de Fernando de Herrera* (Seville, 1580), p. 323. Cf. Américo Castro, *La realidad histórica de España* (Mexico, 1962), p. 148; Otis H. Green, *Spain and the Western Tradition* (Madison, 1965), III, 312-324. For the European renaissance of Stoicism in the sixteenth century, cf. Léontine Zanta, *La Renaissance du Stoïcisme au XVIᵉ siècle* (Paris, 1914).

[83] R. G. Collingwood, *The Idea of History* (New York, 1956), p. 57. Américo Castro insists, of course, that Spaniards, including Quevedo (one of the most commonly mentioned in this connection), are not Stoics although they express admiration for certain classical Stoic philosophers. The inevitable conflict with the hope of the Christian always drastically modified the Stoic posture. «Pero sin apatía y sin suicidio, ¿qué queda de la moral de Séneca?» *La realidad histórica de España,* p. 148. Cf. Otis Green, III, 312-324. As Collingwood indicates, it is not merely a question of Spaniards.

[84] Felix Gilbert, *Machiavelli and Guicciardini* (Princeton, 1965), p. 218.

[85] Myron P. Gilmore, *Humanists and Jurists* (Cambridge, Massachusetts, 1963), p. 28.

the power of man's prudence or foresight («providentia») to control.[86] Even the propitiousness of God could not dispossess the cruel Goddess of all her influence. Herrera warns in the *Relacion* of the possibility of sudden changes in human affairs when the League's generals debate their future course of action:

> y decian que no era prudencia juzgar unas cosas por los efectos de otras, que muchas veces se habia visto suceder mal fin á las cosas bien aconsejadas, y bueno á las mal consideradas, porque esto no procedía del consejo sino de la mudanza del estado de las cosas, que las trocaba.[87]

Yet while the «mudanza de las cosas» tosses about man and his hopes for success, divine will, not Fortune, is the ultimate arbiter of Herrera's universe. For Diego Hurtado de Mendoza, God's purpose can resist human understanding, almost as Fortune does for Guicciardini. In the *Guerra de Granada,* he writes of the conflict: «Vitoria dudosa y de sucesos tan peligrosa, que alguna vez se tuvo duda si éramos nosotros o los enemigos a quien Dios queria castigar; hasta que el fin della descubrió que nosotros éramos los amenaçados y ellos los castigados.»[88] In this period, Herrera's predilection is for heroes who resist mightily the apparently impossible or the inevitable itself. For the drama of history, as Machiavelli says in *Il Principe,* lies in defining the extent of man's ability to stave off Fortune and Fate.[89] Because of the nature of Herrera's God, man does control his destiny in some sense, not through the pure workings of the intellect, but through the purity of his passion for honor and justice, insofar as this perfect passion is able to sway men and ultimately God. The *Relacion* records an event in which human passions actually shape history.

The comparisons Herrera chooses in the course of the *Relacion* make it clear that the criteria for judging an historical event are overwhelmingly human ones. Furthermore, the historical present takes the limelight. It is true that he curses the moral laxity into which the nations of Christendom have fallen; but this does not affect the question of potential greatness. Only

---

[86] Gilbert, p. 289.
[87] Herrera, *Relacion,* p. 335.
[88] Hurtado de Mendoza, p. 3.
[89] Gilmore, p. 60; Machiavelli, *Il Principe,* in *Tutte le opere storiche e letterarie,* ed. Guido Mazzoni and Mario Casella (Florence, 1929), pp. 48-49.

once does the author speak of his hero's imitating past greatness, in comparing Don Juan to Alexander the Great.[90] In summing up the unequalled significance of Lepanto in the course of all history, Herrera permits the «illustrious victory» of Augustus Caesar over Marc Anthony a position nearly equal to the Christian triumph of 1571.[91] Yet he does not elect to compare Don Juan to the Roman Emperor. Don Juan is primarily the spiritual heir of his father.[92] Herrera's attention does appear to focus on the historical heroes of empire —Alexander, Caesar Augustus, Charles V— in harmony with his vision of a united Europe. (In this view, as well as in numerous questions of technique, Herrera's historical prose in the *Relacion* is naturally far removed from the most outstanding Italian Renaissance historians, many of whom were apologists of the Florentine Republic and enemies, in their political and historical thinking, of the claims of empire.[93]) The absence of extensive comparisons with figures of Greek and Roman antiquity is striking for two reasons: one, the presence of so many such allusions in the prose of Mosquera's Preface, which seems to situate the work in an atmosphere of humanistic activity; the other, the elaborate display of classical erudition which overwhelms one in the *Anotaciones*. True, a trace of this background can be seen in the hasty geographical references of the *Relacion*,[94] which we find expanded many times in the *Anotaciones*, replete with chapter and verse citations from Strabo as well as historical and imaginative writers of antiquity. Nor does Herrera mention any Biblical figures in particular, although the force of Old Testament diction is such that the intended scriptural context could not fail to be evident to the reader. Herrera doubtless deemed the allusions of the hymns to Jehovah, Pharaoh and the Israelites to belong to those «ficciones de la poesía» which deny legitimate historical writing its value.

Herrera's *Relacion* is indeed distant from the historical mode represented by another narrative of Lepanto which Daru found in the Bibliothèque du Roi in Paris: *Relazione delle cause e principio della guerra mossa dal Turco in Cypro contro Veneziani*

---

[90] Herrera, *Relacion*, p. 348.
[91] *Ibid.*, p. 373.
[92] *Ibid.*, p. 370.
[93] Hans Baron, *The Crisis of the Early Italian Renaissance* (Princeton, 1966), pp. 47-75.
[94] Herrera, *Relacion*, p. 347, on the «Islas Cuzorales».

e del trattato, eseguito della lega frà il papa, il rè cattolico e detti veneziani, col negozio della conclusione di essa lega, per il signor Marc'Antonio Colonna in Venezia... Comparazione di due battaglie navali memorabili, l'una de Romani con Cartaginesi, appresso Sicilia ad Einomo, e l'altra de' Cristiani con Turchi appresso Lepanto a Curzolari a 7 ottobre 1571. [95]

Normally, as we have seen, Herrera employs recent events as his standards. Within the sphere of the sixteenth century, there is no question for Herrera that history has moved in a crescendo toward Lepanto. This perspective, of course, requires revision in other works, most obviously for us in the poetry, where room for such events as the defeat at Alcázarquivir must be found. Yet doubt is never cast on the fundamental principle that modern history can equal ancient lore and even surpass it in magnificence. History for Herrera is neither static, nor circular in its trajectory. He has inherited from Judeo-Christian tradition a linear view of history. The promise of ultimate perfection for mankind lies in the future, and the world progresses toward that ideal.

Herrera reserves the final pages of his account to weigh the victory of the armada of the League at Lepanto against great naval forces and triumphs of all time: «Desta suerte tuvo fin la mayor batalla que ha habido en mar, porque ninguno de los antiguos se le puede comparar.» [96] He compares sixteenth-century Christians with ancient Greeks, Romans and Goths, according to the importance of the ideals for which they strived, the sophistication of military arts and the degree of danger involved in their battles. In this brief mention of the Goths, Herrera makes them out to be a primitive sort, certainly inferior to the Turks in weaponry, «porque las flechas de los turcos pasan un peto, que nunca pudieron pasar los arcos armados por aquellos fuertes brazos de los godos, porque los antiguos no tuvieron la fineza y temple de los arneses de la edad presente». [97] The Goths's virile strength does not stand comparison with the sophisticated, more modern arsenal of the Turks. In the entry on the elegy in the *Anotaciones,* Herrera imputes the decline of classical civilization to the Goths:

[95] Daru, IV, 183-184.
[96] Herrera, *Relacion,* p. 373.
[97] *Ibid.,* p. 374.

> Porque como despues de la felice i gloriosa edad de Augusto perdiesse la poesia parte de su simplicidad i pureza, i entrase despues en Italia la barbara, pero belicosa nacion de los godos; i destruyendo los sagrados despojos de la venerada antigüedad, sin perdonar a la memoria de los varones esclarecidos, como si a ellos solos tocára la vengança de todas las gentes sugetas al yugo del imperio Romano; se mostrassen no menos crueles enemigos de las disciplinas i estudios nobles; que de la grandeza i magestad del nombre Latino; fue poco a poco escureciendo i desvaneciendose en la sombra de la inorancia la eloquencia i la poesia con las demas artes i ciencias, que ilustran el animo del ombre, i lo apartan de la confusion del vulgo; i si quedò alguna pequeña reliquia de erudicion; parecia en ella el mesmo trato i corrompido estilo que traxo la gente vencedora.[98]

What decides the question for Herrera is the technical superiority of modern weaponry, which makes an enemy more fearful than ever, and individual survival still more tenuous. Cristóbal de Virués, in the *Monserrate,* published in 1588, echoes Herrera's interpretation. His hero Garín, as he looks over the battles sculpted on the front of his ship, decides that Lepanto is the most deserving to be immortalized:

> Pues es muy cierto, que, aunque igual no fuera
> La famosa batalla de este dia,
> En número ó en fuerzas, á cualquiera
> De las cuatro que alli pintado habia,
> ¿Cuál furia dellas igualar pudiera
> A la infernal de tanta artillería,
> De tanto fiero y tempestuoso rayo,
> Del celestial tan infernal ensayo?[99]

The lengthy description of modern armaments recalls a number of similar quasi-scientific entries in the *Anotaciones* on artillery and such, and reveals his many-sided curiosity. In the present context, however, Herrera makes use of the new technology to prove that, if there is now greater cause for fear in battle, so fearlessness and heroism are the more to be praised:

> Pues las batallas de mar, ¿quién duda que no sean ahora mas peligrosas?... Esto es, si yo no me engaño, lo que confirma mi

---

[98] Herrera, *Anotaciones,* p. 291; ed. A. Gallego Morell (Granada, 1966), pp. 396-397.
[99] Cristóbal de Virués, *El Monserrate,* in *Poemas épicos, B.A.E.,* Vol. XVII, ed. Cayetano Rosell (Madrid, 1851), p. 515.

opinión. Otros juzgarán otra cosa, pero no negarán, si la pasión de ánimos enemigos de nuestro tiempo no lo impide, que la grandeza desta vitoria no sea mayor y mas justamente merecedora de la inmortalidad de la memoria.[100]

In the *Anotaciones,* Herrera traces dozens of references to artillery in various Latin European histories (Polydore Vergil, for example); Italian accounts in history and in a dialogue of Petrarch, and in Spanish chronicles from those of Alfonso X to Zurita. The passage is typical of the sort of technique he practices throughout the work, comparing multitudinous historical accounts in quest of the most convincing solution. Herrera sets aside the legend according to which an alchemist friar would have first discovered the principle of «aquel cruel[i]simo linaje de maquina militar»,[101] deciding that «el caso, maestro de casi todas las cosas, fue autor desta maquina».[102] He then proceeds to reconstruct the scene in which the friar or anyone else, in the process of mixing chemicals in a lidded jar, would have been astounded when by accident the mixture exploded: «conocio cuan grande era la fuerça de aquellos polvos que levantaron en alto una piedra... con tan terrible furor que con ningunos vinculos, ni impedimentos se pudo refrenar el impetu de aquella materia incendiaria.»[103] That this remarkable spectacle should be of interest to Herrera in his commentary does not come as a surprise after his descriptions of the spectacle of Lepanto. Furthermore, Herrera's attention in the *Anotaciones* turns on artillery as subject matter for poetry, citing and translating Latin and Italian poets including Fracastoro, Ariosto and Minturno.

The evident wonderment and admiration of Herrera for the military arts of his day stand out in striking contrast to the thoughts of many men of his century. Erasmus railed against all armaments through which man sought to defy his God-given nature as an unarmed creature.[104] Machiavelli saw artillery as a scant threat to ancient modes of valor, and the author of the *Viaje de Turquía* did not find the new weapons especially formidable.[105] Yet for Don Quijote, all firearms are evil. The

[100] Herrera, *Relacion,* p. 374.
[101] Herrera, *Anotaciones,* p. 149 ff.; ed. Gallego Morell, p. 332.
[102] *Ibid.,* p. 151; ed. Gallego, p. 333.
[103] *Ibid.,* p. 151; ed. Gallego, p. 334.
[104] Erasmus, *Querela,* p. 11 ff.
[105] Machiavelli, *Discorsi sopra la Prima Deca di Tito Livio,* in *Tutte le opere,*

displaced knight-errant looks longingly to a utopian past, in which man's true strength provided his only defense. Today, he says, any coward can kill many more brave men than he.[106] Herrera and Cervantes share the medieval notion that «the exercise of arms elevates the one who devotes himself to it».[107] Yet for Don Quijote, the new arms diminish courage, while Herrera feels that this factor has only raised the requirements of daring and fearlessness. (Herrera's disciple and prologuist, Mosquera de Figueroa, evidently took his side, for in his *Comentario en breve compendio de disciplina militar* [1594?] he evinces great admiration for the heights to which military arts have risen.[108]) Herrera's fascination for artillery is perhaps the more curious in view of the relative reluctance with which the Spanish forces adopted its systematic use. The Spanish infantry, renowned for its persistence in hand-to-hand combat, and still clinging to the custom of dueling, perpetuated perhaps through the influence of the romances of chivalry, had to be educated into the new tactics. The great efforts made to implant the use of artillery led to the establishment of academies for its study in Madrid, Seville and Naples; and a flurry of manuals on the subject appear in the 1590's.[109] For Herrera, this relative novelty is part of man's artful progress toward a perfection in the future, while Don Quijote looks backward to his «Paradise Lost» in an «Edad de Oro» where men feasted innocently on acorns.[110]

---

p. 162 ff.; and Maravall, *El humanismo de las armas en Don Quijote* (Madrid, 1948), pp. 142-143.
[106] Maravall, pp. 62-63.
[107] *Ibid.*, p. 119.
[108] *Ibid.*, p. 146.
[109] Felipe Picatoste, *Los españoles en Italia* (Madrid, 1887), II, 52 ff.
[110] Miguel de Cervantes Saavedra, *Don Quijote de la Mancha*, ed. Martín de Riquer (Barcelona, 1958), pp. 104-105. For Cervantes' own position, cf. the prologue of Ramón Menéndez Pidal to Maravall's *El humanismo*. That Cervantes did not share Don Quijote's nostalgia is evident in the prologue to *La Galatea*, ed. Avalle-Arce (Madrid, 1961), I, 6-7. There he describes the role of the poet in enriching his own language:

> para empresas altas y de mayor importancia, y abrir camino para que, a su imitación, los ánimos estrechos, que en la brevedad del lenguaje antiguo no quieren que se acabe la abundancia de la lengua castellana, entienden que tienen campo abierto, fértil y espacioso, por el cual, con facilidad y dulzura, con gravedad y elocuencia, pueden correr con libertad descubriendo la diversidad de conceptos agudos, graves, sotiles y levantados que la fertilidad de los ingenios españoles la favorable influencia del cielo con tal ventaja en diversas partes ha producido y cada hora produce en la edad dichosa nuestra.

If artillery proves the special status of the battle of Lepanto, this most glorious victory of his own day promises «nuevo imperio á la religion cristiana», [111] a new Golden Age of empire. Herrera rebels in history as in literature against the notion that one cannot aspire to do more than equal the feats of antiquity. This opinion belongs to the grudging «enemies of our time». [112] For Herrera, each of life's ventures —be they military, literary or amorous— belongs to an ascending path in which ever new human perfections may be obtained:

> Mas el valor, el noble entendimiento,
> el espirtu, el intento generoso
> aciende a la region de luz serena. [113]

Herrera's linguistic theories, as expressed in the *Anotaciones*, bear the very same stamp. As we observed in his attitude toward the development of military arts. Herrera does not bemoan his own times. He would not, like Don Quijote, wish to recall a Golden Age of harmony with nature, where man's artifice had no place or necessity. For this most artful of poets, harmony with nature consists of producing a richness and variety worthy of her. Of poetry he says, «es el primer loor suyo parir variedad, de que es muy estudiosa la naturaleza mesma». [114] If Herrera speaks admiringly of «Todos los que vivieron en la edad de Tulio, i gozaron de aquel dichosissimo tiempo en que florecio la eloquencia mas que lo que parecio ser posible al ingenio i fuerças de los ombres», [115] and of the «pureza i castidad antigua» of the Latin language before her bifurcation into Spanish and Italian, he does not intend his remarks to disparage the achievements of his own era. For Herrera, language enjoys a

The diction and sense of the passage appear to have been strongly influenced by Herrera's *Anotaciones*, which appeared only a few years earlier.
[111] Herrera, *Versos*, Bk. II, sonnet 64.
[112] The «ánimos enemigos de nuestro tiempo» seem to refer to the Italian historians —Giovio, Sabellicus and Bembo among them— whom Herrera accuses of slander against Spain in the *Anotaciones*, p. 611; ed. Gallego, p. 536. Cf. Benedetto Croce, *La Spagna nella vita italiana durante la Rinascenza*, Chapter VI, «La protesta della cultura italiana contro la barbarica invasione spagnuola», pp. 98-121. For a discussion of the «quarrel of the ancients and moderns» among Spanish sixteenth-century historians, see José Antonio Maravall, *Los factores de la idea del progreso en el renacimiento español* (Madrid, 1963); among poets, see Andrée Collard, *Nueva poesía* (Madrid, 1967).
[113] Herrera, *Versos*, Bk. II, sonnet 64.
[114] Herrera, *Anotaciones*, p. 295; ed. Gallego, p. 400.
[115] *Ibid.*, p. 294; ed. Gallego, pp. 397-399.

tremendous dynamism: a living language undergoes a constant, irrepressible evolution. He warns his contemporaries of the consequences of this for Spanish, «sin alguna comparacion mas grave i de mayor espiritu i manificencia que todas las que mas se estiman de las vulgares».[116] Spain's men of letters should neither be overwhelmed with despair nor stagnate in complacency:

> i no piense alguno que està el lenguage Español en su ultima perfecion, i que ya no se puede hallar mas ornato de elocucion i variedad, porque aunque aora lo vemos en la mas levantada cumbre que jamas se à visto, i que antes amenaza declinacion que crecimiento; no estan tan acabados los ingenios Españoles, que no pueden descubrir lo que hasta aora à estado ascondido a los de la edad passada i desta presente. porque en tanto que vive la lengua, i se trata, no se puede dezir que à hecho curso; porque siempre se alienta a passar i dexar atras lo que antes era estimado.[117]

In the *Anotaciones*, this sense of the potentialities for the present and the future goes hand in hand with a critical independence which separates Herrera from those of his contemporaries who preach unquestioning imitation of the ancients. In answer to El Brocense's «digo, y afirmo, que no tengo por buen poeta al que no imita los excelentes antiguos»,[118] Herrera adds what he believes to be an essential qualification:

> No puedo comigo acabar de passar en silencio esto, que el animo me ofrece a la memoria tantas vezes. porque me enciende en justa ira la ceguedad de los nuestros, i la inorancia, en que se an sepultado; que procurando seguir solo al Petrarca i a los Toscanos, desnudan sus intentos sin escogimiento de palabras i sin copia de cosas; i queriendo alcançar demasiadamente aquella blandura i terneza, se hazen umildes i sin composicion i fuerça. porque de otra suerte se à de buscar o la floxedad i regalo del verso, o la viveza; que para esto importa destreza de ingenio i consideracion de juizio.[119]

Not only imitation but judgment and an agile imagination are required of the true poet. Herrera himself would combine the study of Italian and ancient poets: «hiziera mi lengua copiosa i

---

[116] *Ibid.*, p. 292; ed. Gallego, p. 397.
[117] *Ibid.*, p. 294; ed. Gallego, p. 399.
[118] A. Gallego Morell, *Garcilaso de la Vega y sus comentaristas*, p. 25.
[119] Herrera, *Anotaciones*, p. 71; ed. Gallego, p. 285.

rica de aquellos admirables despojos i osára pensar, que con diligencia i cuidado pudiera arribar a donde nunca llegaràn los que no lleven este passo.» [120]

This is Herrera's exuberant affirmation in an age all too prone to looking backward in its attempt to capture or recapture perfection. For him, perfection, perhaps in quite new manifestations, is very much the prerogative of the present and the future. Just as the ancients did not witness any naval battles to compare with Lepanto, neither did they scale the ultimate heights of poetry. Cicero's prose surpassed what appeared possible in his time. The implication is similar to Herrera's assertion about poetry: «i sè dezir, que por esta via se abre lugar para descubrir muchas cosas. porque no todos los pensamientos y consideraciones de amor, i de las de mas cosas, que toca la poesia; cayeron en la mente del Petrarca i del Bembo i de los antiguos.» [121] Boundless possibilities for achievement remain:

> porque es tan derramado i abundante el argumento de amor, i tan acrecentado en si mesmo, que ningunos ingenios pueden abraçallo todo; antes queda a los sucedientes ocasion para alcançar lo que parece impossible aver ellos dexado. i no supieron inventar nuestros precessores todos los modos i osservaciones de la habla; ni los que aora piensan aver conseguido todos sus misterios, i presumen posseer toda su noticia; vieron todos los secretos i toda la naturaleza della. [122]

Herrera's ideal poet, like the soldier-prince in search of ever more glorious deeds, must always remain restless: «asi devemos buscar en la elocucion poetica, no satisfaziendonos con lo estrenado, que vemos, i admiramos, sino procurando con el entendimiento modos nuevos i llenos de hermosura.» [123] His poet resembles the lover of his verse, for he must hold before him the Platonic conception of the beauty he seeks, «formada de lo mas aventajado que puede alcançar la imaginacion; para imitar della lo mas hermoso i ecelente». [124] All should be able to exclaim with the lover of the sonnet:

---

[120] *Ibid.*, pp. 71-72; ed. Gallego, p. 286.
[121] *Ibid.*, p. 72; ed. Gallego, p. 286.
[122] *Ibid.*, p. 72; ed. Gallego, p. 286.
[123] *Ibid.*, p. 295; ed. Gallego, p. 399.
[124] *Ibid.*, p. 295; ed. Gallego, p. 399.

> Que yo en essa belleza que contemplo
> (aunqu'a mi flaca vista ofende i cubre),
> la immensa busco, i voi siguiendo al cielo. [125]

Whether his subject be arms or letters, then, Herrera seeks to present himself as a man of his own time. However great his admiration for the achievements of antiquity, he reaffirms the belief that the present not only ranks equal to the past, but in many ways continues to surpass it. Herrera suggests that this succession of heroic feats in all areas will stretch far into the future. The past, then, becomes a means both of enriching the present and of measuring its extraordinary newness.

---

[125] Herrera, *Poesías,* p. 75, sonnet 38; cf. Menéndez y Pelayo, *Historia de las ideas estéticas* (Madrid, 1946-1947), II, 70 ff.

CHAPTER FOUR

HISTORY AND POETRY

The *Relacion,* while concentrating on moral and political aspects of the subject, indulges in some descriptive passages which reveal the plastic orientation familiar from Herrera's work in verse. The visual and auditive conception of the actual conflict makes itself evident at every turn: «que ya no *se oia* otra cosa que el sonido dellas [arcabuces, escopetas y flechas], ni *se via* sino las astas clavadas por árboles, jarcias y antenas.» [1] And as Don Juan's men fire for the first time at the enemy flagship, «una rociada de arcabucería... les derribó la presunción y braveza, porque á la segunda carga parecieron pocos turbantes en la popa y crujía, de los cuales venia ántes muy poblada». [2] These isolated passages point up several of Herrera's characteristic techniques, which are developed more fully later. In the first passage cited, we find the preference for series of substantives, often triple («arcabuces, escopetas y flechas», etc.). Related to this is a suggestive concision of description which strikes us as a modern device: the mention of a group of meaningful objects to evoke an entire scene. This device in the first passage resembles the plastic metonymy of the second: «pocos turbantes» for «pocos turcos». Finally, the Biblical echoes appear in even the most minute details of description. The «turbantes» make the most of oriental «local color», while the phrase «les derribó la presunción y braveza» ties the very first fall of the Turks to the divine vengeance of which they are to fall victims.

[1] Herrera, *Relacion de la guerra de Cipre,* in *C.D.I.,* XXI (Madrid, 1852), 358. My italics.
[2] *Ibid.,* p. 357.

Soon, amid specific information concerning the roles of particular combatants, Herrera indulges himself in a panoramic view of the spectacle:

> y así entre unos y otros se trabó una dudosa batalla con grandísimo ímpetu y furia, y con tan grande estruendo que no solo pareció que las galeras se hacian pedazos y quebrantaban, pero el mesmo mar, no pudiendo sustentar aquel ruido espantable, bramaba, revolviendo las ondas llenas de espuma que poco ántes estaban sosegadas y atronados los hombres que no se oian, y el cielo se arrebató de los ojos de todos con la humosa oscuridad de aquellas llamas.[3]

Finally, when victory is won, another such description appears:

> Duró el rendimiento y saco de las galeras hasta la noche que se arrimó á la tierra, quemando muchos bajeles enemigos con espectáculo alegrísimo, porque la noche sucedió oscurísima y con grande pluvia; parecia el mar ardiendo en llamas un monte de fuego, y en todo el espacio de la batalla se vió teñido en sangre infiel y cristiana, llenos de cuerpos muertos y despedazados de varias maneras, y cubierto de bajeles rotos, de fuegos, de remos, de astas y armas, que ningun suceso se pudo ver de mayor terribilidad, ni mas dina consideracion de la miseria humana.[4]

After these excursuses, Herrera returns to statistics of ships lost, destroyed and captured.

The resemblance here to Herrera's poetry is striking. In the sonnet composed to the victory of Lepanto, the sea roars and blazes:

> Hondo Ponto, que bramas atronado
>   con tumulto i terror, d'el turbio seno
>   saca el rostro, de torpe miedo lleno;
>   mira tu campo arder ensangrentado,
> I junto en este cerco i encontrado
>   todo el Cristiano esfuerço, i Sarraceno,
>   i, cubierto de humo, i fuego, i trueno,
>   huir temblando el impio quebrantado.[5]

The same vision of war's horror appears again and again in reference to other bloody battles: in the sonnet celebrating Charles V's Algerian campaign:

---

[3] *Ibid.*, p. 358.
[4] *Ibid.*, p. 370.
[5] Herrera, *Versos,* ed. Pacheco (Seville, 1619), Bk. II, sonnet 87.

> Bramava el mar ardiendo en ira estraña,
> bramando ardia airado el mar perjuro,[6]

in the sonnet to the battle of Muhlberg:

> i rebossò espumoso su corriente
> en la esparzida sangre d'Alemaña[7]

and in sonnet XV of the 1578 unpublished collection:

> Vereys el fiero y aspero tirano
> dexar del largo Eufrates esta parte,
> por fuerça y sangre y hierro y fuego y muerte.[8]

Finally the sonnet to the crushing defeat of Castelnuovo in 1539:

> Esta desnuda playa, esta llanura
> d'astas i rotas armas mal sembrada,
> do acabò al vencedor la Ibera espada,
> es d'España sangrienta sepultura.[9]

This sonnet resembles almost exactly the one for the defeat of Alcázarquivir.[10] Surprisingly, we find few descriptions of this type in the *canciones*. The examples above derive exclusively from the sonnets, where we can observe Herrera's repeated essays in condensing this material into the abbreviated contours of that form. The material takes on a more terse, almost telegraphic, character as it is converted into poetry, the prosaic «cuerpos muertos», «bajeles rotos de fuegos, de remos, de astas y armas» recast into simply «humo, fuego y trueno» or «fuerça y sangre y hierro y fuego y muerte» — lines which place Herrera particularly close to Góngora or Sor Juana Inés de la Cruz.

The sonnet on Lepanto, instead of the literal description in the prose version, addresses itself to the sea («Hondo Ponto») personified. In the prose selection, the men are «atronados»; here the sea, «que bramas atronado», reacts like man to the fearful

---

[6] *Ibid.*, Bk. II, sonnet 7.
[7] *Ibid.*, Bk. I, sonnet 13.
[8] Herrera, *Rimas inéditas*, ed. J. M. Blecua (Madrid, 1948).
[9] Herrera, *Poesías*, ed. V. García de Diego (Madrid, 1914), sonnet 9; *Versos*, Bk. I, sonnet 84.
[10] Herrera, *Versos*, Bk. III, sonnet 18.

spectacle and reluctantly raises its head to gaze upon the bloody «field» afire. The sonnet removes the spectator of the battle from the immediate perspective of the fighting men to that of a sort of sea deity, to a more transcendental perspective.

The «Canción en alabança de la divina magestad por la vitoria del Señor Don Juan» uses the same device, only changing the personification to apostrophe of God: «Tú, Dios de las batallas, tú eres diestra, / salud y gloria nuestra.» [11] The poet addresses the Lord of battle and sings psalm-like his victory over «Faraón, feroz guerrero».[12] A large part of the poem gives the words of Pharaoh's insolent challenge, and the poet counters with the tale of God's vengeance, always directed toward the same «tú». The spectacle of war's horrors takes second place to the mythical confrontation of Jehovah and Pharaoh. It appears in impressionistic details, as when the infidels plan war:

> ¡Venid! dixeron: y en el mar undoso
> hagamos de su sangre un grande lago; [13]

or in God's promise to the wayward:

> Babilonia y Egito amedrentada
> del fuego y asta temblará sangrienta,
> y el humo subirá a la luz del cielo. [14]

The battle itself, however, has become clearly secondary. The Biblical theme, cast now in a characteristic Old Testament form, dwells less on events, and has omitted altogether the subject of Christian heroic valor so prominent in the *Relacion*. It concentrates on extracting the ultimate significance of the battle: the Lord of Hosts has used his chosen people to castigate the proud in the imagination of their hearts.

Herrera's Dedication to the Duke of Medina Sidonia lays down the guidelines for the way history is to be written. Infinite respect for the Truth and the difficulty of ascertaining it make up Herrera's historical credo. He speaks in the Dedication of «cuán incierta es la voz de la verdad traida de partes tan remotas

---

[11] Herrera, *Poesías*, p. 1.
[12] *Ibid.*, p. 2.
[13] *Ibid.*, p. 8.
[14] *Ibid.*, p. 13.

y de lenguas tan varias»; [15] and later in the main body of the account, as he evaluates a piece of evidence, of «la fama incierta y amiga de acrecentar los hechos». [16] Mosquera's Preface, as we have seen, elaborates on the difference between poetry and history. [17] If Herrera's intention were to «dilatarse y hacer largos discursos», he could write in heroic verse, «tan grave y numeroso que viniera á igualar su estilo con la grandeza del sugeto». [18]

Heroic verse may claim certain stylistic advantages over prose, especially for treating grandiose themes, but it is not history. History remains forever on the opposite side from the «ficciones de la poesia». [19] This means that Herrera cannot allow himself in the *Relacion* to be carried away from the facts, either by the enticements of description or by the broad Biblical parallels he might wish to draw. The overall scheme, nonetheless, which informs the poet's vision and diction as well as the historian's interpretation of diverging facts, must be present to a greater or lesser degree in both. For it is related to the Truth which both seek in different ways. History, without such a backbone, would be an amorphous mass of trivial details. For the Christian, history, like life, has a point. This point, the direction in which all life seems to move, forms the basis for the historian's judgment of events, his «loor y vituperio» which Mosquera deems so essential. History must work through particulars to get to universals, whereas poetry is free to manipulate the universals as she likes.

Mariana's entry for the year 1571 in the *Historia de España* makes it appear likely that he had either read Herrera's *Relacion,* or the same sources from which the latter was born. Included in the record of Lepanto in Mariana we find a similar description of the battle scene:

> Era un espectáculo miserable, vocería de todas partes, matar, seguir, quebrar, tomar y echar á fondo galeras; el mar cubierto de armas y cuerpos muertos, teñido de sangre; con el grande humo de la pólvora ni se veia sol ni luz casi como si fuera de noche. [20]

[15] Herrera, *Relacion*, p. 248.
[16] *Ibid.*, p. 370.
[17] *Ibid.*, pp. 255-256.
[18] *Ibid.*, p. 255.
[19] *Ibid.*, p. 256.
[20] *Obras del Padre Juan de Mariana*, in B.A.E., Vol. XXXI (Madrid, 1854), «Año 1571» of *Historia de España*.

The space occupied by the description is smaller, commensurate with the reduced attention given to the entire episode. Many words and phrases are echoed, but the spirit animating the description has been altered. Mariana begins by denouncing the grim spectacle, whereas Herrera is first drawn by the visual contrast of fiery light and darkness, «un espectáculo alegrísimo», [21] created by the burning ships in the black, rainy night. During the battle, Herrera's sea roars with the splitting of ships. Mariana, too, lets loose an avalanche of words to represent the chaotic situation, but the forms are verbal: «matar, seguir, quebrar, tomar y echar á fondo galeras». In contrast, Herrera's vision expresses itself in adjectival forms. The prose is more deliberately pictorial. Herrera evokes a tableau of the sea, «cubierto de bajeles rotos, de fuegos, de remos, de astas y armas», concentrating on the plastic qualities of the bloody conflict's aftermath, unlike Mariana, who views the scene in terms of the action of pursuit and destruction. Yet this passage in the *Relacion,* as we have seen, while displaying poetic leanings, remains nonetheless well within the domain of prose, adding no embellishments which would lead the seeker of Truth astray.

Herrera felt himself drawn toward two aspects of Lepanto, the facts and their transcendence. Yet his feeling for the limits of genre kept his two impulses in neatly separated literary channels. Although the description of each poetic form in the *Anotaciones* furnishes copious evidence of this, the first entry which accompanies Garcilaso's second eclogue is perhaps the most striking. He condemns the piece as an admixture of various genres:

> Esta egloga es poema Dramático, que tambien se dize ativo, en que no habla el poeta, sino las personas introduzidas, porque δρᾶν es lo mesmo que hazer i representar. tiene mucha parte de principios medianos, de comedia, de tragedia, fabula, coro i elegia; [22]

and describes the resulting loss of poetic distinction: «ái de todos estilos, frases llanas traidas del vulgo, *gentil cabeça, yo podrè poco, callar que callaràs;* i alto mas que conviene a bucolica,

---

[21] Herrera, *Relacion,* p. 370.
[22] *Obras de Garci Lasso de la Vega con Anotaciones de Fernando de Herrera* (Seville, 1580), p. 537; ed. Gallego Morell (Granada, 1966), p. 482.

convocarè el infierno, i variacion de versos como en las tragedias.»[23] Because of these flaws, he concludes that while the poem has its moments, it is not perfect. Each time-honored form walks the straight and narrow path broken before by the ancient writers. Herrera belongs with those writers of the Spanish Golden Age who found their most fertile terrain in complying with the classical precepts and pushing the implications of these strict rules to their logical conclusion. Compared with Cervantes, who strains in *La Galatea* at the limits of even the sixteenth-century canons for the pastoral,[24] and mocks in *El coloquio de los perros* the poet who proudly cites Horace's instructions from *Ars poetica* that «primo ne medium, medio ne discrepet imum»;[25] and Lope, who mocks the rules he knows so well as a barrier to popular success,[26] Herrera seems exceptionally interested in surpassing the classical writers at their own game.

Among classical preceptors there is considerable discussion of the place of descriptive ornaments in historical writing. All speak of the need for clarity of style, for smooth and flowing periods.[27] Like the style which Lucian suggests for the historian, Cicero's epideictic style falls short of oratorical brilliance, but it comprises almost an apprenticeship for oratory: «quasi nutrix eius oratoris quem informare volumus.»[28] The epideictic style requires not simple blandness, but also «bright conceits and sounding phrases»: «Dulce igitur orationis genus et solutum et fluens, sententiis argutum, verbis sonens est in illo epidictico genere.»[29] This style can adequately furnish the occasional descriptions and harangues which Cicero would include in history.[30] Both Lucian and Cicero insist on moderation of such

---

[23] *Ibid.,* p. 537; ed. Gallego, p. 482.
[24] Juan Bautista Avalle-Arce, *La novela pastoril española* (Madrid, 1959).
[25] Quintus Horatius Flaccus, *Satires and Epistles,* ed. Edward P. Morris (Norman, Oklahoma, 1968), Epistle II, 3, 1. 152; Miguel de Cervantes, *Novelas ejemplares,* ed. F. Rodríguez Marín (Madrid, 1917), II, 330-331.
[26] Lope de Vega Carpio, «Arte nuevo para hacer comedias en este tiempo», in *Obras escogidas,* ed. Federico Carlos Sainz de Robles (Madrid, 1964). For a discussion of the quarrel of ancients and moderns in Golden Age poetics, see Andrée Collard, *Nueva poesía* (Madrid, 1967).
[27] Lucian, *The Way to Write History,* in *The Works of Lucian,* trans. H. W. and F. G. Fowler (Oxford, 1905), III, 130.
[28] Cicero, *Orator,* ed. H. M. Hubbell (Cambridge, Massachusetts, 1930), pp. 332-333, 336-337.
[29] *Ibid.,* pp. 336-337.
[30] *Ibid.,* pp. 354-355.

ornaments, an excess of which, like too many spices in cooking, ruins the entire confection.[31] Yet history should, Lucian insists, «have a touch of the poetical»:

> It needs, like poetry, to employ impressive and exalted tones, especially when it finds itself in the midst of the battle array and conflicts by land or sea; it is then that the poetic gale must blow to speed the vessel on, and help her ride the waves in majesty. But the diction is to be content with *terra firma,* using a little to assimilate itself to the beauty and grandeur of the subject, but never startling the hearer, nor forgetting a due restraint.[32]

The nature of description, its place in the *Relacion,* and its proximity to poetry on the same subject, suggest that Herrera had taken Lucian's advice to heart. His description of the sea battle, far more poetic than Mariana's, conforms equally well to the recommended modes of historical prose.

What is perhaps curious, then, is that Herrera should have felt the need to immortalize the Spanish victory in these two different ways. Many others, wishing to commemorate deeds of the house of Austria, found poetry a perfectly adequate vehicle. Juan Rufo, in the *Austriada,* followed in verse the footsteps of D. Diego Hurtado de Mendoza.[33] Poems such as Luis Zapata's *Carlo famoso* parallel Mexía's history of the reign of Charles V.

Juan Rufo's poem makes the most interesting subject for comparison with Herrera. The *Austriada,* whose composition began, its author informs us, in the same year of the publication of Herrera's *Relacion* —«gasté diez años de perpetuo estudio en

---

[31] Lucian, p. 130.
[32] *Ibid.,* p. 130.
[33] Due to the late posthumous publication of the *Guerra de Granada,* critics have long disputed the direction of this influence. G. Cirot defended in 1920 the primacy of the *Guerra de Granada* against the attacks on Hurtado de Mendoza by Lucas de Torre. Cf. Cirot, «La Guerra de Granada et l'Austriada», *Bulletin Hispanique,* XXXV (1915), 476-538. Ángel Valbuena Prat tends to side with Cirot; Antonio Papell («La poesía épica culta de los siglos XVI y XVII», in *H.G.L.H.,* ed. G. Díaz-Plaja [Barcelona, 1949], II, 761) adduces the evidence presented in the earlier polemic, which indicates that Hurtado de Mendoza's editor, Luis Tribaldos de Toledo, filled in some gaps in the original manuscript with excerpts from the epic poem. My own view agrees with this, and for one further reason: the evident borrowing in the *Austriada* from Herrera and other later sources (perhaps Paruta). If this is true, then the *Austriada* could not have been composed before 1572 (perhaps even 1574) at the earliest, which would require Hurtado de Mendoza to have seen a manuscript copy of it and borrowed from it during his last year(s) of life.

componer y limar este trabajo» [34] — appears to draw on Hurtado de Mendoza for the events of the Moorish uprising and on Herrera for material concerning Lepanto. Significantly, he draws on both the *Relacion* and the *Canción* to the victory of Lepanto which appeared with it and finds no reason not to mold them together into one *poetic* work. The words of Selim, the Turkish monarch, have evidently been copied from the *Canción* and considerably extended to include more factual information, thus betraying the careful separation Herrera had insisted on. The boasting of Herrera's hymn is drawn out into many stanzas, as part of a kind of council of war.[35] Likewise, Herrera's prose description of the fractious state of Christendom has passed into the *octavas reales* of the longer poem. For example, Rufo laments in the first canto the apostasy of France:

> No viéramos á Francia, que solia
> Resplandecer con fe tan poderosa,
> Que á las otras naciones excedia,
> Y en tierra y cielo se hacia gloriosa,
> Andar agora por diversa via,
> De suerte que la vida licenciosa
> Inficiona y corrompe con malicia
> La importante salud de la justicia.[36]

Rufo also paraphrases Herrera's battle hymn from the psalms in Canto 24:

> Agradeciendo á Dios gracias tamañas,
> Se cantaron: «Señor á tí alabamos,
> A tí por señor nuestro confesamos.
>   «Gloria á tí solo sea en las alturas,
> Alábente los hombres de la tierra;
> Tú solo domas las cervices duras,
> Tu virtud sola vence cualquier guerra.»[37]

The battle description itself is largely similar.

Yet Rufo, like Ercilla, is far more conscious than Herrera of his classical models. Both place many more invented harangues in the mouths of their characters and make frequent al-

---

[34] Juan Rufo, *La Austriada,* in *Poemas épicos,* ed. Cayetano Rosell, B.A.E., Vol. XXIX (Madrid, 1851), p. 2.
[35] *Ibid.,* pp. 57-58.
[36] *Ibid.,* pp. 4-5.
[37] *Ibid.,* p. 135.

lusions to classical heroes. Rufo even manages a reference to Cleopatra.[38] He also makes his own cosmic view even more conspicuous than Herrera's. To Herrera's Old Testament God is added a very active medieval devil on whom the responsibility for Christian troubles often falls. All of these elements walk a perilous line between prose and poetry. For both Rufo and Ercilla, the problems of making poetic so much anecdotal material and concrete detail are manifest. If he was at all concerned about the influence of poetry on the Truth, Rufo seemingly found it sufficient to invoke at the outset the divine grace of «God three in One» in place of the pagan muses and the «vana pompa del hablar fingido».[39] Ercilla (who also writes of Lepanto in a digression in the middle of *La Araucana*) evinces no qualms about writing his tale of South American conquests in verse.

Herrera, as far as we know, never conceived a narrative epic poem of great length.[40] His heroic verse confines itself to *canciones,* elegies and sonnets. Why should this be? It seems evident, in the light of the reservations expressed in Mosquera's Preface, that he felt unwilling to compromise the nature of either poetry or history. Poetry serves the purpose of lending grandeur and magnificence; history serves to record events as they actually happened, not colored by any one extreme interpretation, nor even mildly distorted by the demands which verse makes on vocabulary and syntax. To try to pour history into an epic mold sacrifices something, the best, of both. As syntax and meter stretch the Truth, so facts and figures tend to dilute the rich texture of heroic conception. Here again Herrera appears to conform his own practice to classical prescripts: Aristotle's affirmation in the *Poetics* that «imitation» is more fundamental to poetry than meter;[41] and Horace's self-criticism in the *Satires,* where, excluding himself from the number of true poets on the grounds that his poems are merely versified talk, he requires more of poetry than simple meter.[42]

Finally, having discussed Herrera's concept of history on the

---

[38] *Ibid.,* p. 122.
[39] *Ibid.,* p. 4.
[40] There was possibly a fictional epic on the Amadís theme, mentioned by Rioja in the preface to Pacheco's edition of the poetry, but lost even at that time.
[41] Aristotle, *Poetics,* in *Introduction to Aristotle,* ed. Richard McKeon (New York, 1947), pp. 624-625.
[42] Quintus Horatius Flaccus, Bk. I, 4; cf. Menéndez y Pelayo, *Historia de las ideas estéticas* (Madrid, 1946-1947), II.

basis of the *Relacion,* we must face for a moment a perplexing affirmation made by Pacheco in his portrait of Herrera. He is speaking of the lost universal history:

> la cual mostrò acabada i escrita en limpio a algunos amigos suyos, el año 1590. en ella repetia segunda vez la batalla Naval, i preguntado porque? respondio que la impressa era una relacion simple, i que esta otra era istoria, dando a entender que tenia las partes i calidades convenientes. [43]

Since Pacheco also declares that the *Istoria general* covered Spanish history up to the age of Charles V, which would not then include Lepanto, we can reasonably doubt the accuracy of this reference to Herrera's words. However, we are still left to deal with the question of what might have been the difference between the two works. The *Istoria general* might seem to fit one of the prevailing patterns of sixteenth-century historiography, actually, a vestige of the Middle Ages: the universal chronicle, beginning with Adam and Eve, which may have a particular national slant and which, as it approaches the present, is likely to be organized in arbitrary annalistic fashion. Mariana's *Historia de España* belongs essentially with this type. Its length and scope make it of necessity far less detailed than a more limited account, its prose quite unadorned with flourishes of humanistic erudition. [44]

If this were the case, how would Herrera have proceeded to deal with times before his own? For relatively recent periods, Herrera's technique in the *Anotaciones,* that of culling a number of sources contemporary to the events he relates (where possible) and giving his balanced judgment as to the most probable truth in case of conflict, is visible in its roughest form. Like all but a few of his Italian contemporaries, Herrera gives us no reason to believe that he used archival material or original documents of any sort in the process of his investigation. Guicciardini carried on this modern type of research toward the end of his career in the *Storia d'Italia* without appearing to consider it an especially

---

[43] Pacheco, *Libro de descripcion de verdaderos retratos,* reprint of the Seville 1599 edition (Seville, 1881-1885).
[44] Cf. Georges Cirot, *Les histoires générales d'Espagne entre Alphonse X et Philippe II, 1284-1556* (Paris, 1904); and *Mariana historien* (Bordeaux, 1905).

important development, so that we cannot expect his contemporaries to have realized its significance either.[45]

But beyond a certain point in the past, the historian is obliged to have recourse to materials of a literary or mythological nature, that is, to basically non-historical information. The *Anotaciones* to Garcilaso furnish copious evidence of Herrera's familiarity with this sort of material, which doubtless formed part of the vast fund of knowledge which Herrera was storing up for the composition of the general history. Much of his subject matter there, designed to elucidate Garcilaso's abundant mythological allusions, derives from the Latin poets and from sources of real and legendary geography like Strabo. Herrera's quest for this sort of information becomes not so much a search for the Truth, as an attempt to evoke the richness of the poetic tradition which surrounds these creatures of the imagination. He has an incipient sense of the possibilities for metaphor creation inherent in this wealth of detail, possibilities most fully exploited by the Góngora of the *Polifemo*. Thus his effort in the *Anotaciones* is aimed at recapturing a literary rather than an historical past.

What we should like to know more about are Herrera's views on the origin of Spain. To what extent would he have borrowed the fabulous etymologies for Spanish toponyms to which so many sixteenth-century Spanish historians looked in order to fill the unknown gaps in peninsular history?[46] Would he, like Ocampo, have adopted the twenty-four kings «discovered» by Annius of Viterbo?[47] Or would he, like Juan de Valdés in the *Diálogo de la lengua,* have roundly condemned this misguided patriotism?[48] Or, are his own pronouncements that truth is the backbone of history to be received with the same skepticism as Mariana's in the *Historia de España,* whose voiced scruples do not prevent him from preserving Annius' kings —albeit he calls them «los reyes fabulosos de España»— and a number of other legendary personages (e.g., Tubal), whose prehistoric visits lend prestige to their supposed descendants?[49]

---

[45] Felix Gilbert, *Machiavelli and Guicciardini* (Princeton, 1965), p. 296.
[46] Georges Cirot, *Les histoires générales,* Part I, Chapter 2.
[47] *Ibid.,* Part II, Chapter 1.
[48] Juan de Valdés, *Diálogo de la lengua,* ed. José F. Montesinos (Madrid, 1964), pp. 180-181.
[49] Mariana explains in the first chapter of Book I that the «atrevimiento de escribir y publicar patrañas en esta parte, y fábulas de poetas más que verdaderas historias; ... a mí despertó para que con el pequeño ingenio y erudición

Herrera, like Mariana, felt a high degree of patriotism, of which his literary efforts were a deliberate manifestation. The *Relacion,* Mosquera declares in his Preface, is the first stage in a literary enterprise which he urges Herrera to continue, «celebrando la honra y valor de España». [50] In the *Anotaciones,* Herrera makes a show of modesty over his own literary talents and excuses the faults of his work, begging the reader to believe «que la onra de la nacion, i la nobleza i ecelencia del escritor presente me obligaron a publicar estas rudezas de mi ingenio, i no esperança de alguna estimacion». [51] But we cannot say what form this loyalty would have taken in a discussion of Spain's ancient and medieval past. Pacheco describes the «istoria general del Mundo», [52] in which stress was given to events involving the participation of Spanish arms, as a rebuttal of accounts «que escrivieron con injuria o invidia los escritores estrangeros».

Herrera does come to the rescue in an entry found near the end of the *Anotaciones* in which he explains the phrase «el osado español» of the second eclogue. He seizes on these words, a transparent pretext for the impassioned defense of Spain which follows: «Porque no sè que animos se pueden hallar tan pacientes, que toleren los oprobrios i denuestos con que vituperan a los Españoles los escritores de Italia.» [53] Herrera is not afraid to condemn Italian historiography: «antigua costumbre es suya, i eredada, de los Romanos, alabar con grande ecesso las hazañas de su gente, i cansar en esto con importunacion molestissima a los que leen sus escritos, i olvidarse de las cosas bien hechas de las otras naciones.» [54]

Not only has Italian historiography suffered a kind of chronic myopia, thereby committing countless sins of omission. Lately they have added slander to neglect, deliberately focusing attention on «tales vicios, que estuviera mejor a su reputacion no averse acordado dellos». [55] The arch-offender is Paolo Giovio, once

---

que alcanzo, acometiese a escribir esta historia, más aína con intento de volver por la verdad y defendella que con pretensión de honra o esperanza de algún premio». *Obras del Padre Juan de Mariana.* Cf. Cirot, *Mariana historien.*

[50] Herrera, *Relacion,* p. 257.
[51] Herrera, *Anotaciones,* p. 66; ed. Gallego, p. 282.
[52] Pacheco, *Libro de descripcion.*
[53] Herrera, *Anotaciones,* p. 611; ed. Gallego, p. 536.
[54] *Ibid.,* p. 611; ed. Gallego, p. 536.
[55] *Ibid.,* p. 611; ed. Gallego, p. 536.

admirer of Charles V, but subsequently moved in his disillusionment to the most acid criticism of the Emperor.[56] Opening a barrage of indignant interrogatives, Herrera exclaims:

> quien ái tan olvidado de su naturaleza, del respeto que se deve a la cortesia i a la mesma verdad, que sufra sin indinacion en aquella manifica i abundosa istoria del Iovio las injurias con que afrenta a los Españoles? las cosas ilustres suyas que dexa de tratar, i las infames que con tanta insolencia trae a la memoria? por ventura es lei istorica publicar los delitos i callar las cosas bien hechas?[57]

Gonzalo Jiménez de Quesada less than ten years earlier had likewise defended Spain's honor in the name of truth against this dangerous enemy.[58] Guicciardini, Bembo and Sabellicus are numbered among the other offenders. How can they call Spain barbarous, if the two nations are virtually identical in religion, language and letters?[59]

Herrera attempts to do battle for Spain against a quite understandable Italian literary reaction to the Spanish presence in Italy as a foreign ruler. Many of the outstanding Italian humanists nurtured an ill-concealed hatred for Spanish imperial domination which led them often to blame the foreign presence for the decline of pristine Roman virtues.[60] That the invader should also be an emperor further aroused their republican sympathies to wrath. These historians, in despair over their historical moment, cast sixteenth-century Italy in the image of Rome, threatened with destruction from without. In this context Spain assumes the role of the invading Gothic tribes. Machiavelli closes his instructions for the perfect prince by serving notice that the «barbarian invader» must be expelled if Italy is to enjoy political wellbeing of the kind he envisions.[61]

It is to Herrera's credit that he does not seek to undermine the prestige of Italy. Everywhere in the *Anotaciones* one finds

---

[56] Gonzalo Jiménez de Quesada, *El Antijovio*, ed. Manuel Ballesteros Gaibrois (Bogotá, 1952).
[57] Herrera, *Anotaciones*, p. 611; ed. Gallego, p. 536.
[58] Jiménez de Quesada, Preface.
[59] Herrera, *Anotaciones*, p. 611; ed. Gallego, p. 536.
[60] Cf. Benedetto Croce, *La Spagna nella vita italiana durante la Rinascenza* (Bari, 1949).
[61] Machiavelli, *Il Principe*, in *Tutte le opere storiche e letterarie*, ed. Guido Mazzoni and Mario Casella (Florence, 1929), p. 49 ff.

explicit and implicit acknowledgments of the grandeur achieved in Italian civilization. But Spain too deserves her share of praise. Spain has been endowed with equal dignity, with her own distinguished intellectuals, with military talent beyond comparison.[62] If Spanish scholars cannot match Italians in numbers, it is because until recently arms have taken precedence over letters:

> los Españoles, ocupados en las armas con perpetua solicitud hasta acabar de restituir su reino a la religion Cristiana; no pudiendo entre aquel tumulto i rigor de hierro acudir a la quietud i sossiego destos estudios; quedaron por la mayor parte agenos de su noticia.[63]

The glorious crusade against Islam more than offsets the dark age of Spanish letters: «quien à servido tantos años a la religion con no cansado estudio, acrecentando en ella tantos reinos grandissimos, agenos de su conocimiento?»[64] The answer to Herrera's rhetorical question is plain: Spain has no equal as defender of the faith.

Herrera adduces a long series of examples of this valor to prove his point, from which we glean the only information we have of his conception of Spain's past. Roman historians have neglected this phase of her history, he says:

> quedanos solo un rastro del resplandor despedido de su lumbre con indinacion de la invidia, que no puede sufrir que salgan del sepulcro del olvido las pocas cosas que la fuerça de la verdad compelio con verguença de la eloquencia latina que se contassen desnudamente entre las muchas tan encarecidamente alabadas de los Romanos.[65]

The Spain of antiquity is marked by a consistent, determined resistance to foreign power: did not Spain rise up against Rome? did not Hannibal and Sertorius learn in Spain the military skills they were to use against Rome? did not Spain resist Carthage, Antiochus, Mithridates? But the place of honor is reserved for

---

[62] Herrera, *Anotaciones*, p. 612; ed. Gallego, p. 537.
[63] *Ibid.*, p. 75; ed. Gallego, p. 288. Quevedo, in *España defendida*, makes a similar claim: «Y cuando ... no tuvieran historias copiosas y elegantes todos los reyes de España, era para nosotros gloriosa respuesta que los españoles, más se precian de hacer cosas dignas de ser escritas, que no de escribir sueños o lo que los otros hicieron.» *Obras* (Madrid, 1961), I, 517.
[64] Herrera, *Anotaciones*, p. 612; ed. Gallego, p. 537.
[65] *Ibid.*, p. 613; ed. Gallego, p. 537.

Numancia: «que alabança no sera inferior a la gloria de aquella ciudad que, sin muros i sin torres, pequeña en sitio i en numero, resistio i contrastò en tantos años a los grandes exercitos de Roma?» [66] Numancia, worn by enemy arms and by her own hunger, holds to her honor against incredible odds. Herrera gives his admiration free reign: «no fue vencida Numancia, si no muerta; no rota, si no acabada. no pudo el poder Romano, vencedor de las naciones, la fortuna i destreza del expunador de Cartago, deshazer a Numancia.» [67] After mentioning Trajan and Theodosius, Spain's contribution to the Roman world, Herrera turns to the Reconquest heroes: Pelayo, Bernardo del Carpio, Fernán González, Ruy Díaz, Diego Ordóñez, Garci Pérez de Vargas, Garci Gómez Carrillo, Alonso Pérez de Guzmán, Fernando el Católico and his armies. [68] As if their marvelous deeds («maravillosas, pero semejantes a otras de los grandes príncipes» [69]) would not suffice to demonstrate Spain's glory, Herrera proceeds to name those heroes who have helped make inroads into French power, and who have carried the Crusade to Africa and the New World: the Gran Capitán, Don Alonso de Aguilar, Don Luis Puertocarrero, Antonio de Leiva, Pedro Navarro, Fernando de Alarcón, García de Paredes, and Juan de Urbina. Finally Hernán Cortés, example of perfect manly courage: «que atravessando regiones espantosas, i montes insuperables, quitando a los Españoles la esperança de todo refugio umano, fuera de la que podian tener en la fortaleza de sus braços, se metio en una tierra grandissima.» [70] Spain has never known a lack of heroes, only a scarcity of good historians, «escritores cuerdos i sabios que los dedicassen con immortal estilo a la eternidad de la memoria», and of princes and kings equally wise to use the persuasion of their patronage. [71] Italy can bear no more of the responsibility than Spain herself for the decline of her reputation. The writer has an obligation to defend Spain with his pen; but here, as in the *Relacion,* Herrera does not appear to feel any need to reinforce truth with fiction. That is the province of poetry.

While the *Anotaciones* show Herrera's reverence for the

---

[66] *Ibid.,* p. 613; ed. Gallego, p. 538.
[67] *Ibid.,* p. 613; ed. Gallego, p. 538.
[68] *Ibid.,* pp. 613-615; ed. Gallego, p. 538.
[69] *Ibid.,* p. 614; ed. Gallego, p. 539.
[70] *Ibid.,* p. 615; ed. Gallego, p. 539.
[71] *Ibid.,* p. 615; ed. Gallego, p. 540.

more remote classical sources of information in Greek, Roman and patristic writings, in the *Relacion,* largely because of the nature of the subject, we find him extremely skeptical and cautious. His attitude strikes us as extremely modern, at times even «scientific». His effort in the *Relacion* seems more in tune with the «new» history of detail and precision of Zurita and Morales.[72] It is baffling that, having made such a considerable historiographic advance, he should then have wished to revert to a traditional mold, and furthermore that he should call his step forward a «relacion simple». (To a lesser degree we feel the same sort of suprise as that Cervantes should have written *Don Quijote,* and then have gone on —or back?— to *Persiles y Sigismunda.*) Mosquera's Preface suggests that Herrera will build a more grandiose construction from the terse narrative. True «History» may simply have meant to him «all history». To tell of the present without encasing it in the framework of all of the past becomes the journalist more than the historian. Universal history can perhaps enhance events, giving them a grandeur which less boldly conceived prose is unable to do and which must otherwise be sought separately in the «ficciones de la poesía».

There may, however, be another, more convincing sense to Pacheco's remarks. Repeating Herrera's distinction between the «relacion simple» and actual history, Pacheco explains that the poet meant to say that his longer work had the «partes i calidades convenientes». No change of substance appears to be implied. Herrera's own Dedication affirms that the *Relacion* belongs to history because of its faithfulness to Truth.[73] The «partes i calidades» suggest that the changes will be formal in character. One is struck, when reading the *Relacion* in conjunction with other European accounts of the same episode, as well as the histories of Italian writers who boasted at least the humanistic background of Herrera, by the absence of a number of qualities found in these latter works. Herrera follows a good many of the honored humanist prescripts for the writing of history. As in their classical imitation, he makes war his theme; he gives the background of the campaign, the negotiations which

---

[72] Cf. Cirot, *Les histoires générales* and *Mariana historien*; Benito Sánchez Alonso, *Historia de la historiografía española* (Madrid, 1947).
[73] Herrera, *Relacion,* pp. 248-249.

precede the fighting. In his narrative of the events, he surveys the geography of the place of battle, portrays the military leaders, describes the order of battle, the machinery used, and leaves the actual conflict for his climax. He might also have made eventually the customary division into books and sections.[74]

What then is missing? The most conspicuous absence is that of the lengthy speeches by the protagonists which Thucydides uses and Lucian and Cicero prescribe. Humanist historians followed their ancient counterparts in composing these purely imagined discourses, which were designed to evoke the complexity of a situation, to give insight into the choices faced by a group at a particular time.[75] It is the only form of tampering with the truth that humanist historical theory permits. The historian reconstructs one dramatic moment with the aid of all his acquired knowledge of the situation. This practice had long since been adopted by Spanish historians such as Pero López de Ayala and Pablo de Santa María.[76] Luis Cabrera de Córdoba in his history of Philip II frequently indulges in this technique. Thus in stressing the role of Cardinal Granvelle in the negotiations that led to the formation of the League, Cabrera quotes the Prelate's words «en sustancia».[77]

As we have noticed, these speeches, present in Fougasses and Paruta, have no place in the *Relacion*: Herrera summarizes any spoken arguments of his heroes in the most succinct indirect discourse. We can only speculate as to whether the repetition of the naval battle in his general history would have included additions of this nature. But Herrera's eagerness in the Prologue to plead the stylistic deficiencies of his work suggests that he was thinking of the accepted norms for elegant historical writing among humanists. Whether such a second version would have sacrificed the fruits of his careful investigation to literary

---

[74] Gilbert, pp. 210-211.
[75] *Ibid.*, p. 211.
[76] Cirot, *Les histoires générales*, p. 38 ff.; Robert B. Tate, «An Apology for Monarchy», *Romance Philology*, XV (1961), 111-123; «A Humanistic Biography of John II of Aragon», *Bulletin of Hispanic Studies*, XXXIX (1962), 1-15; «Four Notes on Gonzalo García de Santa María», *Romance Philology*, XXVII (1963), 362-372; «Italian Humanism and Spanish Historiography», *Bulletin of the John Rylands Library*, XXXIV (September, 1951); «Mythology in Spanish Historiography of the Middle Ages and the Renaissance», *Hispanic Review*, XXII (1954), 1-18; «Nebrija the Historian», *Bulletin of Hispanic Studies*, XXXIV (1957), 125-146.
[77] Luis Cabrera de Córdoba, *Filipe Segundo, Rey de España* (Madrid, 1876), II, 74 ff.

polish remains an enigma. Felix Gilbert has shown that Italian sixteenth-century historiography found its loyalties shared between fact and art.[78] Thus, while Herrera may have been only partially aware of the significance of his investigations on the League of Lepanto for contemporary history, his work does represent an advance (by our standards) over many previous works. Yet history was destined to await much longer the thoroughgoing reverence for original historical documents which animates all modern historical investigation.

[78] Gilbert, p. 271 ff.

PART TWO

Tomas Moro

CHAPTER ONE

THE EXEMPLARY LIFE

The twenty years which followed the appearance of Herrera's first published work were marked by intense literary and scholarly activity for the author of the *Relacion.* We can judge only imperfectly the fruits of this work, but the loss for the student of Herrera seems to have been equally great in prose and in poetry. The prologuists of the posthumous edition of his poetry point to several longer poems, of a type not represented in his extant verse: an epic poem, *Amadís;* [1] an *Amarilis;* [2] and a tragic poem, *Amores de Lausino y Corona.* [3] All of these Coster would place early in Herrera's career. [4] Yet the *Anotaciones* bear witness to his continuing interest in numerous poetic types, to his enthusiasm for translation. His edition of Garcilaso's poems is replete with translations of the classics, semi-classics and his Italian contemporaries — translations apologetically offered, but a tantalizing source of information, as yet unexplored, concerning the genesis of Herrera's poetic diction. After the striking paucity of literary allusions in his early opuscule, the *Anotaciones* reveal the vast horizons of Herrera's erudition (sometimes pseudo-erudition) as author after author is led forth to bow before the reader and to make his contribution to the vast fund of knowledge which the experienced critic assembles for the

[1] Prologue of Francisco de Rioja to Fernando de Herrera, *Versos,* ed. A. Coster (Strasbourg, 1916).
[2] *Obras de Garci Lasso de la Vega con Anotaciones de Fernando de Herrera* (Seville, 1580), p. 444; and in *Garcilaso de la Vega y sus comentaristas,* ed. A. Gallego Morell (Granada, 1966), p. 481.
[3] Francisco Pacheco, «Fernando de Herrera», in *Libro de descripción de verdaderos retratos de illustres y memorables varones,* reprint of Seville 1599 edition (Seville, 1881-1885).
[4] Adolphe Coster, *Fernando de Herrera* (Paris, 1908).

uninitiated. Dwarfing Garcilaso's economical production, the commentary shows Herrera to have been acquainted with much of the historical, philosophical and literary writing of his age. The names of Bembo, Guicciardini, Guillaume Budé and countless others suggest that he was in touch with the intellectual activity of the Mediterranean basin. The translations which appear render originally Latin, Italian, Catalan and Portuguese texts. What references one finds to Northern European figures have to do with writings Herrera knew in Latin rather than any non-Romance vernacular and which are of a primarily historical nature. All of this information, lovingly gathered, was carefully assembled into two works: the *Anotaciones* to the works of Garcilaso de la Vega, published in 1580, and the *Istoria general,* which Herrera presented in completed form to his friends in 1590, and which was subsequently lost.

To this we must add an intense poetical activity, which almost certainly continued throughout the entire period, and even beyond it to Herrera's death. If one compares the 1578 manuscript copy of the poems with the published Seville version of 1582, and the latter with the posthumous Pacheco edition of 1619, one finds evidence of the unceasing business of correction and revision in the search for «modos nuevos i llenos de hermosura».[5] Herrera's own words about the need to polish one's verse diligently (for example, his censure of Diego Hurtado de Mendoza for carelessness[6]) provide the most convincing proof of his continuing poetic self-discipline.[7]

Where, then, does the *Tomas Moro* fit into this picture? In fact, it is a curiously symmetrical scheme: two spare narratives, equidistant from a slim volume of poems, set against a background of prodigious scholarly exuberance. What is the relation of Herrera's life of More to the rest of his work? Is it, too, like the *Relacion de la guerra de Cipre,* an extract of the lost

---

[5] Herrera, *Anotaciones,* p. 295; ed. Gallego, p. 399. Cf. Herrera, *Rimas inéditas,* ed. José Manuel Blecua (Madrid, 1948); Oreste Macrí, *Fernando de Herrera* (Madrid, 1959); A. David Kossoff, *Vocabulario de la obra poética de Herrera* (Madrid, 1966). Despite errors of copying which Kossoff indicates in the introduction to his *Vocabulario,* I am unwilling to attribute to Pacheco, Rioja and Duarte the more profound syntactical changes which are found in the 1619 edition.
[6] Herrera, *Anotaciones,* pp. 76-77; ed. Gallego, p. 290.
[7] Francisco López Estrada, «Edición y estudio del *Tomas Moro* de Fernando de Herrera», *Archivo Hispalense,* XII (1950), 9.

Istoria, as some would have us think? [8] The second edition of the *Tomas Moro* carries a note to this effect by Don Alonso Ramírez de Prado, but once again the character of the brief narrative argues for its having been an independent piece, as will become evident from our discussion. [9] Since any conclusions concerning its original location must remain conjectural, we shall concentrate instead on making more clear its substantial relationship to the rest of Herrera's work.

The same problems of generic classification arise over the *Tomas Moro* as they did with the *Relacion* or the *Anotaciones.* Was the first true history? Was the second commentary, poetics or miscellany? And is the *Tomas Moro* biography, history or even sermon? In a much-discussed passage, Herrera declares the obvious. [10] In the first place he does not intend to write a history of the demise of English Catholicism. This need had already been filled for the Spanish reading public by Rivadeneira's *Historia eclesiástica del Scisma de Inglaterra,* published only a short time before in 1588:

> Mas porque, para entendimiento destas cosas, es necesario referir otras, dire solamente las que no se pueden escusar, tomando dellas lo que singularmente toca à Tomas Moro. Porque assi como no es mi intento escrivir toda su vida, assi no me parece acertado traer prolixamente todas aquellas cosas, que fueron maravillosas, i como tales an sido tratadas de onbres doctos. [11]

Herrera refers to a streamlining of his work. The affairs of More belong in the foreground; other less immediate matters remain in the distance. Related historical events are the literary property of other «onbres doctos», while the minutiae of More's everyday life are likewise relegated to another place. What Herrera promises is no simple biographical narrative.

It is the very first sentence of his text which offers the best indication of what is to come:

> Cuando me pongo en consideracion de las cosas pasadas, i rebuelvo en la memoria los hechos de aquellos onbres, que se dispusieron à todos los peligros, por no hazer ofensa à la virtud, i es-

---

[8] *Ibid.,* p. 12.
[9] *Ibid.,* p. 12.
[10] *Ibid.,* p. 16.
[11] Fernando de Herrera, *Tomas Moro,* in «Edición y estudio», p. 38.

cogieron antes la onra i alabança de la muerte, que el abatimiento i vituperio de la vida, no puedo dexar de admirarme de la ecelencia i singular valor de su animo, i estimar marauillosamente sus obras.[12]

Thomas More provides Herrera with a stimulus to reconsider the past, to reassess the deeds of brave men, to refresh memory, admiration, esteem. Henry VIII's Chancellor takes his place in the company of the just. His life and death now form one case, one example of virtuous conduct which can serve as a model for imitation: «es Tomas Moro uno de los varones mas ecelentes, que a criado la religion Cristiana, i clarisimo exenplo de Fè i bondad para todos los onbres constituidos en dinidad, i en oficios i grandeza de magistrados.»[13] Francisco López Estrada rightly calls this manner of focusing on the pinnacles of the past «la historia ejemplar»,[14] for it is in fact a review of the perfections which human time has offered. He cites Pero Mexía's prologue to the *Historia Imperial y Cesárea* on history: «La historia verdadera ninguna virtud deja sin loor, ni vicio sin reprehensión; a todo da su perfecto valor y lugar. Es testigo contra los malos y abono de los buenos, tesoro y depósito de las grandes virtudes y hazañas.»[15] He might equally have cited the words of Cristóbal Mosquera de Figueroa in his Preface to Herrera's earlier work, referring to his «cierta y verdadera relacion de cosas pasadas y acontecidas *con loor y con vituperio*».[16] The *Tomas Moro*, like the *Relacion* and Herrera's brief remarks in the *Anotaciones*, is born of a view of history as exemplarity. In the *Anotaciones*, when he springs to Spain's defense against Italian «slanderers», Herrera implies that history ought to preserve for posterity primarily those deeds which are worthy of memory, or at any rate the historian ought to put exemplary deeds in full relief and leave the rest in shadows.[17] Behind this attitude stands a vigorous conviction of history's value and its inevitable impact, sketched by Mosquera as we have already seen. Books will naturally invite emulation: the protagonists of future history will drink in the elixir of glory in the annals of the past

---

[12] *Ibid.*, p. 34.
[13] *Ibid.*, p. 35.
[14] López Estrada, p. 27.
[15] *Ibid.*, p. 28.
[16] Cf. p. 18 above. Italics mine.
[17] Herrera, *Anotaciones*, p. 611; ed. Gallego, p. 536.

and sally forth to fashion the trajectories of their lives according to the models of true histories. Thus, Herrera tells us, Don Juan de Austria «imitated» the deeds of Alexander the Great and those of his own father, the Emperor Charles V. Consequently, the writing of history becomes a very serious affair and a conscious mission for the Sevillian.

However much he may depart from this norm, Herrera is conscious of following an established literary vein with the *Tomas Moro:* «pues no es negocio nuevo, dexar à la memoria de la edad siguiente, los hechos i costumbres de los onbres señalados, aunque no se estime tanbien el valor i merecimiento de la virtud en los tiempos, en que se halla dificilmente.» [18] Once again, today's history belongs to the future, even as classical history has become the property of Herrera's present. It appears likely that Herrera is not thinking of the tradition of saints' lives, although More clearly falls within their number, but of the lives of antiquity, Plutarch's *Lives* in particular, or the Roman historians Sallust and Titus Livius. [19] Perhaps, as López Estrada suggests, the consciousness of classical prototypes led Herrera to forget all «lo que no está al nivel del panegírico clásico». [20] Certainly we must call attention, as he has, to the absence of any information regarding More's personal and emotional life. Herrera describes succinctly the personality and decorum of More:

> Estava en igual conparacion la modestia i suavidad de sus costunbres con la integridad i mesura de su vida, i la festividad de su ingenio, no se dexava vencer de la policia i elegancia de sus letras i erudicion, con que alcançò entre los onbres doctos de su edad opinion grandisima; i asi era amado i reverenciado de los suyos, i admirado con veneracion de los estrangeros. [21]

Not a single example of the Chancellor's sparkling, irrepressible merriment survives the journey south. Herrera evaluates More from a distance, and we cannot and should not expect from him the intimate family anecdotes which lend so much charm to Roper's *Life of Sir Thomas More,* whether or not Herrera had seen that document. As has been shown, Herrera is extremely selective with the material which did come to his attention.

---

[18] Herrera, *Tomas Moro,* p. 35.
[19] Coster, *Fernando de Herrera,* p. 288; López Estrada, p. 27.
[20] López Estrada, p. 27.
[21] Herrera, *Tomas Moro,* pp. 35-36.

Once again it is López Estrada who has delineated various reasons originating in Herrera's own personality to show why he might not have chosen to recount any of the episodes dealing with Margaret, More's favorite daughter, which appear in the work of Nicholas Sander.[22]

López Estrada has opened up new possibilities for the examination of the *Tomas Moro* by indicating its close borrowing from Sander's *De origine ac Progressv Schimatis Anglicani,* which appeared in Rome in 1586.[23] This same volume, widely read in Roman Catholic Europe as a reliable account of the English heresy, provided the point of departure for Rivadeneira's *Historia eclesiástica,* previously mentioned. It is one of the manifold delights of the Spanish Golden Age to note what different products have been engendered by a single source. (I refer the reader to R. O. Jones's article, which compares the two works.[24]) In comparison with the total extension of his work, Herrera borrows very little indeed from Sander. He appropriates, in fact, the very barest skeleton of narrative to give his incomplete report of the events in question, and on this slim framework erects an elaborate tribute to More. It almost seems that the Chancellor is only incidentally a part of England's history. For, through Herrera's fashioning, he emerges as the perfect Christian gentleman and, in political terms, as the perfect counselor of state, unhappily paired with an all too imperfect monarch. Herrera makes More's life a point of departure for exalting the virtues and exposing the vices of good and evil men of his day, even as he made the heroes of Lepanto models of conduct for quite different circumstances. We shall return in another chapter to the direct comparison of *Tomas Moro* and the *Relacion.*

---

[22] López Estrada, p. 27.
[23] López Estrada, «Las fuentes históricas del *Tomas Moro* de Fernando de Herrera», *Revista bibliográfica y documental,* III (1949), 237-243.
[24] Royston O. Jones, «El *Tomas Moro* de Fernando de Herrera», B.R.A.E., XXX (1950), 423-438.

CHAPTER TWO

A RECURRING THEME: VIRTUE EMBATTLED

1. The Struggle Against Human Weakness

If there is one theme which Herrera pursues unceasingly throughout his literary career, it is the theme of human virtue, sustained in the face of overwhelming odds against its survival. The heroes of Lepanto are truly virtuous men, that is, men who have overcome first apathy and passivity among their own ranks, and then have boldly pitted themselves against superior infidel forces. A worthy life connotes struggle, to master self, to purify one's own conduct, and to provide a model of active virtue for lesser men. Thus, in the *Anotaciones,* as we have seen, Hernán Cortés achieves the ultimate perfection of heroic virtue when he has cut himself and his men off from all help beyond the power of their own wills: «quitando a los Españoles la esperança de todo refugio umano, fuera de la que podian tener en la fortaleza de sus braços.»[1] This resembles a lengthy entry in which Herrera accounts for the Spanish defeat at Gelves. The historian condemns the utter imprudence of the venture and does not shrink from describing the rashness of the inexperienced Spanish commander Don García. Herrera even admits to Don García's fright when the Moors charge his thirst-crazed troops. Yet this very cowardice heightens the value of his eventual rallying:

> en aquel subito caso lleno de confusion i temor, hizo entonces oficio de fortissimo soldado i capitan mananimo; porque peleando primero a cavallo, se apeò, i con una pica en las manos se puso

---

[1] *Obras de Garci Lasso de la Vega con Anotaciones de Fernando de Herrera* (Seville, 1580), p. 615; ed. Gallego Morell (Granada, 1966), p. 539.

> delante los soldados, esortandolos a combatir con valeroso animo, i a cobrar fuerça i osadia de la necessidad presente. I aunque vio, que no lo seguian mas de aquellos 60. cavalleros, i algunos otros pocos, en quien pudo mas la verguença que la sed i el miedo; no desmayò, antes dio con ellos tal carga a los Moros, que los hizo retirar cuanto una carrera de cavallo. [2]

The diction of this 1580 panegyric is identical to that of 1572. Among many, we could recall Herrera's praise of Philip II's persistence in the face of misfortune: «mas que no por eso habia desmayado el Rey Filipo.» [3]

Oreste Macrí, in his invaluable study, first called attention to the cross-fertilization of heroic and erotic diction in the poetry of Herrera. [4] The protagonists of both types of adventure aspire to timeless realms of light where reigns the purest immortal beauty of soul. If their goals resemble one another, so does their struggle. In the sixth elegy of the 1582 collection of his verse, Herrera portrays the conflict between love (passion) and virtue:

> D'aquel error en que viví engañado
> salgo a la pura luz, i me levanto
> tal vez del peso que sufrí cansado. [5]

The next lines begin to outline a traditional conflict between «los dañados gustos del sentido» and Reason, but farther into the poem Herrera returns to his concept of heroic virtue:

> Quien sabe en qué se goza, i nunca entrega
> su buena dicha en el poder ageno,
> de la virtud a l'alta cumbre llega.
>   Estos deleites, tras quien fuí sin freno,
> qu'al fin tan caro cuestan, me traxeron
> siempre de confusión i temor lleno.
>   Ni fueron firmes, ni fieles fueron;
> dañáron [me] huyendo; i si uvo alguno
> que no huyó con cuantos me huyeron.
>   Seguro gozo puede ser ninguno,
> ninguno puede ser perpetuo cuanto
> la tierra cría, i cerca el gran Netuno.

---

[2] *Ibid.*, p. 594; ed. Gallego, p. 524.
[3] Herrera, *Relacion de la guerra de Cipre*, in *C.D.I.*, XXI (Madrid, 1852), 338.
[4] Oreste Macrí, *Fernando de Herrera* (Madrid, 1959).
[5] Herrera, *Poesías*, ed. Vicente García de Diego (Madrid, 1914), p. 126.

> Sola virtud, tú sola, puedes tanto,
> qu'el gozo dar perpetuo i bien seguro
> puedes, si en amor tuyo me levanto. [6]

Virtue and the struggle it entails provide the only possible human certainty. Herrera then bewails human «flaqueza» with an *ubi sunt*:

> ¿Dó está el desseo ya del onor justo?
> ¿dó el amor verdadero de la gloria?
> ¿dó contra el vicio el coraçón robusto?
> Gran hazaña es gozar de la vitoria
> del bravo contendor, i los despojos
> guardar para blasón de la memoria;
> pero es mucho mayor ante los ojos
> que miran bien, por la no usada senda
> caminando entre peñas i entre abrojos
> sobrepujar en áspera contienda
> sus contrarios, i ver[s']en l'ardua cumbre,
> do no alcance el nublado, ni l'ofenda. [7]

Herrera's «no usada senda» does not connote a retreat from the struggle, in the way that Fray Luis envisions a path which would lure him from the «mundanal ruido» of his own combative life. The poet here envisions not withdrawal from the struggle but confrontation:

> Ira, miedo, codicia aborrecida
> nos cercan, i huir no es de provecho,
> que las llevamos siempre en la huída. [8]

Virtue, like a sword blade, must be continually sharpened with use. Every area of life furnishes a battleground where love of honor and glory carry virtue to its difficult triumph over vice and human weakness. Herrera's poetry, far from being simply the exercise in nascent *culterano* techniques or a slight Spanish variation of a Petrarchan *canzoniere*, belongs in the mainstream of his philosophical and moral preoccupations. Numerous poems such as the one cited force us to abandon as artificial and inexact the division of Sevillian poetry of the latter part of the sixteenth century into «esthetic» on the one hand (Herrera) and «philo- sophical» on the other (the author of the «Epístola moral a Fa-

---

[6] *Ibid.*, pp. 130-131.
[7] *Ibid.*, p. 131.
[8] *Ibid.*, p. 130.

bio» and others).[9] It would be a mistake to allow Herrera's radical attitudes about spelling and the archaism to convince us that he was divorced from the intellectual climate of the Seville of his day.

The theme of virtue, so much alive then, ten years after the publication of Herrera's first work, has lost none of its vigor a decade later. Herrera continues, as we have seen in the first sentence of the *Tomas Moro,* to be vitally concerned with the company of the just, those who face any peril to attain immortal honor, those who somehow escape the ravages of human time with their deeds, «mayores que las umanas».[10] While Don Juan de Austria is implicitly measured by the same standards as the medieval crusaders who left hearth and home to defend the cause of the one true religion, Thomas More must be seen against another yardstick, «los gloriosos hechos de los Martires, las penitencias i estrechezas de aquellos, que se ocupavan en contenplacion de las cosas divinas».[11]

Some of Herrera's references to the suffering of Christian martyrs originate in the Sander text. For example, Herrera follows his Latin model in recording an identical conversation between More and the council which has been convoked to pass judgment on him. In this exchange, Sander pictures More growing ever more certain of his martyr's calling and invoking the example of other martyrs and servants of the Church, more powerful to woo him than the English King.[12] But Herrera expands on Sander in this vein as well. When virtually translating the latter's report of the Chancellor's conversations with the visitors to his cell, Herrera adds that More recalled to them the trials of the martyrs, «acordandosele las cadenas de los Santos i Martires, à quien procurava imitar en la muerte, como en la causa. I encendido assi en su amor, aguardava su llamamiento con grandisimo deseo i umildad de coraçon».[13]

Herrera's hero is a soldier only metaphorically. Like the Christian warrior and the afflicted lover, his virtue is pitted

---
[9] Cf. Mario Gasparini, introduction to Juan de Mal Lara, *El libro quinto de la «Psyche»* (Salamanca, 1947).
[10] Herrera, *Tomas Moro,* in Francisco López Estrada, «Edición y estudio», *Archivo Hispalense,* XII (1950), 34.
[11] *Ibid.,* p. 34.
[12] *Ibid.,* pp. 48-49, 55.
[13] *Ibid.,* p. 45.

against forces of human vice and frailty, personified by the rule of Henry VIII and the timid consent of the English people. More's virtue increases in value when compared with the surrounding perdition: «Por eso jùzgo por mayor hecho, que de onbres tan entregados al vicio, levantarse alguno de animo generoso, entre la confusion i ceguedad de tanta gente perdida; i ronpiendo todas las dificultades, llegar al merecimiento de la verdadera gloria.» [14] Again and again Herrera hammers away at his point: the virtue of Sir Thomas More displays itself in the face of dire threats. First, in his reply to Luther's attack on Henry's defense of the Sacraments, More (like Don Juan de Austria and Philip II before the insolent Selim) rebuked the brazen «insolencia i libertad eretica» for its insult to religion and the monarchy as well: «de tal suerte burlò i desbaratò las vanas razones i opinion de aquel onbre, que le pudo quitar el atrevimiento para encontrarse con el.» [15]

Herrera pictures More not in strictly institutional fashion as simply a learned repudiator of heresy, but rather as a gallant Christian, come to the rescue of honor and virtue:

> Mas quien de los que sabian, no avia de acudir à la causa de la religion, contra un cruel i anbicioso enemigo della, que tenia enpañados los ojos de muchos con el velo de su engaño? I quien podia callar en aquella opresion de la virtud? Porque en sazon semejante no tienen lugar los respetos umanos, ni entra en parte alguna consideracion. Pues quien se desvia de tal enpresa i no se ofrece à ella, pudiendo valer à la causa publica, no se deve contar por verdadero siervo de la Religion Catolica. I assi merecieron mucha culpa los onbres sabios, que miraron en ociosidad el peligro, que amenazava aquella fiera à la Iglesia Romana. [16]

These final words, a possible accusation against Erasmus, [17] recall Herrera's condemnation in the *Relacion* of France and other nominally Christian powers who allow petty interests to divert them from their duty to the Church.

As in 1572, verbal profession of Christian values does not begin to satisfy Herrera's ethical requirements. As Herrera

---

[14] *Ibid.*, p. 35.
[15] *Ibid.*, p. 36.
[16] *Ibid.*, p. 36.
[17] López Estrada, «Edición y estudio», p. 28.

pictures his hero almost alone in resisting Henry VIII's wayward will, he comments on those who observed the catastrophe:

> Porque aunque es mui estimado el nonbre de la virtud, i todos se enciende en amor de su gloria, cuando oyen, ò ven algun hecho eroico, i precien el valor i merecimiento de los que no dudaron ofrecer por ella su vida à los peligros i à los tormentos, i à la mesma muerte, i condenan i vituperan à los que se desviaron della, i desanpararon temiendo con vileza i abatimiento de animo las ocasiones, que les obligavan à posponer todos los deleites i onras de la vida: i todos piensan, que, si se hallaran ellos en aquellos casos, no perdieran ocasion para onrar su vida con la gloria de la inmortalidad, por ventura tienen estos pensamientos mas deseo i demostracion de alabança propia, que firmeza de animo. Porque, aunque es amado el nonbre de la virtud, es mui recelado el trabajo, i peligro, i *no se juntan facilmente deseos i obras*. [18]

If there has been a development in Herrera's thinking on this point since he composed the *Relacion,* it is in the direction of greater intensity and greater universality. He does specifically take the English to task for their cowardly submission to Henry's sinful whims. But the condemnation here directs itself more to general Christian frailty. Not just the English, but all («*todos* piensan») would like to attribute to themselves a virtue of which their deeds fall far short. These claims arise more out of egotism than firmness of character, Herrera adds. He pictures More's fellows incredulous at his determination, when submission or even silence would have assured him a comfortable berth in the monarch's court. But More's virtue is worthy of the true Christian and should be valued as such, inspiring others to join the long chain of emulation to which the Englishman belongs:

> Cuando arriba un onbre à tanta fineza de valor, que osa consagrar su vida al amor de la eternidad, bien se deve admirar, como exenplo rarisimo de virtud, i poner en todos un ardor i deseo de imitar aquellas hazañas, que encienden los animos generosos. [19]

For Herrera, the vicissitudes of More's existence seem to be of little importance, and in fact almost no details creep in beyond the accusation and trial. Although he speaks of the «Teatro de

---

[18] Herrera, *Tomas Moro,* pp. 41-42. Italics mine.
[19] *Ibid.,* p. 42.

la Tragedia» in which More's life is played out to its end, there is relatively little suspense, for Herrera's public knows well the outcome, and the author makes his case for the meaning of More's life in the light of his death. But the portrait we gain of Thomas More in reading this brief account seems more like a relief map of human life: More stands stalwart, like a lone island of virtue in a desolate sea of sin and error.

Herrera places More in a special class of men. His former heroes have enjoyed the advantages which their birth among the aristocracy could afford them. But the Englishman, he tells us, is the son of a man «de linage mas onrado que noble», one seemingly of small consequence. Yet More is made to earn stature through strength of character. Herrera tells us: «Pero el grande concurso de dotes corporales i bienes de l'alma, que resplandecieron en su hijo [Thomas], hizieron clarisimo al uno i al otro, i dieron *verdadera nobleza* à su familia.»[20] Considerations of birth have been set aside. While Don Juan de Austria inherited physically the stamp of empire and his crusader's role, Thomas More's is an entirely spiritual inheritance, that of the Christian martyrs whose company he will shortly enter.

Herrera insists on More's naked virtue and natural endowments as the causes of his rise as well as of his tragic fate:

> De la umanidad i regalo de las letras, salio Tomas Moro à las causas forenses, en las cuales resplandecio con tanta igualdad de juizio i tanta prudencia, que el Rey Enrique, que entonces favorecia las letras, i era grande amigo de los onbres doctos, *por solo merecimiento i estimacion de su virtud* lo puso en cargos onrosos.[21]

The wisdom of the king depends upon his ability to appreciate the benefits of learning, acquired at considerable expenditure of effort, and to detect the highest forms of personal worth. A wise man cannot tolerate a hypocritical attitude toward nobility, any more than a true Christian can condone piety composed of empty words. The early King Henry adopts these sound criteria in the selection of his highest counselor: «I finalmente conociendo por luenga esperiencia su entereza i valor, i cuan importante era por l'administracion de la suprema potestad, con maduro consejo

---

[20] *Ibid.*, p. 35. Italics mine.
[21] *Ibid.*, p. 36. Italics mine.

lo escogio i colocò en el mayor grado de dinidad que ai en Inglaterra.» [22]

Furthermore, Herrera continues, the Chancellor himself is not satisfied with the mere name of his office and the dignities which accrue to him as a result of royal favor:

> En el cual [magistrado] se ocupò tan santa i sinceramente, que por universal confesion se le dava grandisima alaba[n]ça de fe, justicia, i prudencia. Porque no sufriendo que pudiese mas el favor que la verdad, i el poder que la inocencia de los pobres i desanparados, ayudava siempre à la causa mejor (cosa dificil i maravillosa en nuestro tiempo) sembrando en los animos de todos una segura opinion de su virtud i bondad. [23]

Herrera pictures More as determined to make virtue and nobility one in his character. Thus, when the tables have been turned, and royalty no longer nurtures nobility, the dignity of office alone no longer conserves its appeal: «viendo Tomas Moro, que no podia conservar ya, como antes, la integridad de su vida, por el Magistrado que tenia, i aborreciendo ser ministro ò participe en la maldad de aquellos consejos.» [24]

More's entire career is described by Herrera as a process of self-discipline directed towards perfecting this virtue. The change in Henry VIII's fancy converts self-discipline into heroism. Much more than Rivadeneira in the *Historia eclesiástica*, Herrera emphasizes More's aloneness in virtue. The others of his fellow English Catholics are mentioned hastily. Rivadeneira accumulates martyr after martyr, to overwhelm his public with the magnitude of the English disaster. But Herrera characteristically finds a solitary hero, one unaided even by human friendships. The King himself clears from the righteous man's path all external supports. Like Numancia's residents, like Hernán Cortés, like Don García, More can rely on nothing but his own strength; and he in fact confronts peril head on:

> Pero nunca el se mostrò mas ecelso, i de animo mas generoso i sin temor, que en aquella tempestad; porque no solo no lo quebrantò, pero ni aun lo movio la furia de aquella violencia espantosa. Antes lleno de vigor, i encendido en aquel amor hermosisi-

---

[22] *Ibid.*, p. 36.
[23] *Ibid.*, p. 37.
[24] *Ibid.*, pp. 58-59.

> mo de la virtud, se opuso à ella con tanta grandeza de coraçon, i con tanta firmeza i seguridad de conciencia, por la obligacion en que se hallava à la religion Catolica, que contrastando a la fuerça i tirania de aquel endurecido i ostinado Rei, alcançó entre los onbres, que juzgan bien de las cosas, nonbre de fortisimo i santisimo. [25]

More derives strength from danger and the absence of all human comforts. Once again Herrera insists that the greatest virtue belongs to the one whose determination resists all assaults, to the «varon de admirable constancia,... i que tenia confirmado su animo, i disupesto à todas las persecuciones i asaltos, asegurado con la conciencia de su buena intencion». [26]

The progress of Herrera's narrative centers around the repeated efforts of the King's advisers to win approval for his deeds from More. With each new attack from these Devil's disciples, the Biblical echoes become still clearer. The true believer has refused to bow down before vain gods: «solo el mostrò el animo i la voz libre, sin espantarse del peligro, que tenia casi à todos tan acobardados, i que el era entre tantos uno, de los que no doblaron la rodilla a Baal.» [27] New Testament phrases ring clear to stress the solitary moral heroism of a strong man surrounded by weakness: «Blessed are they which are persecuted for righteousness' sake: for theirs is the kingdom of heaven.» «Blessed are ye, when men shall revile you, and persecute you, and shall say all manner of evil against you falsely, for my sake.» [28] It is this state of blessedness which More achieves as Herrera concludes:

> I bien creo yo, i comigo quien siente bien de las cosas, que avia hecho asiento la virtud en el animo deste varon con tanta firmeza, que ninguna turbacion de afectos, i ninguna violencia de tenpestades pudiera arrancalla; i que despreciava todas las amenazas, todas las aflicciones, i todos los tormentos, que le podian nacer de la ira de su rei, de tal suerte estava defendido i anparado. Por cierto que no me parece mas dichoso i bienaventurado, el que està libre de las mudanças i trabajos, que el que sufre sin rendirse la fuerça de las adversidades. Porque, no es cosa mara-

---

[25] *Ibid.*, p. 38.
[26] *Ibid.*, p. 44.
[27] *Ibid.*, p. 38.
[28] Gospel according to St. Matthew 5: 10-11.

villosa, estar seguro en la tranquilidad, mas si es, levantarse alguno, donde todos estan opresos, i afirmarse, donde caen todos.[29]

Herrera reserves special mockery for the last royal effort to sway More, the visit of his wife Alice. Herrera naturally does not evince the personal antagonism toward Alice More which makes itself felt in Roper's biography. For Herrera, only More emerges with the stature of an individual personality. His wife becomes a kind of symbolic figure. She represents the call of hearth and home, of paternal and conjugal affection, and finally, the weakness of a woman's tears. More rises above this last temptation: «como si por ven[t]ura pudiera mover à un varon constante i sin temor, i anparado i favorecido de Dios, ocasion tan liviana, despues de tantos trabajos i afliciones.»[30]

Those who «consider things well», who «think rightly», can well understand More's choice. This wisdom is grounded in the Church's teachings concerning value. Life on earth must be weighed in the balance with immortality. More responds to the confiscation of his books by turning his attention to Christ: «despreciando todas las cosas, se retirò consigo ocupado todo en Cristo, i en la contenplacion del martirio, que esperava, i ardiendo en deseo de aquella gloria, considerava el valor, i grandeza de aquella hazaña, i cuan pequeño era el precio que se aventurava.»[31] The final step toward martyrdom can be taken only by a chosen few (Herrera and Sander picture More fearful that he might not be found worthy of it), by one «anparado i favorecido de Dios».[32] Herrera will stress, as did Juan de Valdés in the *Diálogo de doctrina cristiana*,[33] and the Sevillian Doctor Constantino Ponce de la Fuente in his *Suma de doctrina cristiana*,[34] a generation or more before Herrera, that man alone cannot be the final arbiter of his fate. Thus More prays to God for strength of soul to repulse all temptations in order to deserve the greatest honor: «Porque nunca esperò de si, ni confiò el varon justo,

---

[29] Herrera, *Tomas Moro*, p. 45.
[30] *Ibid.*, p. 47. Cf. R. O. Jones, «El *Tomas Moro* de Fernando de Herrera», *B.R.A.E.*, XXX (1950), 423-438.
[31] Herrera, *Tomas Moro*, p. 48.
[32] *Ibid.*, pp. 46-47.
[33] Juan de Valdés, *Diálogo de doctrina cristiana*, ed. Domingo Ricart (Mexico, 1964); and Marcel Bataillon, *Erasmo y España* (Mexico, 1966), p. 339 ff.
[34] Constantino Ponce de la Fuente, *Suma de doctrina cristiana*, ed. Luis de Usoz, *Reformistas Antiguos Españoles*, Vol. XIX (Madrid, 1863); and Bataillon, pp. 535-540.

antes reconocio sienpre todo el buen suceso de sus obras, por beneficio de la grandeza divina.»[35] From the apparently limitless trust in the power of good works, exemplified in Don Juan de Austria's buoyant confidence that God never abandons a just cause, Herrera has evolved to a greater humility in his sense of virtue. All of man's deeds are powerless without the intervention of divine grace. Perhaps it had become more possible to insert in the midst of narrative so vivid an echo of a once passionately voiced, passionately silenced credo which Herrera had learned from a Valdés or a Doctor Constantino. Or it might constitute but another facet of the revisions maturity has imposed on youthful convictions. What part has the course of twenty years of Spanish history played in shaping Herrera's thought? We shall reserve these questions for a later part of our study.

And what of the role in the *Tomas Moro* of the thirst for fame and immortality which prompted the strivings of the *Relacion's* protagonists? For the Herrera of 1592, the truly virtuous man must not be blinded by fame in the sense of renown in his own time, among his own countrymen. The perfect public official will be endowed with sufficient independent moral worth so that «no lo desvanezca i deslunbre l'alteza i resplandor de aquella dinidad».[36] For the public servant there will come a time when duty will oblige him to «posponer los deleites i onras de la vida».[37] Herrera concerns himself with a fame beyond the superficial considerations of reputation or fame as conceded by society. He prays to God to grant his kingdoms a prince «que procura mas *ser,* que *parecer* bueno».[38] When Thomas More is blamed by his former colleagues for having abandoned his advisory post and the influence he might have been able to wield, his biographer justifies him: «Pero el, que mirava antes su juizio, que era lo que devia hazer, no parava en lo que avian de alabar, ò vituperar los otros.»[39] Opinion and reputation in the eyes of men are associated with ambition, security, worldly authority, wealth. All these must be laid aside.

[35] Herrera, *Tomas Moro,* p. 48.
[36] *Ibid.,* p. 37.
[37] *Ibid.,* p. 42.
[38] *Ibid.,* p. 40. Italics mine.
[29] *Ibid.,* p. 44.

Yet fame has another, more transcendental meaning, as it did for Herrera in the *Relacion*. The innate desire for glory which Mosquera found to be common to all men attaches to More's religious vocation as well, and to the tenacity of all those righteous Englishmen who have determined to withstand Henry's wrath:

> Mas los que tenian conpuesto su animo para sufrir todos los trabajos i todos los tormentos que sabe allar la furia de un principe indinado i lleno de crueldad i se oponian advertidamente à todos los accidentes, que sucediesen, no desapercibidos, sino prevenidos i sin temor, pensavan, i esperavan perder la vida, i no el premio de aquella contienda... donde se prometian segurisimamente *el favor de los buenos i una inmortal alabança*. [40]

It is the approval of the just and the applause of posterity that serves to uplift the man of courage, rather than the «onras» or the granting of superficial social dignity.

As we have seen, Herrera acknowledges the universality of human desire for glory, but he no longer evinces the ebullience of the *Relacion*, where he pictured all men as actively straining toward that glory. Rather he skeptically suggests the distance which separates desire from deed. And he goes on to show, as both he and Mosquera had done twenty years before, the effects of fame on the unjust. More's resolve to remain firm in his conviction serves, if not to reform Henry, at least to confound him and his ministers, so that they vacillate between letting their prisoner go free or condemning him to death, this «clara i resplandeciente lunbre del orbe cristiano». [41] Herrera explains their fear of the judgment of Fame: «porque muchas vezes, aun los onbres declaradamente malos, sirven à la opinion, i temen la voz de la fama, à quien se inclinan tan bien, i rinden no pocas vezes los buenos por ostentacion de virtud.» [42] Fame, then, is likened to Truth, a kind of monitor, not always effective, on the actions of even those who do not experience the positive impulse to merit immortal praise.

The «gloria i alabança» which Sir Thomas More seeks and is accorded carries two connotations. [43] The first asserts that the

---

[40] *Ibid.*, p. 44. Italics mine.
[41] *Ibid.*, p. 46.
[42] *Ibid.*, p. 46.
[43] *Ibid.*, pp. 49-50.

judgment of posterity will vindicate the just. Even among those who oppose him, More's deeds spread shame and fear of the reputation he will attain: «Tanta fuerça tiene la verdad en la boca del bueno, i tanto averguença el sonido della à los malos.» [44] Herrera allows Henry to have reaped the just deserts of his actions in the unfavorable judgment of posterity:

> No entiendo yo, que avra alguno... que no confiesse, si da algun lugar a la verguença, i respeta el juizio de los onbres... que no alcançò el rei Enrique fruto de su maldad, pues padecio las injurias i afrentas hechas tantas vezes a su onra, i no siendo poderoso, para vencer la firmeza de un vassallo, aviendo vencido tan facilmente todo su reino, dexò al cabo de su vida vna miserable memoria de su apostasia. [45]

Fame is a minister not only of Truth but of Justice. The second is of course glory in the Christian sense, immortality which is not dependent on human but on divine judgment, the glorious union of the faithful for everlasting life: «la gloria eterna, que promete Cristo à los que lo siguen verdaderamente.» [46] More, Herrera says, «aviendo hallado con liviana costa de tiempo, como se hiziesse inmortal, goza en seguridad la bienaventurança con Cristo.» [47] Although the classical concept of the search for personal fame, through which the individual personality can survive the ravages of time, has not disappeared, still, in a sense, it has been surpassed. [48] Glory for More does not furnish a substitute for immortality: it is immortality.

2. Virtue and Government

If Herrera presents the figure of Thomas More to us as a paragon of human virtue which remains intact despite any assault directed against it, it is also true that he has a particular context in mind. While the *Relacion* focuses on military virtues and international politics, the later work speaks to the question of

---

[44] *Ibid.*, p. 49.
[45] *Ibid.*, p. 52.
[46] *Ibid.*, p. 46.
[47] *Ibid.*, p. 52.
[48] María Rosa Lida, «Salustio», in *La idea de la fama en la Edad Media castellana* (Mexico, 1952), pp. 33-35.

internal affairs of state, of government, and how a nation's affairs are to be conducted. Herrera's final words to his reader indicate that the lesson of *Tomas Moro* must read this way: «I sea exenplo à los que tienen por uso admirar las cosas ilicitas, i entiendan que puede aver, i se hallan varones grandes, i dinos de toda alabança en el inperio de malos Principes.» [49] He fashions his version of More's life into a set of principles by which a man can remain good even if forced to live under an evil ruler.

Henry VIII becomes nothing more or less than the prototype of the good prince who has erred in his ways. For our Spanish observer, the problems of divorce and adultery are minor ones. Herrera seems to be saying that they are merely symptoms of a more far-reaching problem. The King's plan to marry Ann Boleyn at the expense of his legitimate wife Catherine of Aragon receives scant attention. If we had expected the Spanish critic to launch into a lengthy diatribe with the end of defending the Spanish royal house in Europe, we can find none of this. Catherine belongs to a line of good kings, «aquellos gloriosos Reyes i nunca dinamente alabados, don Fernando i doña Isabel». [50] Yet her worth is of a primarily moral order:

> La cual, si miramos à la piedad i religion, si à las costunbres i vida, si à la claridad i ecelencia del linage, aventajado sin alguna conparacion al de todos los Principes Cristianos, era la mas esclarecida Reina de su tienpo, i merecedora de mejor fortuna en la suerte que le ocupò. [51]

The Queen hereafter disappears from view, a virtuous Christian to whom Fortune has shown herself unkind. Likewise, Herrera passes with very little comment over the details of the controversy itself. The King's transgression is simple: «puso los ojos en Ana Bolena, i procurò obligarse con ella en casamiento.» [52] Herrera chooses to add nothing to the common knowledge of the sordid affair. With extraordinary restraint, he declines even to review the case: «Las causas, que mostrava tener, para repudiar su mujer legitima, por ser comunes à todos, i escritas de muchos,

---

[49] Herrera, *Tomas Moro*, p. 52.
[50] *Ibid.*, p. 38.
[51] *Ibid.*, p. 38.
[52] *Ibid.*, p. 38.

no las refiero.» [53] Herrera finds no reason to take up these supposed causes. Henry has already been judged.

López Estrada has already pointed to the affinities between the thought of Herrera in the *Tomás Moro* and the literature of the early sixteenth century which theorized on the nature of the perfect prince and his equally perfect counselors. [54] The diffusion of Castiglione's *Libro del cortegiano* [55] and the *Enchiridion* and *Institvtio principis Christiani* of Erasmus was achieved at an early date, [56] and Spanish writers too began to concern themselves with deducing models of perfection from these prototypes, from Boscán's translation-adaptation of *El Cortesano* and so on throughout the Golden Age. In the years surrounding the publication date of Herrera's biography, there was a new flurry of this kind of literature. In 1595, Pedro de Rivadeneira, the Jesuit, published in Madrid a *Tratado de la religión y virtudes que debe tener el príncipe cristiano para gobernar y conservar sus estados, contra lo que Nicolás Maquiavelo y los políticos deste tiempo enseñan.* [57] The volume was dedicated to Prince Philip, soon to become Philip III, and enjoyed a great popularity, testified to by the fact that three new editions appeared in the ten years following its original publication. [58] By means of a Latin translation and subsequently a French one, the work became general European property. Juan de Mariana's *De rege et institutione regis,* which appeared only slightly later (1599), provoked a still more clamorous reaction beyond Spanish borders, including an *Antimariana,* [59] primarily because of its defense of regicide in cases of tyranny.

The differences between this kind of literature and the earlier manuals arise, in part at any rate, from the events which have filled the intervening years. These events are both literary and political in nature. For one thing, as Rivadeneira's title suggests,

---

[53] *Ibid.,* p. 38.
[54] López Estrada, «Edición y estudio», pp. 21-22.
[55] Baldassare Castiglione, *Il libro del cortegiano,* ed. Vittorio Cian (Florence, 1947); Juan Boscán, trans., *Los quatro libros del Cortesano,* ed. Menéndez y Pelayo (Madrid, 1942).
[56] *Erasmo y España,* p. 190.
[57] Pedro de Rivadeneira, *Obras escogidas,* ed. Vicente de la Fuente, in B.A.E., Vol. LX (Madrid, 1868).
[58] Rivadeneira, p. 450.
[59] *Del Rey y de la institución real,* in *Obras del Padre Juan de Mariana,* B.A.E., Vol. XXXI (Madrid, 1854). Cf. Roussel, *L'Antimariana, ou réfutation des propositions de Mariana* (Paris, 1610).

literature of princely perfection had taken two directions. Machiavelli appeared to the Christian moralists to undermine their sense of value with his description of a purely political virtue, one designed to reap not the rewards of heaven, but those of secure power. This writers like Mariana and Rivadeneira found unconscionable, and they set about to prove with all the arms they could muster from Scripture, classical philosophy and history that a king could keep peace and faith with his subjects as well as with God by one and the same means. The monarch must raise ordinary Christian virtues to the dimensions which his special position requires.

Where Machiavelli had reared up imaginary princely devils, history too had produced her share: Henry VIII, Elizabeth I and the French Henry's III and IV, who all managed to fuse the conceptions of heresy and tyranny in the minds of their orthodox critics. They applauded the French for having risen from apathy and oppression to strike down their tyrant rulers. England, however, was more resistant to reform. Philip II, in a last, glorious impulse of crusading fervor, sent an invincible force to avenge the death of Mary Queen of Scots at the hands of her diabolical cousin. But the Grand Armada, fitted out with gleaming moral armor, was no match for the more realistic forces of «evil».[60] The time, then, was ripe for a reassertion of the power of virtue against the ways of the world. However, we ought not to expect, nor do we find, the rosy flush of ebullience of a Castiglione. These later moralists do not seem to share the optimistic hopes of those lords and ladies at Urbino who summoned up the figure of the perfect courtier, Pygmalion-like, hoping to blow life into their new creation. No longer does a Christian emperor hold out for them, as perhaps Charles V once did for Erasmus, the hope of a Europe united as one flock under one single shepherd. The exuberance of Hernando de Acuña's famous sonnet contrasts with the skepticism of these preceptists and historians:

> Ya se acerca señor, o ya es llegada
> La edad gloriosa, en que promete el cielo
> Vna grey, y vn pastor, solo en el suelo,
> Por suerte a vuestros tiempos reseruada.

[60] Garrett Mattingly, *The Defeat of the Spanish Armada* (New York, 1965).

Ya tan alto principio en tal jornada
  Os muestra el fin de vuestro santo zelo,
  Y anuncia al mundo para mas consuelo,
  Vn monarca, vn Imperio, y vna Espada. [61]

The new model prince is painted with a negative shadow. Mariana concerns himself with what he should not do as much as with what he should do. To discuss the nature of the righteous king, he must say that he is *not* a tyrant («Diferencia entre el rey y el tirano»). [62] The subsequent chapters deal not with obedience to the former, but with eliminating the latter: «¿Es lícito matar al tirano?» and «Si es lícito envenenar a un tirano.» They explain what the King may not do: «El príncipe no puede legislar en materias de religión», «El príncipe no está dispensado de guardar las leyes.» [63] By 1592, building an ideal monarch meant erecting an edifice on the ruins of transgression.

Herrera belongs very much, as we shall see in detail, with the currents of thought Mariana and Rivadeneira exemplify. But he does not belong with them in either method or style. The two Jesuit writers set out to compose a complete guide for the prince who would avoid the manifold perils confronting him. On a bold, solid framework of laudable virtues and maxims are hung the threads of historical fact and philosophical opinion which weave the fabric of argument tight. Herrera, as author of a life rather than a treatise, proceeds in the opposite direction. One real man's existence, one pressing testimony for virtue, suggests itself as a model, and the author must only draw the general conclusions which each virtuous deed urges on him. The comparison with these other works of a distinctly didactic and non-historical character (insofar as history in them is subservient to generality) helps us to perceive the special nature of the *Tomas Moro*. It still belongs in the camp of history rather than that of philosophy. Herrera's soaring meditations are at the service of history: they comprise the «loor y vituperio» which Mosquera de Figueroa, following Cicero, had found indispensable. They

---

[61] Hernando de Acuña, *Varias poesías,* ed. Elena Catena de Vindel (Madrid, 1954), p. 342.
[62] Mariana, *Del Rey,* Part I, Chapter 5.
[63] *Ibid.,* Part I, Chapters 6, 7, 9, 10.

ponder the lessons of history, rather than glimpsing history through lessons.

It is true, nonetheless, that Herrera's own models of monarch and magistrate bear upon his conception of history. We have had occasion to note earlier some of the conspicuous omissions from the prevalent accounts of Thomas More's life: reference to his wit and paternal affections, and Herrera's silence on the question of adultery. Perhaps, as some have suggested, this partiality can be traced to the personality of the biographer, that is, to his own gravity and solitary existence.[64] This is as plausible as it is unsusceptible of proof. It seems perhaps less speculative to note that Herrera concentrates on those features of More's life and Henry's behavior which relate to the moralist's arsenal of precepts. Adultery is not the primary evil which threatens monarchy, nor is fatherly devotion the most relevant virtue for an ideal royal counselor.

The life of Thomas More thus stands not only as an example of Christian virtue, but of those particular traits required of a public official: «clarisimo exenplo de Fè i bondad para todos los onbres constituidos en dinidad, i en oficios i grandeza de magistrados.»[65] What are these virtues? «Fè i bondad» occupy the position of honor: religious purity and chastity. More, like the exiled Juan Luis Vives, occupies himself with the poor («la inocencia de los pobres i desanparados»).[66] He is a man of letters, the humanists' ideal of the thoughtful member of the ruling class, and has earned his position largely through demonstration of his learning. Herrera reflects on the most remarkable trait of all, the Chancellor's rare humility:

> I aunque suelen estragar el animo umilde i tenplado las onras grandes, i lo levantan i ensoberbecen, mudando las costunbres, como si no le tocara aquella estimacion i alabança, que le davan todos, medía la grandeza del estado presente con la llaneza del pasado. I en aquel animo no sobrado por dones, ò anbicion i lisonjas, se via una singular igualdad, i assi no era fastidioso, ni pesadamente severo en su trato; antes de tal manera tenplava la severidad de aquel magistrado, con la blandura i facilidad de su condicion, que no era menos amado, que temido.[67]

---

[64] López Estrada, «Edición y estudio», pp. 26-27.
[65] Herrera, *Tomas Moro*, p. 35.
[66] *Ibid.*, p. 37; cf. Juan Luis Vives, «De subuentione pauperibus», *Opera* (Basel, 1555).
[67] Herrera, *Tomas Moro*, p. 37.

Herrera insists on his hero's refusal to take advantage of his new position:

> I por ventura pensava tanbien, que no devia atribuirse las onras devidas a su oficio, como si se devieran a su persona, conociendo que nacia del abuso dellas, el odio i la indinacion que tenian los onbres por la mayor parte a los que no son propios i naturales señores. I no es verdadero aquel respeto, sino temor de su insolencia i tirania. I es cosa aspera, que quiera merecer el ministro violentamente por si, lo que tiene solo del ministerio que representa. [68]

Everywhere the restrained conduct of Thomas More urges the limitations of official power, for magistrate and king alike, of which treatises such as Mariana's are full.

Herrera's portrait of the perfect magistrate evinces especially close affinities to Erasmus' instructions about the selection of public officials in the *Institvtio principis Christiani.* Here the counselor of Charles V, having quoted Seneca's distinction between the nobility of virtue, of training and of genealogy (the latter being synonymous with wealth), advises that «magistratus non censu, non imaginibus nec annis est eligendus, sed potius sapientia et integritate». [69] Erasmus mentions as well the importance of age, but only as a function of the experience through which Herrera shows More attaining to high office.

The *Tomas Moro* paints an equally vivid picture of More's opposites, the misguided public officials («estos animos anbiciosos i terribles» [70]) driven not by reason or charity but by their own appetite for power:

> Porque aquella enfermedad interna, que padecen, no les dexa lugar libre, para aprovechar la causa agena, que está necessitada de favor, i es menos poderosa. I aunque no parece inabil para el cuidado i modestia del govierno el onbre anbicioso, no todas vezes desocupa su animo, para acudir libre i derechamente a los negocios de los otros onbres. [71]

Mariana, in the *De Rege,* blames most corruptness in magistrates on the «avaricia inmensa» of the self-seeking man, and cautions

---

[68] *Ibid.,* p. 37.
[69] Desiderius Erasmus, *Institvtio principis Christiani saluberrimis referta praeceptis* (Basel, 1518), p. 107.
[70] Herrera, *Tomas Moro,* p. 37.
[71] *Ibid.,* p. 37.

infinite care in appointing them.[72] Herrera and Erasmus both seem to place the onus of the magistrate's conduct on the prince himself. The *Institvtio* advises:

> Pure creabuntur magistratus, si princeps eos asiscat, non qui plurimo emant, non qui improbissime ambiant, non qui cognatione coniunctiores, non qui ad illius mores aut affectus cupiditatesque maxime sint accomodi, sed qui moribus sint integerrimis, & ad functionem mandati muneris aptissimi... At qua fronte puniet princeps iudicem, qui muneribus corruptus pronunciauit aut pronunciare noluit, cum ipse iudicandi munus aere uendiderit, & hanc corruptelam prior suum docuerit iudicem?[73]

Erasmus quotes Aristotle in his *Politics* as advising that «super omnia cauendum esse, ne ex magistratibus lucra proueniant, iis qui ea gerunt».[74] Herrera follows the same path when he makes the well-being of a kingdom depend on the providential selection of counselors by the king:

> Mas cuando aviene, que por señalado favor del Cielo, acierta el Principe à escoger a[l]gun onbre de tanta grandeza i confiança de animo, que no lo desvanezca i deslunbre l'alteza i resplandor de aquella dinidad, antes atienda al provecho i conservacion de todos, sin acudir a si solo; entonces se puede llamar dichosa i bienaventurada aquella region, como desdichada i miserable, la que tuvo en suerte, iuezes i governadores tiranos i enemigos de sus pueblos.[75]

Herrera, more caught up (because of the nature of his subject, a magistrate) than Erasmus or Mariana with the character of the king's advisers, borrows the Erasmian attributes of the prince himself in his description of More. The *Institvtio* urges the prince to put godliness first:

> Deus cum nullis tangatur affectibus, tamen optime mundum administrat iudicio. Ad huius exemplum princeps in omnibus quae gerit, exclusis animi motibus, rationem & animi iudicium debet adhibere.[76]

---

[72] Mariana, *Del Rey*, Part II, Chapter 11, p. 518 ff.; and Part III, pp. 531-535.
[73] Erasmus, pp. 108-109.
[74] *Ibid.*, p. 109.
[75] Herrera, *Tomas Moro*, pp. 37-38.
[76] Erasmus, p. 51.

The prince's tutor will hold a picture of this ideal before him:

> Deliniet igitur caeleste quoddam animal, numini quam homini similius, omnibus virtutum numeris absolutum, omnium bono natum, imo datum a superis subleuandis rebus mortalium, quod omnibus prospiciat, omnibus consulat: cui nihil sit antiquius, nihil dulcius republica, cui plusquam paternus sit in omneis animus, cui singulorum uita charior sit quam sua.[77]

And everywhere in his treatise, Erasmus insists that royal authority must temper justice with mercy, that the good ruler must attempt, like a father, to inspire love rather than fear,[78] even as Herrera sees Thomas More «que no era menos amado que temido».[79]

Henry VIII has evidently undergone a radical evolution in Herrera's eyes. Once a defender of the holy sacraments against Lutheran heresy, once «grande amigo de los onbres doctos», he seemed almost to realize Plato's ancient dream of the philosopher king, which had also informed Erasmus' standards for the wise ruler:

> Ne putaris temere dictum a Platone & a laudatissimis laudatum uiris, ita demum beatam fore rempublicam, si aut philosophentur Principes, aut philosophi capessant principatum. Porrò philosophus is est, non qui dialecticen, aut physicen calleat: sed qui contemptis falsis rerum simulacris, infracto pectore, uera bona & perspicit & sequitur. Vocabulis diuersum est, caeterum re idem esse philosophum & esse Christianum.[80]

For Erasmus as for Herrera, knowledge and the truth carry the inevitable connotation of Christ's truth revealed and guarded over by the Roman Church. Thus, Henry's friendly association with «wise men» and the purity of his Catholic conviction are but two aspects of one and the same state of well-being.

Herrera envisions this monarchy under the guidance of a Christian philosopher king with his carefully chosen adviser as a harbinger of felicity: «Parecia, que entrava por el [Thomas More] en Inglaterra la felicidad, que prometian los antiguos à los reinos, cuyos principes i governadores amavan las letras, i se-

---

[77] *Ibid.*, pp. 34-35.
[78] *Ibid.*, p. 43 ff.
[79] Herrera, *Tomas Moro,* p. 37. Cf. p. 138 above.
[80] Erasmus, p. 21.

guian la ciencia, que enseña à los onbres, i modera sus afectos.» [81] Once again Herrera echoes Erasmus' faith in learning as a moral force. The entire weight of the *Institvtio* rests on the premise that education, begun early and pursued with unceasing diligence, will nurture integrity: «Et quamquam nonnulla boni principis spes in emendatis moribus ac moderatis affectibus est sita, praecipua tamen est in rectis opinionibus.» [82]

Yet in fact, this new Golden Age is rapidly eclipsed by the King's determination to divorce Catherine, and Henry's exemplarity as king is exchanged for that of a tyrant:

> Mas el Rei, que fue un portento de naturaleza, en quien mostró la inconstancia de las cosas umanas, i lo poco que se deve fiar de los buenos principios, cuando se dexan vencer los onbres de sus apetitos, queriendo hazer cierta aquella sentencia, que los ecelentes ingenios suelen produzir grandes virtudes i vicios juntamente, puso los ojos en Ana Bolena. [83]

Henry has teetered between his passions and justice, and fallen inexplicably:

> Avia servido el Rei Enrique à la Iglesia Romana con las fuerças de su Reino, i con las de su ingenio, escriviendo en defensa della contra Martin Lutero, e mereciendo ilustrisimo titulo por estas cosas, parecia aver alcançado los terminos de la felicidad, si quisiera, ò supiera contenerse en los limites de lo justo i onesto. Mas es mui dificil la conjetura del animo del onbre, i engaña muchas vezes las esperanças de los que piensan, que no responde diferentemente al credito della. Porque no reprimiendo sus deseos ilicitos, i no estimandose por principe, si no obligava todas las cosas à su gusto, se dexò arrebatar de sus apetitos tan inconsideradamente, que dio en todos los vicios, que suele seguir la licencia de los poderosos. [84]

Herrera's ideal monarch in the *Relacion,* Philip II, rose to his greatest heights when he put down personal interest and private passion, in that case his anger with the Venetians who had failed to come to his aid. Henry VIII falls from virtue when he loses control, willingly or otherwise, of his own passions. Felicity becomes possible only with moderation: «lo justo i ones-

---

[81] Herrera, *Tomas Moro,* p. 37.
[82] Erasmus, p. 66.
[83] Herrera, *Tomas Moro,* p. 38.
[84] *Ibid.,* p. 39.

to» imposes limits on a man's actions.[85] Herrera poses the antithesis *justo-gusto* which will continue to absorb Spanish authors (and others!) for many years. Fuenteovejuna's Comendador and Calderón's Segismundo will face in fiction the same dilemma as Henry VIII in history. And the dramatists will conclude with Herrera that the greatest victory is that which one wins over one's self.[86]

Not only does Herrera's admiration for restraint and victory over passion recall his chaste devotion for the Countess of Gelves, as López Estrada suggests.[87] There appears in the passage just cited the suggestion of another aspect of his literary production. Beyond the standard rebuke of unbridled passion, Herrera seems, through the English King, to be gazing in wonderment into the depths of human character: «Es mui dificil la conjetura del animo del onbre, i engaña muchas vezes las esperanças.»[88] Human behavior may be easily categorized, but it is not summarily explained. Herrera's *cancionero* records an endless tug-of-war between the forces of passion and the impulse to virtue in an accelerating rhythm of determination and despair. The poet lover, wholly cognizant of his position, is nonetheless incapable of sustaining his progress toward the gleaming realms of Light, Beauty, Virtue, Truth. Human affairs, existence in time, betray their inconstancy when men let themselves be overcome by their passions. If Thomas More furnishes Herrera with evidence that they can vanquish this uncertainty, Henry evokes his despair.

While suggesting a link with modes of thought in very different modes of literature by the same author, we must situate Herrera's portrait of the tyrant in the mainstream of political thought in his day. Erasmus followed the ancient Greeks and Romans and Holy Scripture in setting forth the antithesis king-tyrant. The King —Erasmus culls his adjectives from Julius Pollux's *Onomasticon*— is lauded as «Pater, mitis, placidus, leuis, prouidus, aequus, humanus, magnanimus, liber, pecuniae contemptior, haud obnoxius affectibus, sibiipsi imperans.»[89] The tyrant, on the other hand, is a monster, a «portento de naturaleza»:

---

[85] López Estrada, «Edición y estudio», p. 19.
[86] Pedro Calderón de la Barca, *La vida es sueño*, in *Obras completas* (Madrid, 1966-1967), ll. 3255-3258.
[87] López Estrada, «Edición y estudio», p. 19.
[88] Herrera, *Tomas Moro*, p. 39.
[89] Erasmus, p. 45.

«crudelis, efferus, uiolentus, ... superbus, elatus, ... turbulentus, uoluptatum seruus, intemperans, immoderatus, ... intolerabilis.»[90] These epithets summarize the endless harangues, often ostentatiously documented from the philosophers, in which Erasmus expounds on the qualities of the ruler. Mariana and Rivadeneira incorporate these same antithetical portraits into their discussions, which stress, as we have seen, the monarch's role with respect to his subjects and the Church.[91]

Herrera includes in his account of More's life and death references to most of the questions raised by the moralists: the role of religion in a monarchy and the monarch's jurisdiction in religious affairs, the question of popular allegiance to a ruler, the scourge of flatterers and the duties of a royal adviser. The reflections are often embroidered onto the very phrases of Herrera's principal source, Sander, and the comparison of the two texts reveals Herrera's especial concern with these questions. But he does not, as he had in the *Anotaciones,* or in the manner of a Mariana or a Rivadeneira, give in to the impulse to provide support from the philosophers for his assertions. In fact, nowhere in the *Tomas Moro* is one referred to any other source. What he presents us with is an historical account with his own evaluation of its significance, Cicero's «how and why».[92]

Many of the concerns voiced by Spanish historians and moralists of Herrera's time constitute a direct reaction to Machiavellian ideals of government. Pedro de Rivadeneira informs the reader of his *Tratado de la religión y virtudes que debe tener el príncipe cristiano* that he writes precisely «against what Niccolò Machiavelli and politicians of our time teach».[93] Sixteenth-century Catholic philosophers probably did the Florentine's political thought a certain injustice. Machiavelli in his own particular wisdom expressed as much concern as they did over the relationship between a prince and his subjects. He devotes a special chapter of *Il Principe* to the question of avoiding hatred of one's subjects, and insists on the need for a prince to curry the approval of his subjects, for his ability to rule ultimately

---

[90] *Ibid.,* p. 46.
[91] *Ibid.,* p. 34 ff. Cf. Mariana, *Del Rey,* Part I, Chapter 5; Rivadeneira, *Tratado del Príncipe Cristiano,* Bk. II.
[92] Marcus Tullius Cicero, *De Oratore* (New York, 1847), p. 137.
[93] Rivadeneira, p. 449.

depends on them.[94] Yet Machiavelli does not envision the monarch in a paternal capacity. Addressing himself to the question whether it is better to be loved or feared, he admits the possibility that even the good prince will have to resort to cruelty to keep his kingdom together.[95] God does not, as in the view of a Mariana or an Herrera, automatically reward the good prince with a peaceable kingdom and the evil one with chaos. God's power over man appears tempered by fortune and man's own will.[96] Thus, the prince must act decisively, but he also must «procedere in modo, temperato con prudenzia e umanità, che la troppa confidenzia non lo facci incauto».[97] Machiavelli's reply to the question «s'egli è meglio essere amato che temuto o e converso» is:

> che si vorrebbe essere l'uno e l'altro; ma perchè egli è difficile accozzarli insieme, è molto più sicuro essere temuto che amato, quando si abbia a mancare dell'uno de' dua..... Debbe nondimanco il principe farsi temere in modo che, se non acquista lo amore, che fugga l'odio.[98]

Machiavelli requires principally of the good ruler that he make all of his subjects entirely dependent on him for their well-being, so that they will never experience the temptation to eliminate him. Erasmus on the other hand insists that the prince imitate God, who «ne coactis imperaret, & angelis & hominibus liberum dedit arbitrium».[99] Rule through fear is the right of the pagan prince, not the Christian. Mariana and Herrera echo the concern that a ruler should be loved rather than feared.[100] Thomas More himself behaves so that «no era menos amado, que temido».[101] Any other approach cannot produce true respect: «no es verdadero aquel respeto, sino temor de su insolencia i tirania».[102]

Machiavelli builds his entire philosophy on a pessimistic view of human nature. Neither a king's subjects nor his allies behave

---

[94] Niccolò Machiavelli, *Il Principe*, in *Tutte le opere storiche e letterarie,* ed. Guido Mazzoni and Mario Casella (Florence, 1929), Chapter XIX, pp. 35-41.
[95] *Ibid.,* pp. 32-34.
[96] *Ibid.,* pp. 48-49.
[97] *Ibid.,* p. 33.
[98] *Ibid.,* p. 33.
[99] Erasmus, pp. 52-53.
[100] Mariana, *Del Rey,* Chapter 14, Part III, p. 565 ff.
[101] Herrera, *Tomas Moro,* p. 37.
[102] *Ibid.,* p. 37.

in the manner of tractable and loyal children. While Mariana can rail against deceit and proclaim the necessity of «amor a la verdad y el odio a la mentira», [103] the pragmatist takes a different view in his pronouncements on keeping faith. In Chapter XVIII of *Il Principe,* he advises the ruler to abide by his promises only when it is in his interest to do so, explaining his stand in this manner: «E se gli uomini fussino tutti buoni, questo precetto non sarebbe buono; ma perchè sono tristi, e non la osserverebbono a te, tu etiam non l'hai ad osservare a loro.» [104] The most successful of princes then are naturally the ones «che della fede hanno tenuto poco conto». [105] Here Machiavelli adds the bait to which Herrera will rise. Speaking of the appropriate virtues of the prince he says:

> A uno principe, adunque, non è necessario avere in fatto tutte le soprascritte qualità, ma è bene necessario *parere* di averle. Anzi ardirò di dire questo, che avendole e osservandole sempre, sono dannose; e *parendo* di averle, sono utili; come parere pietoso, fedele, umano, intero, religioso, ed essere; ma stare in modo edificato con l'animo, che, bisognando non essere, tu possa e sappi mutare el contrario. [106]

Herrera's position on this point is clear, as we had occasion to note in our discussion of the *Relacion,* and thoroughly Erasmian: to be a nominal Christian is never enough. Erasmus found it better to be a sincere Turk than a hypocritical Christian. [107] Without mentioning names —Spain and her monarch remain curiously in the background— Herrera applauds the kingdom whose ruler embodies true goodness:

> Pero lo que en esta sazon se me ofrece à la consideracion, como una cosa maravillosa i de estimacion grandisima, es la buena suerte i particular merced, que haze Dios al reino, que es governado de principe, que procura mas ser, que parecer bueno, i cuan agradecidos deven estar los onbres, en cuya edad reluze con la Magestad Real la virtud i ecelencia de costunbres. [108]

---

[103] Mariana, *Del Rey,* Part II, Chapter 10, pp. 516-518.
[104] Machiavelli, p. 34.
[105] *Ibid.,* p. 34.
[106] *Ibid.,* p. 35.
[107] Erasmus, *Dulce bellum inexpertis* (Brussels, 1953), pp. 90-91.
[108] Herrera, *Tomas Moro,* p. 40.

Rivadeneira devotes several chapters of the second part of his *Tratado* to refuting Machiavelli on this point: «Que las virtudes del príncipe cristiano deben ser verdaderas virtudes, y no fingidas, como enseña Maquiavelo.» [109] Machiavelli did not indulge himself in this sort of nostalgia for a state of innocence in which goodness would become synonymous with power.

In many individual instructions, Machiavelli appears far less distant from the Christian political theorists. He expends considerable attention on the problem of flatterers, following the ancients. [110] Similar chapters are to be found in Erasmus' *Institvtio*, in Rivadeneira and in Mariana. [111] But while Erasmus concentrates on the folly of the prince who falls prey to the vainglory of lofty titles, and Rivadeneira decries any private counsel which does not consider the will of God, Machiavelli concerns himself with the problem of the prince's independence. A prince must not wholly turn himself over to anyone, for to do so would be to surrender a part of his power. On this subject as well, Machiavelli's advice incurs the righteous indignation of the orthodox. Machiavelli steers what he thinks a middle course between the deceit of flatterers and an attitude so removed that even the faithful are discouraged from proffering advice. The wise prince will choose a council of wise men and seek its opinions, but only when he wishes to. He must make it clear that unsolicited opinions are not welcome, and he must ultimately come independently to his own decisions through absolutely private deliberations. [112] But the wise ruler ought to be «largo domandatore, e di poi circa le cose domandate paziente auditore del vero; anzi, intendendo che alcuno per alcuno respetto non gnene dica, turbarsene». [113]

Rivadeneira, perhaps the most hypersensitive interpreter of Machiavelli among his contemporaries in the last decade of the sixteenth century, infers from this insistence on the ultimate autonomy of the prince a denial of the importance of advice. Accordingly he sets aside a chapter in which he extols the willingness of a ruler to seek counsel as one of the requisites of true prudence and indicative of the Christian virtues «blandura

[109] Rivadeneira, p. 520.
[110] Machiavelli, pp. 46-47.
[111] Erasmus, *Institvtio*, p. 66 ff.
[112] Machiavelli, p. 46.
[113] *Ibid.*, p. 46.

y docilidad».[114] Rivadeneira's prince is no more than a man: he participates in human frailties and inadequacies. Thus humility best becomes him. Mariana's advice falls somewhere between these two positions. He warns, in his remarks on the education of a royal heir, that the young prince should not allow too close a familiarity with his companions to develop.[115] Later in his treatise, he cautions against listening always to one counselor rather than balancing the contributions of many.[116]

Herrera's special preoccupations in the *Tomas Moro* seem to follow the lines of Erasmian thought more closely than any other. The royal counselor has a moral obligation to offer his honest opinion regarding any of the king's affairs:

> Deven ser los amigos i consegeros de los Principes (si algunos tienen con ellos este lugar) buscados i escogidos entre todos, para que puedan dezilles libremente lo que conviene, i advertir con modestia i respeto de las cosas, que mandan mal.[117]

He assuredly need not wait, as Machiavelli would have him, to be asked his feelings. Instead, the courage to offer one's objections becomes a mode of heroism. The problems of advice-giving are twofold. On the one hand, the fault belongs with the advisers themselves: «Mas casi ninguna, ò pocas vezes sucede, que aya quien ocupe bien aquel puesto, i ose acudir à otra cosa, que à la voluntad buena, ò mala del señor.»[118] In the case of Henry, his new counselors are no better than common flatterers, corrupt creatures of weakness, passion, ambition, who devise support and encouragement for the King's most vulgar caprices, which they should instead devote themselves to restraining:

> Esforçaron la opinion del Rei, los ministros i consegeros, i los aduladores, pestilencia perpetua de las casas reales. Estos, como pensavan crecer i valer por este camino, olvidando el respeto i el temor, devido à los onbres i à Dios, le aconsejaron, que pusiese su intento en execucion, i *con razones coloradas i conpuestas à su gusto,* lo incitaron de tal suerte, que hizieron despeñar al que corria sin freno en seguimiento de su voluntad. Tanto es pode-

---

[114] Rivadeneira, p. 553.
[115] Mariana, *Del Rey*, pp. 513-516.
[116] *Ibid.*, pp. 565-570.
[117] Herrera, *Tomas Moro*, p. 39.
[118] *Ibid.*, p. 39.

> rosa la lisonja, i tanto es dañosa en los onbres, que trastornò à aquel principe sabio i de grande animo tan violentamente, que dexandose sobrar de sus passiones, cayò en tantos defetos.[119]

The flatterer leads the king on to share in his own moral ruin. Yet the monarch himself shares heavily in the responsibility for this self-delusion:

> Pero lo que es mas miserable deste vicio, siendo los que lo siguen de animo vil i corronpidas costunbres, i llenos de inorancia, i dañosos conocidamente à los reinos i à los reyes, son los que valen i tienen estimacion entre ellos, quedando olvidados i aborrecidos los onbres de sano consejo i de valor i prudencia. Porque casi nunca sufrio cerca de si la grandeza real el resplandor de la virtud agena.[120]

The passage resembles uncannily one which is found in Erasmus' chapter on legislation in the *Institvtio,* where he contrasts loyalty and treason, and the rampant confusion between them:

> Proditorem uocant (nam id uocabulum odiossimum esse uolunt) qui principem ad ea deflectentem quae nec ipsi decora sunt aut tuta, nec patria conducibilia, liberis consiliis ad meliora reuocat. Atque illum plebeiis opinionibus corrumpit, qui in uoluptates sordidas, qui in comessationes, in aleam, & alia id genus dedecora praecipitat, num is dignitati principis consulit? Fidem uocant, quoties per assentationem stulto principi mos geritur, proditionem, si quis turpibus coeptis obsistat. Imo nemo minus amicus est principi, quis qui turpiter assentando dementat & abducit a recto..... Haec est uera proditio, & non uno supplicio digna.[121]

The prudent monarch always moves in an ascending path toward virtue and perfection. Herrera seems to envision an ideal situation in which the King and his magistrates would engage in a kind of mutual emulation, where each would find strength in the other's virtue. For this to be possible, all must take on the dimensions of heroes in fearlessness and confidence:

> Pero es cosa cierta, que nunca amò la lisonja aquel, cuyo animo estuvo lleno de verdadero valor, i conocio i dio su entero precio à las cosas. Porque jamas favorecio à los lisongeros, otro que

---

[119] *Ibid.,* pp. 39-40.
[120] *Ibid.,* p. 40.
[121] Erasmus, *Institvtio,* pp. 105-106.

> el onbre de poca virtud, i que no constituyò su felicidad en la bondad de las obras, sino en la opinion falsa. Mas quien, que tenga algun espiritu de varon, darà credito, à los lisongeros, sino el que lisongea à si mismo? [122]

Such a man is a creature of appearance, rather than substance, whose passion for virtue is illusory, who cares only for the fruits of public opinion. He is no more a real man than a real Christian. As in the *Relacion*, Herrera has no sympathy for empty displays of virtue. He contrasts the «ánimo... lleno de verdadero valor» of the Chancellor with the cowardice and cruelty of the King. [123] More's experience exemplifies the great perils public life holds for a virtuous man:

> cuan peligroso es para los que siguen la virtud el trato con los principes i poderosos, que olvidan como ingratos i desconocidos todos los servicios i merecimientos de sus vassallos i criados,... cuando se atraviesa alguna cosa de su gusto, sin atender, si es derecho seguir en los casos injustos la violencia de sus desatinos. [124]

Herrera foresees a number of objections which he attributes to More's friends. First, some claim that by objecting to the King, the counselor can only precipitate more violent upheavals than were caused by the original transgression. Furthermore, as the saying goes, time cures all things. Others maintain the need for a certain cunning: the royal adviser should remain silent on one point so that he will retain at least a moderating influence over the King's passions («afectos»). [125] Finally there is the problem of respect for royal authority, of which Machiavelli was so conscious. Should not a certain restraint inhibit even the king's intimates? If not, how is order to be maintained? The kind of situation in question clearly provides the key: «Estos consejos humanos son provechosos en otros casos, i no es onbre de buen seso, el que desprecia el respeto i obediencia, que debe a su Rei. I ninguno, que repunase a su inperio, se pudo alabar derechamente.» [126] Ordinary circumstances require respect for

---

[122] Herrera, *Tomas Moro*, p. 40.
[123] *Ibid.*, p. 40.
[124] *Ibid.*, pp. 50-51.
[125] *Ibid.*, p. 51.
[126] *Ibid.*, p. 51.

royal authority. Herrera does not attempt to make a virtue of disobedience to a monarch, except in this one circumstance:

> Pero donde se pone en aventura la verdad i la religion, no sè, por cual razon devan ser admitidos. Apartese de los animos cristianos opinion tan peligrosa, i llena de tantos inconvenientes. No puede en ellos lisonja, o temor, para seguir voluntades de onbres apassionados i sugetos à sus vicios, contra las leyes del cielo. [127]

When a ruler through his sins would persuade his subjects to disobey divine laws, his authority over them ceases. Tyranny, in the minds of Herrera and his contemporaries, seems to carry with it the implication of a transgression of divine laws. In fact, the historical examples of tyranny in their own era which prompt their concern involve the desire of a monarch to influence the religious practices of his subjects. As with Henry VIII of England, so with the Henrys of France. For Herrera, virtue possesses ultimately greater strength than vice. The fall of tyranny obeys an historical as well as a religious inevitability: «no fue, ni podra ser poderosa la tirania, para establecer en la tierra su inpiedad.» [128]

The virtue which man owes to God belongs to a higher order than that which is due to one's country. A hero then finds a more glorious death in the cause of religion than in the service of a king:

> I si es gloriosa muerte, la que se recibe en servicio de los reyes, i en defensa de la patria, cuanto serà mas gloriosa i mas bienaventurada la que padece el onbre, por no assentir cosa agena i contraria à la religion? Quien se halla ofrecido en ocasion semejante, i no satisfaze a la obligacion, en que nacio, i por flaqueza de coraçon, o cualquiera otro respeto umano, no se muestra firme, seguro, i sin temor, dexa tan desobligada la fè, que se puede dezir, que no la tuvo, o no quiso tenella. [129]

Defense of religion strikes right at the core of human dignity. Herrera insists, too, on the fact that his tyrant has already transgressed all the laws of human dignity, as he has those of true religion. When Henry's will is opposed by his theologian

[127] *Ibid.*, p. 51.
[128] *Ibid.*, p. 51.
[129] *Ibid.*, p. 51.

counselors, Herrera describes his wrath turned to cruelty: «ardio en ira, i como andava apartado del camino, i no acertava, determinò mostrar contra ellos la crueldad i fiereza de su animo.» [130] Henry becomes a kind of savage, subhuman beast, recalling Herrera's own description of the infidel tyrant Selim and Erasmus' portrait of human ferocity. In the *Querela pacis* Erasmus stressed the savagery of war among Christians by claiming that like animals do not combat one another. Herrera resorts to a similar comparison to describe the English King's conduct toward his more virtuous magistrate:

> Ninguno de todos los animales quitò al otro el mejor lugar, ò le hizo injuria, siendo su inferior. Pero al onbre bueno se prefiere el malo, i el adulador al verdadero, i usurpa el vicio los grados de la virtud, por miserable suerte desta edad, en que reinan abundantemente todas las pasiones del animo. [131]

Like Mariana's tyrant, and many since Aristotle, Henry VIII knows the plague of fear and mistrust of his advisers and subjects. [132] Herrera records Sander's description of the death of Bishop John Fisher; but where Sander merely notes that the Bishop's head was removed from a spike on London Bridge, Herrera adds that this measure was taken so that «no acresentase [sic] el rumor, i abraçasen algunos aquella ocasión para hazer movimientos». [133] Herrera goes on to elaborate the guilty fear of the wanton sinner: «Porque nunca pierde el temor el injusto, i ninguno asegura la conciencia, que no ai cosa mas eficaz que ella, ni tormento, que descubra mejor el maleficio, ni verdugo alguno, que castigue mas cruelmente.» [134] Likewise, the advisers who have encouraged their king's misguided will burn in secret guilt: «los que le sirvieron en ministerio tan inpio, se atormentavan secretamente, por aver seguido i alentado aquella opinion, i no aver osado imitar al que avian ellos mismos condenado i muerto.» [135]

Unlike Herrera and his Spanish contemporaries, Machiavelli

---

[130] *Ibid.*, p. 43.
[131] *Ibid.*, p. 43.
[132] Mariana, *Del Rey*, p. 479.
[133] Herrera, *Tomas Moro*, p. 46.
[134] *Ibid.*, p. 46.
[135] *Ibid.*, p. 50.

did not consider tyranny as essentially immoral or antireligious, but rather as singularly inexpedient. In the *Discorsi,* he criticizes tyranny because it provides neither happiness for the people nor security for the ruler.[136] Excessive cruelty always turns out to be counter-productive and imperils the preservation of the state. But it is basically the state which concerns the author of *Il Principe.* The integrity of the state constitutes a virtue in itself. In the *Discorsi,* he preaches the defense of one's country, whether it bring glory or ignominy.[137] Any methods whatever are sanctioned to promote this end.

Machiavelli's view involves the premise that there are times when the state's interests of self-preservation and the dictates of Christian morality will find themselves at odds. Thinkers such as Herrera, Mariana and Rivadeneira rebelled violently against this notion. If God is in fact the ultimate arbiter of human events, then His laws will either preserve or damn human undertakings. In a divinely ordered universe, there can be no conflict between virtue and necessity. Just as tyranny is doomed to failure, so must virtue triumph, and therefore she belongs intimately bound up with the apparatus of government. Thus we find that Erasmus, Mariana, Rivadeneira, all concern themselves with molding the young prince's character so as to inculcate in him all the Christian virtues of piety, charity and humility. Machiavelli commented specifically on this very type of upbringing in the *Discorsi,* and in so doing, further fed the fires of indignation, especially in Rivadeneira. In Book Two, where he discusses the expansion of the Roman Republic, Machiavelli pauses to reflect on why men were more fond of liberty in ancient times than in his own day. The answer he finds in the difference of education, and consequently in the difference of religion. Christianity,

> avendoci... mostro la verità e la vera via, ci fa stimare meno l'onore del mondo.... La nostra religione ha glorificato più gli uomini umili e contemplativi, che gli attivi.... E se la religione nostra richiede che tu abbi in te fortezza, vuole che tu sia atto a patire più che a fare una cosa forte.[138]

---

[136] Machiavelli, *Discorsi sopra la Prima Deca di Tito Livio,* in *Tutte le opere,* p. 74.
[137] *Ibid.,* p. 256.
[138] *Ibid.,* p. 141.

To make weakness a virtue is in reality to turn the world over to the wicked. But this cowardly resignation arises from a misinterpretation of Christian teaching, Machiavelli claims, for religion actually permits us «la esaltazione e la difesa della patria». [139]

In Part Two of the *Tratado del Príncipe Cristiano*, Rivadeneira vehemently reproaches Machiavelli's attitude toward strength, his reading of the passage apparently having been stopped by anger before he arrived at the main thrust of the Florentine's remarks. [140] For Rivadeneira there can be no difference between strength spiritual and political. The strength which Machiavelli appears to him to desire is «una bárbara e inhumana fiereza». [141] Rivadeneira devotes the entire first part of his treatise to demonstrating the necessity of the one true religion in the constitution of a state, and the destruction visited upon those kingdoms and republics which have not taken Christ into account. Where the responsibility for punishment and reward of human enterprise lies with God, there can be no question that the king must cultivate virtue above all other things. Herrera and Rivadeneira both rail against the misuse of religion fostered by the author of *Il Principe*: «no ai tirania mas dura i aborrecible, que la que se cubre i ajusta con pretesto de religion, de quien se sirven muchos poderosos, segun les cae à cuento para sus intenciones.» [142] Rivadeneira details the dire fates which have befallen such rulers.

The fall of the tyrant, and particularly the tyrant who threatens religion, only manifests a general law of God's will for his creation. Juan de Mariana speaks most explicitly of the tyrant's deserved fate. Tyrants fall within two general classes: those duly constituted in authority, and those who have usurped power for themselves unjustly. With the latter, the people's right to eliminate the monarch is not questioned. As to the former, God desires that they be tolerated as long as possible, that is, until their hardness of heart brings them to break divine law. Then the tyrant must fall. [143] Herrera does not address himself

---

[139] *Ibid.*, p. 141.
[140] Rivadeneira, pp. 567-569.
[141] *Ibid.*, p. 567.
[142] Herrera, *Tomas Moro*, p. 40; Rivadeneira, p. 459 ff.
[143] Mariana, *Del Rey*, pp. 479-483.

directly to the question of tyrannicide, but it is evident that Henry has, in his eyes, forfeited any real right to continue on the English throne. If Herrera did share Mariana's views on regicide, such elimination of a tyrant is permitted in any case only as a last resort. Before such measures become permissible, all possible steps must be taken to divert the tyrant from his course.

The *Tomas Moro* clearly implicates those surrounding the monarch for England's current distress. Henry's ambitious advisers have fed his passions rather than restraining him. Herrera seems to be advocating disobedience rather than tyrannicide, rejection of the King's unreasonable desires rather than flattery, and Erasmus' favorite method — persuasion by Christian example:

> Mas atendamos i juzguemos si por la floxedad i tibieza de los prelados, i por la cobardia i lisonja de los grandes i de toda la nobleza, ganò y mejorò, algo Inglaterra, i si por el sacrilegio i abominacion del Rei se hallò, mas grande i mas gloriosa, i si perdio alguna caridad i ecelencia por la entereza i constancia de Tomas Moro. [144]

Had the English nobility and the specifically accused clergy simply opposed their monarch, they might have averted all the ills they currently suffer:

> Creamos, pues, como es justo, en estas cosas, que si resplandeciera en los coraçones de los Principes Ingleses, i de la gente señalada la caridad, i el zelo ardiente de la religion, que no dudàran oponerse con respeto i lealtad al error de Enrique, i estorvàran los daños que sucedieron. [145]

As over against these weaklings, Herrera praises the resistance:

> Porque sè bien que ai muchos, en quien no pudo hazer mudança alguna de las persecuciones, que tanto an afligido, i angustiado à Inglaterra. Antes los estimo por mayores i mas ecelentes, i conozco en ellos la grandeza i misericordia divina, pues vemos onbres perseguidos i desanparados, desnudos de todo favor i de toda esperança umana, que contra las fuerças i la ira de una Reina que procura establecer los ritos abominables de su eregia, i derri-

---

[144] Herrera, *Tomas Moro*, p. 51.
[145] *Ibid.*, p. 52.

> bar la religion santissima, contra todos los engaños i tiranias de los privados i consejeros, i contra los tormentos, que hallan los ministros del error, se descubren sin temor de la muerte con generosidad de animo, i muestran cuanto mas se deven respetar los derechos i ordenacion de la Iglesia, que los antojos i desafueros de los tiranos. [146]

We find not a word which would allow us to conclude that Herrera favored the systematic elimination of either Henry or his equally abominable daughter, Elizabeth. In the passage we have just cited, he offers an ethic of suffering and of perseverance. The faithful will not permit the tyrant or any other force to bend their consciences in matters of religion. Before they submit to the king on questions of faith, they will suffer martyrdom. Herrera seems to regard Henry's aberration almost positively, as an opportunity for the virtuous to display their true mettle. In this case the seat of honor is left vacant: «dexaron todo el lugar libre i desenbaraçado a quien no temio perder la gracia de su Rei, i osò ofrecer por Dios su vida en sacrificio.» [147] True virtue requires disadvantage and sacrifice up to the most extreme limit. Human nature is the tyrant's closest ally, «Porque somos faciles à lo peor, sin que para ello nos falte guia, ò conpañero». [148] The tyrant's persistence in power clearly indicates God's will to punish his people for their unquestioning submission:

> puede conocer por castigo de sus culpas, i por ultima infelicidad el reino, que tiene administrador vicioso, porque ninguno ai, que le aconsege cosa estraña de su gusto, antes parece que se conforman todos a sus costumbres. [149]

While Herrera seems to suggest (or simply hope) that conscientious and upright counseling might have averted disaster, and offers no other plan of resistance, he declares as well that «no son obligados los pueblos à la infidelidad, o eregia de sus superiores». [150] The monarch, as becomes more than evident in the case at hand, is subject to error in questions of doctrine. Mariana and Rivadeneira insist on the separation of ecclesiastical and political power to the extent that they strip the king of the

---

[146] *Ibid.*, p. 41; cf. *Relacion*, p. 269.
[147] Herrera, *Tomas Moro*, p. 52.
[148] *Ibid.*, p. 41.
[149] *Ibid.*, p. 40.
[150] *Ibid.*, p. 41.

right to legislate or have jurisdiction over church affairs and religious conviction.[151] Mariana further asserts —as did Erasmus and Machiavelli (with reservations)— that the prince is not excused from abiding by the laws of his kingdom.[152] Thus Herrera shows the monarch and his people measured by one and the same yardstick. The error of the one can never serve to condone that of the other. Rivadeneira takes great pains to demonstrate that God has punished both peoples and princes for tolerating the heresy and immorality of one another.[153] Likewise for Herrera, the present tribulation of England inevitably springs from guilt on the part of the people. God's justice never fails. We leave the implications of this for Herrera's view of history to the following chapter.

---

[151] Rivadeneira, pp. 485-487; Mariana, *Del Rey,* pp. 491-495.
[152] Erasmus, *Institvtio,* p. 103; Machiavelli, *Discorsi,* pp. 115-116; Mariana, *Del Rey,* pp. 488-491.
[153] Rivadeneira, *Tratado del Príncipe,* Part I, Chapters 27-29.

CHAPTER THREE

THE DIRECTION OF HISTORY

Herrera published the *Tomas Moro* in 1592, four years after Pedro de Rivadeneira had completed his adaptation of Nicholas Sander's work on the crisis of the English Church, and two years after Pacheco claims that Herrera circulated a complete manuscript of the *Istoria general* among his friends.[1] In addition to these literary events, the years which separate Herrera's last work of certain date from his earlier historical writings had wrought vast changes in the Spanish spiritual landscape. Spain's military might had suffered the ultimate humiliation. It was no casual rout that the English inflicted, but rather a crushing defeat of the culminating effort of Philip II's dream for a united Christendom. The expedition had been thwarted in its widely advertised purpose of avenging the honor of Christ and the death of Mary Queen of Scots. When the last battered ships straggled home, having been blown clear around Scotland and assaulted by the inclemencies of the Northern seas, the stain of dishonor had still not been washed away. The Grand Armada, self-appointed savior of Christendom, was a punctured illusion. England's strength forced a reluctant recognition of the tenacity of the Anglican heresy and of the scant likelihood that further crusades would meet with more success than the first. Spain continued to be weighed down by the related problems of France and the Low Countries. Nor could even Spain's Mediterranean destiny, so seemingly glorious in the first flush of optimism after Lepanto, offer any consolation. The League of Lepanto had fallen victim to more pressing concerns and to the divisive character

[1] Pacheco, *Libro de descripción de verdaderos retratos* (Seville, 1881-1885).

of individual national interests. Christian forces under the youthful King of Portugal had sustained a defeat in North Africa which claimed the flower of knighthood. In short, the great crescendo of Christian history, as it appeared to countless writers and poets in 1572,[2] must have seemed to Herrera's contemporaries of twenty years afterward to have been abruptly halted.

Ascetic writers found their clear cue in the events of history, and their messages were primarily two. In the first place, all human affairs are ultimately in the hands of God. Thus, although we may be unable to perceive it, or if at all, we see it through a glass darkly, there must exist in the divine mind a plan for history of which these events are a part. Furthermore, since God is the fountainhead of all justice, disaster provides the inescapable proof of human transgression. If mankind wishes to enjoy any hope for the future, it must cleanse itself of all iniquity. The literary result: a new barrage of didactic literature designed to lead God's people back to the path of righteousness. In the particular historical situation which they faced, the principal guilt appeared to attach to the role of the prince. Evil rulers bore the responsibility for leading England and France astray. Hence the most useful didactic enterprise would consist in warning of the perils faced by a monarch and his subjects. The presence of pernicious teachings, conspicuously those of Machiavelli, spurred them on in their task, in the hope of being able to bring human activity into harmony with the designs of Providence. Pedro de Rivadeneira, addressing himself to Prince Philip in 1595, refers to the difficulties of ruling in the world, availing himself of the age-old metaphor of the ship of state. But his words conjure up a sea which belongs as well to sixteenth-century political reality:

> Es tan peligrosa esta navegación, son tan alterados estos mares, tan varios y tan contrarios los vientos, tan altas las rocas, y los bajos tan ciegos y tan mudables, y tantos y tan crueles los cosarios que la infestan, que para que la nave llegue al deseado puerto, es necesario que el mismo Dios lleve el gobernalle, y sea luz, guía y amparo de los príncipes.[3]

---

[2] José López de Toro, *Los poetas de Lepanto* (Madrid, 1950).
[3] Rivadeneira, *Tratado del Príncipe Cristiano*, in *Obras escogidas*, ed. Vicente de la Fuente, B.A.E., Vol. LX (Madrid, 1868), p. 452.

Surely no contemporary reader could have failed to be struck with the applicability of this image to Spain's historical situation. Mariana ascribed the origin of his own *De Rege* to the presence of even greater perils and trials which his day posed for the monarch compared with those he had faced in the past. Otherwise it would not have been necessary to address Europe's most pious king.[4]

The writings of Pedro de Rivadeneira, also the principal Spanish historian of the English crisis, exemplify both reactions to the hostility of events. The first we have already considered: the reform of conduct as directed in a manual for the prince. The other response is the way of resignation to the trials which God in his infinite wisdom sends to men. This is the message carried in the *Tratado de la tribulación,* published in 1589, only a year after the *Historia eclesiástica* appeared in Spain.[5] The treatise contains almost no historical references. Particularly absent is anything but the most general allusion to the book's own time. After a work of history, necessarily submerged in time, Rivadeneira removes to a more detached sphere. While the heresies which he mentions as among the most rigorous of God's means to torment men are clearly related to the sixteenth-century history he had concentrated on earlier, his allusions draw overwhelmingly on previous periods. The point seems to be not to emphasize the ruin of «our time» over all previous eras, but to show the unchanging nature and purpose of tribulation throughout history. Men of Rivadeneira's day suffer as Job did and for the same reasons. Present-day sufferings are simply a renewed test of faith.

We must look elsewhere for specific comment on contemporary history. Various remarks in Mariana's *De Rege* give us evidence of a changed view of history and Spanish history in particular. In a chapter on military art,[6] Mariana continues to proclaim that profession as the sole hope of the nation's honor, but at the same time, he laments the decay of ancient military arts in his own time. For this he ascribes no fault to men themselves, but rather to the times, which no longer encourage such pursuits.

---

[4] *Del Rey y de la institución real,* in *Obras del Padre Juan de Mariana,* B.A.E., Vol. XXXI (Madrid, 1854).
[5] Rivadeneira, *Tratado de la tribulación,* in *Obras escogidas.*
[6] Mariana, *Del Rey,* p. 545.

Mariana goes on to describe the plight of Spain, no longer the awe of other nations as she had been so little time before. Rivadeneira shows himself to be by far the most vindictive of his day with regard to Spain's enemies and the architects of her defeat. The *Historia eclesiástica* dwells obsessively on every sordid detail that can be mustered for England's condemnation, including tales which delve into the history of Henry VIII's libertinism and succeed in making simple adultery into incest. To record a breach of divine law is not enough: Rivadeneira's Ann Boleyn is made a prodigy of nature, a six-toed freak with buck teeth, all designed to create a being repugnant on the most superficial level, to arouse the primitive emotions of disgust for physical deformity.[7] Rather than retrace his steps, we refer the reader to the excellent study of R. O. Jones which contrasts the attitudes of the authors of the *Historia eclesiástica* and the *Tomás Moro*.[8]

In the light of Rivadeneira's perspective, we ought to be surprised not by what Herrera has said, but by what he has not, as Cervantes once urged his public. R. O. Jones has suggested that the *Tomás Moro* lacks the *Historia*'s vituperative fury and its graphic evocation of the horrors of martyrdom. Herrera, too, appears to treat England herself with considerably greater equanimity. She is not simply the locus of a hated heretic infestation. Herrera describes London, More's birthplace, as a «nobilisima ciudad de Inglaterra, que puesta en luengo à la ribera del Tamisa, se estiende tanto, que parece no tener fin, i por lo ancho se ensangosta i recoge estrechamente».[9] When Herrera speaks of England's troubles, they do not seem to be fully part of her nature, but rather something which has suddenly befallen her:

> Pues vemos aquella Isla nobilisima entre todas las que cerca el Oceano, padecer amargamente todos los trabajos i daños, que suelen nacer de la mudança de las costunbres, i del perdimiento de la religion catolica.[10]

---

[7] Rivadeneira, *Historia eclesiástica del Scisma de Inglaterra*, in *Obras escogidas*, pp. 192-193.
[8] R. O. Jones, «El *Tomas Moro* de Fernando de Herrera», B.R.A.E., XXX (1950), 423-438.
[9] Herrera, *Tomas Moro*, in Francisco López Estrada, «Edición y estudio», *Archivo Hispalense*, XII (1950), 35.
[10] *Ibid.*, p. 39.

England is a nation which, like any other human institution, at times falls prey to error.

Herrera always surrounds his comments on England's fall with reflections on the frailty of human nature — «la flaqueza umana.»[11] Henry VIII is portrayed, as we have seen, as a veritable monster («portento de naturaleza»[12]), but his monstrosity is offered as proof of a general law: «la inconstancia de las cosas umanas, i lo poco que se deve fiar de los buenos principios, cuando se dexan vencer los onbres de sus apetitos.»[13] This rule has nothing in particular to do with England, but with all mankind. Ann Boleyn is nothing resembling Rivadeneira's and Sander's English whore, nor is all of Britain a brothel. The second wife of Henry VIII loses her individuality in Herrera's narrative even more thoroughly than the first. Ann Boleyn is merely the personification of temptation, unsuccessfully resisted by Henry. She need be put in no sharper focus than Thomas More's wife and daughter. Herrera's concerns are completely universalized. England's plight is not the worst to be found in history: she simply represents all such types.

Nor have flatterers singled out England as their special target. English flatterers belong to a knavish international brotherhood, «pestilencia perpetua de las casas reales».[14] Likewise the most current scourge, Elizabeth I, is spared all the calumnies which would make her the illegitimate fruit of an adulterous, even incestuous union. Her role in history as Herrera sees it is that of «una Reina que procura establecer los ritos abominables de su eregia, i derribar la religion santissima»,[15] and one who is served in her efforts by «los ministros del error». The lesson of history clearly states that England has been lost «por culpa de su principe»,[16] and has remained so because Englishmen, as others would likely have been, proved too weak to rise to an invitation to glory.

Herrera confirms the neutrality of his observations by refusing to hold out —as Rivadeneira does in his preface to the *Tra-*

---

[11] *Ibid.*, p. 39.
[12] *Ibid.*, p. 38.
[13] *Ibid.*, p. 38.
[14] *Ibid.*, pp. 39-40.
[15] *Ibid.*, p. 41.
[16] *Ibid.*, p. 41.

tado del Príncipe Cristiano [17]— Spanish monarchs as the personification of his ideal ruler. Only the early figure of Henry VIII, present in the author's nostalgia of better days, offers the desired characteristics. Spain appears to hold out no longer the promise of regal perfection which Herrera saw in Philip II, Don Juan de Austria and their father, the Emperor, in the *Relacion de la guerra de Cipre*. Spain's glorious past, more distant in the *Tomas Moro,* injects only a fleeting ray of light in the persons of «aquellos gloriosos Reyes i nunca dinamente alabados, don Fernando i doña Isabel». [18] But the legacy of that past, Queen Catherine, though deserving of a better fate, has been wretchedly treated by luck. [19] It is tempting to view her disappearance from the narrative as symbolic of an eclipse of Spain's royal house.

Herrera's strange silences do not stop here. In a work in whose sense of disillusion one is inclined to see the sad inheritance of the Invincible Armada, we find no mention of this or any other of the recent chain of disheartening events. Herrera mentions Elizabeth I, but he does not comment on her reign any further than those passages we have pointed out. The *Istoria general,* as Pacheco described it, [20] would have reached only through the reign of Charles V. We search the extant poems of Herrera in vain for any trace of «La Invencible». The last historical events recorded in Herrera's poetry take place in 1578: the disaster of Alcázarquivir which inspired the first *canción* of the 1582 edition, «Voz de dolor, i canto de gemido», and several sonnets of the posthumous verse; [21] and the death of Don Juan de Austria. [22] After 1578, there is a *canción* for the reinterment of San Fernando, [23] the poems for the death of the Countess of Gelves and a sonnet for the death of the Marqués of Santa Cruz. [24] The impossibility of fixing any other poems at a later date led Coster to conclude that Herrera had abandoned poetry after the publication of the 1582 edition of

---

[17] Rivadeneira, pp. 452-453.
[18] Herrera, *Tomas Moro,* p. 38.
[19] *Ibid.,* p. 38.
[20] Pacheco, *Libro de descripción de verdaderos retratos.*
[21] Herrera, *Versos emendados i divididos por el en tres libros* (Seville, 1619); *Versos,* ed. Adolphe Coster (Strasbourg, 1916): Bk. I, 67; Bk. III, 18, 20 and 21.
[22] Herrera, *Poesías,* ed. Vicente García de Diego (Madrid, 1914), sonnet 69.
[23] *Ibid.,* Canción V.
[24] Herrera, *Versos,* Bk. III, 57.

his verse.[25]   Others have come to the same conclusion by another route. With the death of his Muse, Herrera, unlike Petrarch, turned away from the profane sphere of poetry and, in a return to his historical vocation, set his thoughts on more sober matters.[26]   This is not the place to argue various theories as to the chronology of Herrera's poetry, and we leave that question for another occasion. Yet, if in fact we possess a piece of prose writing dated after 1588 and find no reference to recent history in it, then surely we cannot use the same absence from the poetry to conclude that Herrera was no longer composing verse after 1582. What we find interesting for our purposes in this study is that, as far as we know, Herrera's silence was complete.

It is difficult, perhaps impossible, to make binding statements about Herrera's later career on the basis of these few scant pages. Even where Herrera the historian is concerned, we know that the *Tomas Moro* can only represent the most minute fraction of the results of Herrera's literary-historical activity. We do not know whether the *Tomas Moro* would have evidenced a sharp departure from the criteria of the *Istoria general,* finished only two years before. And even if such a shift were observable, the differences might be due in rather arbitrary fashion to the diversity of subject matter, without necessarily implying any contradiction in what the author has said on other subjects. With the *Tomas Moro,* the problem is this: for the first time that we know of in Herrera's historical prose, we have a work which does not use military exploits as a preferred raw material for history. Although Pacheco's testimony cannot replace a first-hand knowledge of the *Istoria,* in which we might search for subtle indications of change, we do have his evaluation of its contents: «las acciones donde concurrieron las armas Españolas» up to the end of the age of Charles V.[27]   Thus Thomas More appears to be Herrera's first non-military hero. Both the *Anotaciones* and Herrera's own verse bear out this theory. The heroes of the *Anotaciones,* as we have seen, are the leaders of Spain's crusade against Islam. Herrera addresses poems to the military heroes of his time: Don Álvaro de Bazán, the Duke

---

[25] Coster, *Fernando de Herrera* (Paris, 1908), Chapters 6-7.
[26] López Estrada, «Edición y estudio», p. 9.
[27] Pacheco, *Libro de descripción de verdaderos retratos.*

of Medina Sidonia, Don Juan de Austria and to the many heroes of particular battles. He addresses kings and princesses and poets, but we find no poems directed to saints (with the exception of San Fernando) or martyrs or ascetic figures like Thomas More. One possible exception is a sonnet addressed to Charles V, referring to his abdication in favor of his son Philip.[28] Herrera there glorifies this withdrawal from worldly preoccupations and Charles's decision to attend to the needs of his immortal soul. We have noted, too, sonnet 65 of the 1582 edition, which deals exclusively with virtue, giving no hint of a military bias. Finally, we have tried to stress the common language and conception of virtue shared by soldier and saint alike in Herrera's view.

We must ask ourselves whether the *Tomas Moro* indicates that Herrera had completely reshaped his interpretation of history. Classical historiographical precepts, which Herrera venerated to some degree, made war history's central theme. Here, Herrera speaks of civil martyrdom. Before the *Tomas Moro*, his interests are distinctly nationalistic, although we have seen that the *Relacion* goes beyond Spanish exploits to propound a general theory of heroic virtue. But in the brief account of More's life, nations and national pride are all but completely submerged in the universality of Christendom. In the *Relacion* and the *Anotaciones*, Herrera's protagonists participate in a timeless community of heroes of the Spanish crusade. Thomas More belongs to another eternal brotherhood, that of saints and martyrs of the Church. Do these two visions continue to exist side by side, or are they mutually exclusive? Perhaps events or even Herrera's own autumn years have stripped the historian of his sanguine vision of the course of military and political ventures.

The author of the *Relacion* saw modern history as not only having equalled ancient civilization, but as having completely surpassed it. The heroes of Herrera's day were called upon to display greater valor in wars made more spectacular by the presence of modern weaponry, particularly artillery. The *Anotaciones* preach a vision of history which moves always forward to greater heights of achievement. Language, considered as a gauge of national importance, has been steadily improved by the

---

[28] Herrera, *Versos*, Bk. III, 33.

efforts of its users and holds inexhaustible possibilities for future perfection. Should anyone dare to claim that he had reached the highest possible point, he would thereby merely confess his own ignorance and lack of courage.[29] The relevance of this last factor will shortly become clear.

The opening phrases of the *Tomas Moro* appear to take the opposite view. Herrera's thoughts, first of all, concentrate on the past: «Cuando me pongo en consideracion de *las cosas pasadas,* i rebuelvo en la memoria los hechos de aquellos onbres, que se dispusieron à todos los peligros, por no hazer ofensa à la virtud.»[30] «Aquellos onbres» belong to another era, to the preterite tense. They are separated from Herrera by a gulf of years that memory must strive to bridge. They belong to a Christian Golden Age of virtue:

> Porque parece, que florecio la virtud en *aquella edad,* i crecio en toda la grandeza i fuerça, que se pudo esperar, i los animos de los onbres estavan llenos de vigor, i deseavan mostrar su fortaleza en los casos dificiles. I como los que se hallaban en la sazon mas entera y robusta del mundo, i tenian casi frescas i rezientes las hazañas, los trabajos, i las predicaciones de los Discipulos de IESVCRISTO, reparador de la salud umana, i verdadero Dios i Señor nuestro, i vian presentes los gloriosos hechos de los Martires, la penitencia i estrecheza de aquellos, que se ocupavan en contenplacion de las cosas divinas, imitando generosamente sus obras, procuravan, si ya no podian aventajarseles, descubrirse no inferiores, ò a lo menos no mui desviados dellos.[31]

Restated in Christian terms, this is the classical theory of the pristine perfection of the world, «la sazon mas entera i robusta del mundo». Here the single point at which history's perfection is manifest seems to be the life of Christ. All things subsequent to his existence have brought decay. Even the martyrs whom Herrera describes cannot achieve such perfection. They seek to imitate a model, hoping first to equal it if they cannot surpass it, then not to fall far from the mark, if they cannot reach it. The gulf between men and pristine virtue continues to widen:

> Mas como sean flacas las fuerças de los onbres, i la naturaleza umana se canse sienpre, siguiendo en esto su condicion, como en

---

[29] *Obras de Garci Lasso de la Vega con Anotaciones de Fernando de Herrera* (Seville, 1580), p. 294; ed. A. Gallego Morell (Granada, 1966), p. 399.
[30] Herrera, *Tomas Moro,* p. 34. Italics mine.
[31] *Ibid.,* pp. 34-35. Italics mine.

> las otras cosas, de tal suerte à ido desfalleciendo el amor i estimacion de la virtud, que ninguna cosa ai mas despreciada, i ninguna mas aborrecida. [32]

The law of human nature seems here to be perpetual decay, and thus history has followed a path from love of virtue to the opposite. How far we seem now from the *Relacion,* in which nature dictates instead that man pursue glory and virtue in accordance with a kind of inner need!

Thus, Thomas More stands as «exenplo rarisimo de virtud» [33] at a moment in history when «usurpa el vicio los grados de la virtud, por miserable suerte desta edad, en quien reinan abundantemente todas las pasiones del animo». [34] Herrera insists that the world is in its declining years («la vegez del mundo» [35]) and that nature seems no longer to bring forth virtuous men in the numbers she once produced: «la naturaleza olvidada de produzir onbres, aborrecedores de las costunbres deste tienpo, i que justa i libremente osen sacrificar su vida por la onra de Dios, i por el amor de la virtud.» [36] He contrasts again and again «la miseria de nuestra edad» [37] and the scant signs of virtue («cosa dificil i maravillosa en nuestro tienpo» [38]) with the times «cuando florecia mas la caridad en los coraçones de los onbres». [39] Government naturally has suffered along with so many spheres of human endeavor. Thus a virtuous king results from «la buena suerte i particular merced, que haze Dios al reino», [40] and the subjects of such a monarch should acknowledge this unusual divine favor. The good magistrate is equally a rarity. Thomas More, Herrera says, «mas parecia nacido en la edad, donde tuvo mas lugar la virtud, que en la suya, que tan entregada estava al vicio». [41] The way of the world seems to lead not to ever more glorious conquests of man's bravery and reason, but rather to fulfill the grim prophesy of his nature.

As we have seen before, Herrera returns many times to the

[32] *Ibid.,* p. 35.
[33] *Ibid.,* p. 42.
[34] *Ibid.,* p. 43.
[35] *Ibid.,* p. 35.
[36] *Ibid.,* p. 35.
[37] *Ibid.,* p. 35.
[38] *Ibid.,* p. 37.
[39] *Ibid.,* p. 47.
[40] *Ibid.,* p. 40.
[41] *Ibid.,* p. 38.

theme of human weakness: «somos faciles à lo peor, sin que para ello nos falte guia, ò conpañero. Aunque se ofrece sin ellos, i nos halaga, i atrae con la falsedad de sus deleites.» [42] Unlike virtue, vice needs no teacher. We recall the passage in which Herrera speaks of the «popularity» of virtue. [43] But men have only an empty admiration of her and are at a loss to match their words with deeds. Herrera's subject provides him with many occasions to portray man under the influence of his passions, in this slipping away from virtue. Henry VIII, we remember, is the personification of human inconstancy. [44] Good beginnings tend to move toward disappointing ends. Thus, the virtuous man must swim against the current, «i, ronpiendo todas las dificultades, llegar al merecimiento de la verdadera gloria». [45]

Paradoxically, the historical law which decrees the scarcity of virtue is also the circumstance by which true virtue is possible. All of Herrera's heroes, as we have seen, have been purified, and their virtue strengthened, precisely through the presence of seemingly insuperable obstacles. Philip II, Don Juan de Austria and Pope Pius V came to the rescue of Christ's honor at a time when all Europe seemed oblivious of her duties, and the Turks had consequently prevailed. Lepanto itself, Herrera's principal evidence for the «crescendo» of history, is played against a background of Spanish Mediterranean defeats. Herrera's literary heroes, too, must struggle to redeem Spain's language and history from years of neglect. The greater the difficulties, the more pressing the invitation to heroic deeds. Henry's error and the fear of others have created a «vacant place» —«dexaron todo el lugar libre i desenbaraçado» [46]— for heroism.

We search for the view of historical causation which underlies this vision of a decaying civilization. In the *Relacion,* divine providence seems always to be at hand to aid a just cause. Those who conform their conduct to its commandments can be assured of its continuing favor, just as those who transgress divine law will be frustrated. This law applies clearly in the *Tomas Moro* to the English people:

[42] *Ibid.,* p. 41.
[43] *Ibid.,* pp. 41-42.
[44] *Ibid.,* p. 38. See above, p. 142.
[45] *Ibid.,* p. 35.
[46] *Ibid.,* p. 52.

> puede conocer por castigo de sus culpas, i por ultima infelicidad el reino, que tiene administrador vicioso, porque ninguno ai, que le aconsege cosa estraña de su gusto.[47]
>
> Cosa es dina de la consideracion de los onbres cuerdos i piadosos, el castigo que padece Inglaterra, por aver temido i seguido mas los decretos de Enrique, que las leyes del cielo.[48]
>
> I no es maravilla, que sufran estas afliciones, los que desanpararon, ò con miedo ò anbicion umana la causa de Dios, i abraçaron inpiamente el error.[49]

Failure to resist the pressures of heresy counts as a sin for which God inflicts terrible punishment. Thomas More enjoys divine favor through the purity of his virtue, but he does not receive the personal safety of Don Juan de Austria, for example, because of corruption in the ranks.

This much is clear. But one asks oneself why Henry disobeyed God's will in the first place. Some previous guilt of the English is implied in the «puede conocer por castigo de sus culpas»[50] cited above. Father Pedro de Rivadeneira spells out, in the *Tratado del Príncipe Cristiano* and the *Tratado de la tribulación*, many possible reasons to explain the Job-like torments of the righteous along with the punishment of sinners.[51] The most common explanation urges that God has taken it upon himself to test the mettle of a good man's virtue. Herrera points to the «incomprensible abismo de la sabiduria divina» which «nos deslunbra i amedrenta, para que no osemos levantar los ojos al conocimiento destas causas».[52] Which is to say, he pleads the same argument without legislating the details. Perhaps, too, Herrera alludes to the secret working of divine providence when he describes Henry's unexpected disruption of England: «Mas por una fuerça oculta de causas superiores se començò à turbar esta buena suerte.»[53]

---

[47] *Ibid.*, p. 40.
[48] *Ibid.*, p. 41.
[49] *Ibid.*, p. 41. While making the monarch's virtue a condition for divine favor, Saavedra Fajardo and other seventeenth-century writers realized that chance («la ocasión») and prudence used to create chance were also important factors for the survival of even a good monarch. See John Dowling, *El pensamiento político de Saavedra Fajardo* (Murcia, 1957), p. 196 ff.
[50] Herrera, *Tomas Moro*, p. 40.
[51] Rivadeneira, *Obras escogidas*.
[52] Herrera, *Tomas Moro*, p. 41.
[53] *Ibid.*, p. 38.

On the other hand, Herrera may be thinking of the mysterious workings of human existence in general, the factor which made so difficult «la conjetura del animo del onbre»,[54] which determined the «inconstancia de las cosas umanas».[55] There is a strong sense of human fallibility, of human tendency to err. Yet it is looked upon, as we have noted in another context, not simply as a law, but as a kind of unknown quantity, which is in no small degree responsible for the course of historical events. In a real sense, Henry and the English people hold the initiative in their power, as did Don Juan de Austria and his men at Lepanto. God rewards and punishes, but his discipline always appears to respond to a prior human action. Herrera everywhere implies that a definite guilt can be established as having brought on present tribulations, and conversely that certain individuals enjoy the choice of determining the direction events will take. Had the British nobles and clergy opted to resist their ruler's heresy, they could have succeeded in doing so. And, regardless of the fate of entire kingdoms, each individual carries within himself a power over history through his own will to heroism.

Sir Thomas More calls on God for the strength to purify his soul, confessing his own nothingness; and God in some sense is responsible for the selection of the martyrs of his Church.[56] But it is evident from Herrera's narrative that More's personal decision alone can initiate the process. More first rallies the moral forces within him and then seeks God's confirmation of his calling. Thus, not just the world's old age, but men themselves have a role in directing history. Herrera points to nature's «forgetfulness» in producing upright men[57] as though the times were responsible for the decadence of men's character. The times make virtue more difficult: they force men to swim against the current. But they also bestow a greater power on the valor and determination of the individual and place his positive contribution in starker relief.

Therefore, although Herrera proclaims a quantitative demise of virtue, he hints that there may even have been a qualitative improvement. Valor in difficult times («donde caen todos»[58])

---

[54] *Ibid.*, p. 39.
[55] *Ibid.*, p. 38.
[56] *Ibid.*, pp. 47-48.
[57] *Ibid.*, p. 35. See above, p. 168.
[58] *Ibid.*, p. 45.

deserves more praise than virtue in favorable circumstances. The moral of the brief life urges the conclusion: «puede aver, i se hallan varones grandes i dinos de toda alabança en el inperio de malos Principes» [59] and that «ninguna demasia i ninguna insolencia de la malicia puede derribar la virtud, aunque encerrada en ombre de mui pocas fuerças». [60] If history has moved and continues to move away from virtue, then opportunities for virtue have been created at an equal rate and continue to expand. The possibilities for man's virtuous participation in history, like the possibilities for poets and writers to enrich their native tongue, are inexhaustible. [61] The responsibility rests squarely on the shoulders of each man and his willingness to accepts life's manifold invitations to courage. Thus we find that Herrera's interpretations of the direction of history in the *Tomas Moro* persist, if more reflectively, in an essential optimism.

---

[59] *Ibid.*, p. 52.
[60] *Ibid.*, p. 52.
[61] Herrera, *Anotaciones,* p. 294 ff.; ed. Gallego, p. 399.

CHAPTER FOUR

HERRERA AND MORE AS AUTHOR

Herrera's admiration for Sir Thomas More —«l'aficion de mi animo» [1]— had many possible sources. Hitherto we have concerned ourselves with the attraction held out by the Chancellor's character and the nature of his concrete personal situation. More was a perfect Christian gentleman for Herrera, and a perfect hero of pure, disinterested virtue. Yet he was also a man of letters. The brief survey of Garcilaso's life with which Herrera prefaced his *Anotaciones* to that poet's work provides us with another sketch of the perfect gentleman who combines the pursuits of arms and letters. More's life appears as a slight variant of the ideal life in which action is offset by contemplation. In addition to his many gifts of temperament, Herrera tells us, More

> no se dexava vencer de la policia i elegancia de sus letras i erudicion, con que alcançò entre los onbres doctos de su edad opinion grandisima; i asi era amado i reverenciado de los suyos, i admirado con veneracion de los estrangeros. [2]

More belonged to an international community of Catholic humanists, at whose existence Herrera merely hints. We would love to know just how great was his knowledge of the Englishman and the intellectual ambience in which he moved; whether he had any clear understanding of the intimate connection between More and Erasmus; and just how much of More's work he had actually read.

[1] Herrera, *Tomas Moro*, in López Estrada, «Edición y estudio», *Archivo Hispalense*, XII (1950), 35.
[2] *Ibid.*, p. 36.

Herrera's allusions to his own reading in the *Anotaciones* offer no evidence of any familiarity with More's work. And, as we have noted previously, we find no reference whatever to Erasmus. What Herrera tells us in the opening pages of the *Tomas Moro* about his subject's works is at best disappointing. The most conspicuous absence is that of the *Utopia*. Herrera was undoubtedly aware of its existence, for it is discussed at some length in Stapleton's biography, which Herrera quotes on More's other writings. Although More's description of an ideal commonwealth was not translated to Spanish until forty years after Herrera's death, he could have read it in the original Latin.[3] The *Utopia* was published in a half-dozen editions on the continent during More's lifetime,[4] starting with the first in Louvain, late in 1516.[5] Circulation of Latin works in the various humanistic capitals of the Renaissance was not difficult. We know that Spaniards as early as Don Vasco de Quiroga, Bishop of Michoacan in New Spain, had read and taken to heart its lessons.[6] But by 1583, More's name was to be found on the Index of Gaspar de Quiroga, and his work proscribed.[7] Quevedo, as has been pointed out by R. O. Jones,[8] owned a copy of the Louvain edition of 1548, which now resides in the National Library of Madrid and bears the marginal comments of its former owner. Quevedo's «annotations» indicate that he recognized the Erasmist leanings of the document, and he found it necessary to excuse the shortcomings of the book with respect to orthodox Catholicism by supposing that the oppressive situation in England had forced More to «fingir» in order to be heard. There is no question that Herrera would have experienced similar misgivings, particularly over More's controversial notions of religion.

Herrera mentions several other works of Thomas More: his

---

[3] Thomas Stapleton, *The Life and Illustrious Martyrdom of Sir Thomas More*, ed. E. E. Reynolds (New York, 1966), pp. 32-34; López Estrada, «La primera versión española de la *Utopía* de Moro», in *Collected Studies in Honour of Américo Castro's Eightieth Year* (Oxford, 1965), pp. 291-310.

[4] C. R. Thompson, *The Translation of Lucian by Erasmus and St. Thomas More* (Ithaca, 1940).

[5] Thomas More, *Utopia* (New Haven and London, 1964), introduction of Edward Surtz, S. J., p. xvi.

[6] Silvio Zavala, *La «Utopía» de Tomás Moro en la Nueva España y otros estudios* (Mexico, 1937); *Sir Thomas More in New Spain: A Utopian Adventure of the Renaissance* (London, 1955).

[7] López Estrada, «La primera versión», pp. 291-292.

[8] Royston O. Jones, «Some Notes on More's *Utopia* in Spain», *MLR*, XLV (1950), 480 ff.

translations of Lucian's dialogues, some epigrams both translated and original, and a response to an attack by Luther on Henry VIII's defense of the sacraments. His discussion of these works furnishes no real proof that he had any first-hand knowledge of them. Much of what he says appears to come from Stapleton. Perhaps the most likely to have come to his attention were the translated dialogues. Although almost ignored in our time, these were More's most published and most popular works in his own day. Thirteen editions of the translations appeared from the time of their publication in 1506 to the time of More's death.[9] In most of these thirteen, More's translations were offered side by side with those of Erasmus, and logically so, for they had undertaken the project together in a sort of friendly competition. Herrera says this of them: «Traduzio dichosamente algunos dialogos, escogidos por el argumento, entre los que escrivio Luciano.»[10] The phrase «escogidos por el argumento» suggests that Herrera did not feel unqualified admiration for the Greek satirist. Lucian was unquestionably known in Sevillian literary circles, for Mosquera mentioned him, as well as borrowing entire unacknowledged paragraphs from *The Way to Write History*. But the sharp, merciless humor of the dialogues would hardly have appealed to a man of Herrera's gravity. Another sort of Spanish genius would take up the legacy of Lucian for its own use. Herrera seems to give his approval to the subjects treated in the dialogues which More translated, but he does not say what these subjects are.

In fact, Thomas More translated four dialogues of Lucian which went into the joint edition with Erasmus: *Cynicus, Menippus, Philopseudes* and *Tyrannicida* to which he added a *Declamatio*, replying to the arguments of the speaker in the last dialogue as a kind of formal exercise in rebuttal.[11] The *Tyrannicida* is only implicitly a dialogue, being the monologue plea of a man to be recognized as the assassin of a king he has driven to suicide by killing his son. Erasmus and More both composed rebuttals to this argument, but nowhere is there any indication that they dispute the moral right to eliminate a tyrant.[12] Of the four

[9] C. R. Thompson, pp. 2-3.
[10] Herrera, *Tomas Moro*, p. 36.
[11] Thompson, pp. 23-24.
[12] *Ibid.*, pp. 23-24.

dialogues, this one has the most relevance for Herrera's concerns in the *Tomas Moro,* and is the one mentioned in Stapleton, but Herrera, for reasons we cannot deduce, does not refer to More's treatment of the subject. The dialogues *Cynicus* and *Menippus* have to do with a side of More's character and thought that Herrera does not elucidate, although it too may have contributed to the «aficion» which he professes. This is the Englishman's austere life and his rejection of luxury, which would have attracted him to Lucian's dialogues on the subject.[13] Finally the *Philopseudes* hits at another Morean theme, the folly of superstition and the mendacity of philosophers. If Herrera had read the *Tyrannicida,* mention of it seems strangely lacking. Perhaps Herrera felt that his public would understand the reference without any further mention.

Herrera also refers to More's Latin epigrams, some of which were original, while others were translated from Greek authors of rather doubtful identity.[14] Some of them were attributed to Lucian, although subsequently this attribution proved spurious. Herrera seems less interested in the subjects which these epigrams touched upon, than in their general quality:

> I se exercitò con la mesma felicidad en epigramas agudos i graciosos, ò fuesen traidos de aquellos antiguos poetas griegos, ò hallados por el. En los quales guardò la templança, que deven los onbres graves i modestos, no derramandose à las lacivias i desonestidades de los poetas latinos, que cerca de su tienpo florecieron en Italia. Porque no la permitía su modestia i encogimiento escrevir, lo que podia causar verguença aun a los onbres perdidos, sabiendo que no solo deve carecer el bueno de crimen, pero de la sospecha del tanbien. Ni quiso ofender con aspereza i demasia de palabras injuriosas, la vida i costunbres de algunos; antes juntò con la mansedumbre de su animo la facilidad i cortesia, para no ser molesto i enojoso.[15]

These remarks, largely borrowed from Stapleton, recall statements by Herrera in the *Anotaciones.* There Herrera admired the sonnet as the most difficult poetic form, precisely for its similarity with the epigram. The sonnet and the epigram are the most economical forms and thus the most exacting tests of «agudeza».

---

[13] *Ibid.,* pp. 23-24.
[14] *Ibid.,* p. 4.
[15] Herrera, *Tomas Moro,* p. 36.

They had to consist of one unified, striking thought.[16] Yet Herrera appears here to find the merit of the epigrams not so much in their wit as in their sobriety. He clearly thinks of More in these terms, as one of a group of «onbres graves i modestos». He leans toward a view of More as essentially a serious, didactic author, quite different from our present-day conception of the inseparability of wit and wisdom in More's makeup.

Above all, Herrera admires More's work for its decency, its «onestidad» and its eagerness to avoid damaging, biting criticism. He may be implying censure of Erasmus' satirical works. In the *Anotaciones,* Herrera also castigates the presence of «desonestidades» and «lacivias» in poetry. Then, too, the Italians were the worst offenders, beginning with Roman poets like Ovid.[17] Herrera takes Gutierre de Cetina, a fellow Sevillian, to task for the lascivious and effeminate nature of his work, which he has learned from the Italians.[18] Thus More embodies the modesty, gravity, dignity and restraint which Herrera requires of serious literature, both prose and verse. Furthermore, he has used his pen in the service of religion by defending the sacraments, as Herrera himself used his pen to safeguard the honor of the Church by recording the deeds of Christian soldiers and martyrs.

Herrera's remarks, then, leave unanswered the question of just how much of More's work he had read. In short, from these comments alone we do not know for certain that he had read any of it at all. Perhaps he simply used the scant threads of information he had concerning the Englishman's literary production and then cast them into the mold of his highest aspirations for literature. Thus, some critics have concluded that Herrera and Rivadeneira likewise probably had read nothing at all by More, and point to a paucity of references to More's writings during the period when Herrera composed his life.[19] If Herrera had not read even those works which he chose to mention, how are we to suppose that he knew those which he does not so much as name? We should perhaps dismiss the notion that Herrera knew *Utopia,* except for a factor also noticed by López

---

[16] *Obras de Garci Lasso de la Vega con Anotaciones de Fernando de Herrera* (Seville, 1580), p. 67; ed. Gallego Morell (Granada, 1966), p. 282.
[17] *Ibid.,* p. 69; ed. Gallego, p. 284.
[18] *Ibid.,* p. 77; ed. Gallego, p. 290.
[19] R. O. Jones, «Some Notes», p. 479.

Estrada: namely, the uncanny similarity between some of the political preoccupations of the *Tomas Moro* and the «anhelo de la *Utopía* de Moro, hermano político del anhelo de amor platónico de Herrera».[20] We cannot hope to answer the question whether any such likeness owes itself purely to coincidence of interest or to Herrera's knowledge of More. In theory, both are possible. However, the number and intensity of any such resemblances could tend to argue against chance. Let us, therefore, briefly consider the *Utopia* and the *Tomas Moro* each in the light of the other, with other works of the two authors in mind.

The later fortunes of the *Utopia* in the Spanish vernacular may provide us with some indication of the problems surrounding that work for the Spanish reader.[21] When Don Jerónimo Antonio de Medinilla translated the *Utopia* into Spanish in 1637, he offered it to his reader as worthy of the «admiration and imitation» of all in his time.[22] However, he must have felt bound to comment on the religious theories advanced by Hythlodaeus in Book II. Medinilla justifies this part of the work on the grounds that in Christianity, too, one finds a variety of legitimate rites in practice.[23] Quevedo, as we have already noted, felt obliged to explain some of More's unorthodox views as part of a disguise imposed on him by the repressive political situation in England at the time — although this judgment results from an inexact understanding of the chronology of the work's genesis.[24] (In 1516, when *Utopia* appeared, Henry was still a «friend of learned men», as Herrera portrayed him.) In general, Quevedo praised *Utopia* in his introduction to Medinilla's translation, but he was abundantly aware of the author's relation to Erasmus, which he reprehends in his marginal notes, particularly in those details of the treatise where More inveighs against the evils of church property and the monastic life.[25] But the most surprising comment on *Utopia* comes in the form of an omission. In addition to being a conscious condensation

---

[20] López Estrada, «Edición y estudio», p. 18.
[21] López Estrada, «La primera versión», p. 304.
[22] *Ibid.*, p. 305; López Estrada, «Quevedo y la *Utopía* de Tomás Moro», *Actas del Segundo Congreso Internacional de Hispanistas* (Nimega, 1967), pp. 403-409.
[23] López Estrada, «La primera versión», p. 306.
[24] R. O. Jones, «Some Notes», p. 482.
[25] *Ibid.*, pp. 480-481.

of the original, Medinilla's version eliminates Book I entirely, leaving only the fairy-tale description of the island paradise.[26]

Now it is easy to imagine why a translator might have considered it wise to suppress the Dialogue on Counsel in a 1637 edition in Spain. Quevedo's criticisms of the abuses of *privanza* brought him to grief more than once. Book I of *Utopia*, written after Book II, fixes its attention not on a «Nusquama», or never-never land, but on sixteenth-century Europe and its troubles.[27] It is a scathing criticism of the unbridled appetites of European monarchs for power and territorial conquest and their willingness to go to any lengths to achieve their ends, in perfect disregard of the interests or the welfare of the common people.[28] It is in this first book of the *Utopia* that we find a striking community of concern with Herrera's *Tomas Moro*.

In the Dialogue on Counsel, Raphael Hythlodaeus and More wrestle with the question of the place of a Christian humanist in royal administrations. More and Peter Giles suggest to their friend that he should enter royal service and offer the benefit of his learning and travels to a king:[29]

> quorum neminem esse satis scio, cui non sis futurus uehementer gratus, utpote quem hac doctrina atque hac locorum hominumque peritia non obletare solum, sed exemplis quoque instruere, atque adiuuare consilio sis idoneus;... Caeterum uideberis plane rem te atque ist hoc animo tuo tam generoso, tam uere philosopho dignam facturus, si te ita compares, ut uel cum aliquo priuatim incommodo ingenium tuum atque industriam publicis rebus accomodes, quod nunquam tanto cum fructu queas, quanto si a consiliis fueris magno alicui principi, eique (quod te facturum certe scio) recta atque honesta persuaseris. Nempe a principe bonorum malorumque omnium torrens in totum populum, uelut a perenni quodam fonte promanat.[30]

More reminds Hythlodaeus of his favorite author, Plato, who judges «respublicas ita demum futuras esse felices, si aut regnent philosophi, aut reges philosophentur».[31]

---

[26] López Estrada, «La primera versión», pp. 303-304.
[27] J. H. Hexter, *More's «Utopia»: The Biography of an Idea* (New York, 1965), p. 15.
[28] *Ibid.*, pp. 99-155.
[29] Thomas More, *Utopia*, in Latin from the edition of March, 1518, and in English from the first edition of Ralph Robynson's translation in 1551, ed. J. H. Lupton (Oxford, 1895), pp. 34-37.
[30] *Ibid.*, pp. 34-35, 37.
[31] *Ibid.*, pp. 79-80.

Hythlodaeus counters this evocation of an ideal commonwealth where reason and justice prevail, championed by power, with the sad political realities of his day. More's advice, he says, would indeed be excellent, «si hii qui rerum patiuntur essent parati bene consultis parere».[32] But even Plato discovered that unless a king be a philosopher by education, he will shun the advice of real philosophers. Hythlodaeus conjures up an imaginary session of the French King's privy council:

> Age, finge me apud regem Gallorum, atque in eius considere consilio, dum in secretissimo secessu, praesidente rege ipso in corona prudentissimorum hominum, magnis agitur studiis, quibus artibus ac machinamentis Mediolanum retineat, ac fugitiuam illam Neapolim ad se retrahat: postea uero euertat Venetos, ac totam Italiam subiiciat sibi; deinde Flandros, Brabantos, totam postremo Burgundiam suae faciat ditionis, atque alias praeterea gentes, quarum regnum iam olim animo inuasit.[33]

For More as for Erasmus, the greedy, territory-snatching practices of European royalty held up a favorite target. But here, More has Hythlodaeus aim slightly lower, at the advice which buoys up ignoble ambitions. The traveler-observer parodies the contributions of the short-sighted, ambitious adviser. One proposes a treaty which will last only until its usefulness is outlived; another suggests the use of mercenaries; another, bribes; another, a convenient marriage alliance; and still another advises the King to maintain a nobleman in foreign territory who would press an invented claim to the throne in order to keep its current occupant in check.[34]

Where is the place of a disinterested counselor among so much petty ambition, Hythlodaeus asks:

> praeterea si ostenderem omnes hos conatus bellorum, quibus tot nationes eius causa tumultuarentur, quum thesauros eius exhausissent, ac destruxissent populum, aliqua tandem fortuna frustra cessuros tamen; proinde auitum regnum coleret, ornaret quantum posset, et faceret quam florentissimum; amet suos et ametur a suis; cum his una uiuat, imperetque suauiter atque alia regna ualere sinat, quando id quod nunc ei contigisset satis amplum superque esset; hanc orationem quibus auribus, mi More, putas excipiendam?[35]

[32] *Ibid.*, p. 80.
[33] *Ibid.*, pp. 81-82.
[34] *Ibid.*, pp. 82-84.
[35] *Ibid.*, p. 87.

His interlocutor is forced to conclude with him that such a blueprint for public happiness would count for little against such vicious enemies. Hythlodaeus does not, however, stop here, but he proceeds to paint a grim picture of the odds he as a counselor would face. He shows a majority of the councilors expending all their energies to invent new pretexts for taxation, even «ut bellum simulet», in order to satisfy their misguided ruler's craving for the riches of a Midas.[36] He imagines them dredging up old laws which can then be twisted to serve the King's purposes and used as another means to bleed the oppressed populace.[37] They urge the appointment of only such judges as will support the King's will, right or wrong; and they themselves confess the King's «indisputabilem praerogatiuam».[38]

Then, as though reacting to the nightmare he has conjured up, Hythlodaeus gives his prescription for the behavior of a king who would be beloved of his subjects rather than hated by the discontented, trampled masses, and who would rather rule a kingdom than a jail.[39] More, through his speaker, concentrates on the abuses of fiscal and legal power which were of greatest concern to him at the time.[40] Military campaigns had drained huge sums from the poor, and the nobles left farmers bereft of any means of support by the practice of enclosure. As Herrera says of him in the *Tomas Moro:*

> no sufriendo que pudiese mas el favor que la verdad, i el poder que la inocencia de los pobres i desanparados, ayudava siempre à la causa mejor (cosa dificil i maravillosa en nuestro tienpo) senbrando en los animos de todos una segura opinion de su virtud i bondad.[41]

Is it not conceivable, even likely, that Herrera had this section of *Utopia* in mind when he wrote these words? The early pages of the *Tomas Moro* in which this passage occurs are filled with the very same ideas expressed in the portion of the *Utopia*

---

[36] *Ibid.,* p. 88.
[37] *Ibid.,* p. 89.
[38] *Ibid.,* p. 91.
[39] *Ibid.,* pp. 92-94.
[40] Hexter, pp. 99 ff.
[41] Herrera, *Tomas Moro,* p. 37.

which we have been considering. Hythlodaeus has been talking about the duties of a counselor by way of negative example, and about the rarity and unwelcomeness of a good magistrate. Herrera follows the passage just cited with reflections about a Platonic republic, which we cite again for purposes of comparison:

> Parecia, que entrava por el en Inglaterra la felicidad, que prometian los antiguos à los reinos, cuyos principes i governadores amavan las letras, i seguian la ciencia, que enseña à los onbres, i modera sus afectos. [42]

Herrera goes on to describe the way in which «suelen estragar el animo al onbre umilde i tenplado las onras grandes, i lo levantan i enso[r]bervecen», [43] and to contrast this folly with «aquel animo no sobrado por dones, ò anbicion i lisonjas» [44] of his hero.

To continue our parallel, Herrera criticizes the abuse of power and the false respect which it brings: «no es verdadero aquel respeto, sino temor de su insolencia i tirania.» [45] Finally, Herrera, like More in the passage on which we have just now focused, describes the incapacity of «estos animos anbiciosos i terribles» for good government: «Porque aquella enfermedad interna, que padecen, no les dexa lugar libre, para aprovechar la causa agena, que esta necessitada de favor, i menos poderosa.» [46] Then, before relating Henry's change of heart and More's demise, Herrera contrasts the fortunate kingdom with righteous rulers, to the «desdichada i miserable, la que tuvo en suerte, iuezes i governadores tiranos i enemigos de sus pueblos». [47] These repeated references to the downtrodden poor, the means used by kings to pervert laws for their own ends, the vivid portrait of the bad advisers' petty ambitions, even the specific naming of the «iuezes» which were one of More's targets as we have seen — are these points of contact not perhaps too many and too frequent to owe themselves to pure coincidence?

Herrera's ideal counselor would be the free intellect whom Hythlodaeus describes:

[42] *Ibid.*, p. 37.
[43] *Ibid.*, p. 37.
[44] *Ibid.*, p. 37.
[45] *Ibid.*, p. 37.
[46] *Ibid.*, p. 37.
[47] *Ibid.*, pp. 37-38.

Deven ser los amigos i consegeros de los Principes (si algunos tienen con ellos este lugar) buscados i escogidos entre todos, para que puedan dezilles libremente lo que conviene, i advertir con modestia i respeto de las cosas, que mandan mal. Mas casi ninguna, ò pocas vezes sucede, que aya quien ocupe bien aquel puesto, i ose acudir à otra cosa, que à la voluntad buena, ò mala del señor. [48]

Hythlodaeus, like Herrera, insists on the unlikelihood of such a man appearing in the king's councils. All strive to serve the king's will indiscriminately. Even though they may disagree, all will acquiesce from shame or fear,[49] as Herrera shows the majority doing in Henry's councils: «callavan todos los demas, ò por lisongear à su principe, ò vencidos de miedo.»[50] Hythlodaeus complains that as a royal councilor,

> approbanda sunt aperte pessima consilia, et decretis pestilentissimis subscribendum est. Speculatoria uice fuerit, ac pene proditoris etiam, qui improbe consulta maligne laudauerit.
>
> Porro nihil occurrit in quo prodesse quicquam possis, in eos delatus collegas qui uel optimum uirum facilius corruperint quam ipsi corrigantur; quorum peruersa consuetudine uel deprauaberis, uel ipse integer ac innocens alienae malitiae stultitiaeque praetexeris.[51]

In the *Tomas Moro*, Herrera seems almost to echo these very lines in a phrase which he inserts into his translation of a piece of Sander's narrative. More was moved to resign his post, Herrera explains, «viendo que no podia conservar ya, como antes, la integridad de su vida, por el magistrado que tenia, i aborreciendo ser ministro, ò participe en la maldad de aquellos consejos.»[52] More's case demonstrates for Herrera, as for Hythlodaeus,

> cuan peligroso es para los que siguen la virtud el trato con los principes i poderosos, que olvidan como ingratos i desconocidos todos los servicios i merecimientos de sus vasallos i criados,... cuando se atraviesa alguna cosa de su gusto, sin atender, si es

---

[48] *Ibid.*, p. 39.
[49] More, *Utopia* (Oxford, 1895), p. 90.
[50] Herrera, *Tomas Moro*, p. 38.
[51] More, *Utopia*, p. 103.
[52] Herrera, *Tomas Moro*, pp. 38-39.

derecho seguir en los casos injustos la violencia de sus desatinos.[53]

Although Herrera would no doubt have shared Quevedo's reservations about a number of the more controversial aspects of Utopian society, many others of More's glancing blows at European social ills would have fallen on receptive ears. Everywhere, the *Utopia* speaks out against false aristocracies of wealth and inherited position, and sets forth a society which ranks men by their virtue.[54] The governor of *Utopia* normally holds his office for life, but he remains directly accountable to the people, and may be deposed by them should he begin to rule tyrannically.[55] The officials of Utopia are elected, and chosen for their virtue. These officials may not campaign for elections or sollicit votes in any way: «nec magistratus ullus insolens aut terribilis est. patres appellantur et exhibent. iisdem defertur, ut debet, ab uolentibus honor, non ab inuitis exigitur.»[56] We remember Herrera's description of More:

> no era fastidioso ni pesadamente severo en su trato; antes de tal manera tenplava la severidad de aquel magistrado, con la blandura i facilidad de su condicion, que no era menos amado, que temido.[57]

This is followed by the remarks on forceful extraction of respect, which we have already seen. Utopian government, too, is constituted so that «propositis quoque honoribus ad uirtutes inuitant» and keep the memory of great deeds before them «ut calcaret incitamentum ad uirtutem sit».[58] In *Utopia*, Herrera would have seen a description of a whole society embodying the idea of virtue.

Utopia also hits hard, as Herrera had in the *Relacion,* against flimsy treaties of Christian princes which are merely used to suit the purposes of their makers (Machiavelli was at the same time recommending just this[59]) and broken at will. The Utopians

---

[53] *Ibid.,* pp. 50-51.
[54] More, *Utopia,* pp. 174 ff., 182-183, 255, 302 ff.
[55] *Ibid.,* p. 136.
[56] *Ibid.,* p. 233.
[57] Herrera, *Tomas Moro,* p. 37.
[58] More, *Utopia,* p. 233.
[59] Machiavelli, *Il Principe,* in *Tutte le opere storiche e letterarie,* ed. Guido Mazzoni and Mario Casella (Florence, 1929), p. 32 ff.

consider a treaty to be a sign of bad faith and avoid making one if possible.[60] If they should, however, make a pact with another nation, they guard it religiously to the letter.[61] More, like Erasmus, made everywhere evident his loathing for war and condemns it except as a last resort.[62] The Utopians use every means to eliminate bloodshed from their disagreements with other peoples.[63] Perhaps a reading of More, combined with the lessons of recent history, had something to do with the absence in Herrera's last work of any eulogies of military glory.

Hexter, in his illuminating «biography» of *Utopia*,[64] has given a convincing account of the relationship of the arguments put forth in the Dialogue on Counsel of Book I to the dilemmas which Thomas More faced in the years (1516-1519) immediately preceding his entry into Henry's service. Hythlodaeus appears to prevail in the Dialogue, as does his argument against public service in More's mind, until the management of the chancellorship by Cardinal Wolsey seems to offer him the assurance that his ideas can be of some use in the royal councils. Hexter's study exemplifies the best fruits of our twentieth-century concern for chronological precision and close textual analysis. This kind of appreciation would have been less likely in a sixteenth-century reader, although he too would have shared Hexter's desire to relate the literary text in some way to its author's life. Quevedo gives us some idea of the way the *Utopia* might have been evaluated, when he says that oppressive conditions in England forced More to «fingir».[65] Quevedo, writing a century after More's death, superimposes the composition of the *Utopia* on the circumstances of More's martyrdom. Actually, when More composed *Utopia* and somewhat after, Erasmus could still write of the Englishman's good fortune in serving so enlightened a ruler.[66] I am inclined to believe that Herrera would have made, and probably did make, the same interpretation as Quevedo.

If Hythlodaeus' rejection of royal service is puzzling in the context of 1516, it would certainly not have been in 1535. In

---

[60] More, *Utopia*, pp. 238, 241.
[61] *Ibid.*, p. 263.
[62] *Ibid.*, p. 246.
[63] *Ibid.*, p. 247.
[64] Hexter, p. 99 ff.
[65] R. O. Jones, «Some Notes», p. 482.
[66] Erasmus, «Life of More», in Thomas More, *Selections from his English Works*, ed. P. S. and H. M. Allen (Oxford, 1924), pp. 1-10.

1516 More urges his traveler-philosopher to enter the council of a king even despite unfavorable conditions. He condemns his friend's «academic» philosophy («scholastica») and begs him to adopt a more practical («civilior») view of things:

> Si radicitus euelli non possint opiniones prauae, nec receptis usu uitiis mederi queas ex animi tui sententia, non ideo tamen deserenda Respublica est, et in tempestate nauis destituenda est, quoniam uentos non possis. at neque insuetus et insolens sermo inculcandus, quem scias apud diuersa persuasos pondus non habiturum; sed obliquo ductu conandum est atque adnitendum tibi, ut pro tua uirili omnia tractes commode, et quod in bonum nequis uertere, efficias saltem ut sit quam minime malum. [67]

Hythlodaeus rejects the notion on these grounds: one, it is immoral and unchristian to dissemble one's true feelings; two, it would not serve any useful purpose to spend his advice in vain; and lastly, he too should quickly become corrupted. [68]

How easy it would be to transpose such arguments to the case of More himself in the years before his death! Perhaps Herrera was doing just this when he described the arguments with which More's friends urged him to soften his stand on the King's divorce:

> Parecia a muchos onbres sabios i amigos suyos, que deseavan su vida, que no fue acertado oponerse a la tenpestad que sobrevino porque es violenta la ira de los Reyes, i si les resisten sin razon, causan daños de mayor efeto, que el tienpo cura muchos casos, que no se pueden emendar con fuerça alguna; i que son instables las cosas umanas, i siempre varian como ondas..... *Que los que sirven a los Reyes, deven dissimular i sobrellevar algunas cosas, para que si no pudieren conseguir lo que juzgan por mejor, pueden a lo menos moderar en alguna parte sus afectos.* [69]

Thomas More, like his own creation Hythlodaeus, rejects these arguments, for slightly altered reasons, as we have seen. He, too, would not allow himself to be corrupted. But most important, his acquiescence would aid the King to break divine laws. If this sin merits capital punishment in Mariana's view, Herrera could not condone it.

---

[67] More, *Utopia*, pp. 99-100.
[68] *Ibid.*, pp. 100-104.
[69] Herrera, *Tomas Moro*, p. 51.

Still we find ourselves unable to offer indisputable proof that Herrera was acquainted with the writings of More. If he had been, would the presence of More's name on the Quiroga *Index* have sufficed to keep Herrera from mentioning all but the most useful didactic writings among those he found referred to in Stapleton? We might recall in this connection that Herrera leaned heavily on the *Poetices libri septem* of Julius Caesar Scaliger, which is peppered with praise for Erasmus, yet Herrera did not mention that author once in the whole of his work.[70] Nor is Erasmus named in *Tomas Moro,* although the coincidences of theme with the *Institvtio principis Christiani* are considerable, and Erasmus' book was one of the standard works on this subject. Herrera would probably have been exposed in some way to his teachings. There is no denying that most of the ideas that Herrera shared with Erasmus and More belonged to a long tradition of classical lore on the nature of the perfect prince.[71] Perhaps the similarities between the theories of *Tomas Moro* and More's *Utopia* owe themselves to the strong political Platonism of both works. Yet the similarities are so many and occur with such intensity and in unified passages of each work, that we are tempted to believe that Herrera knew More's work personally, had assimilated the forceful message of the Dialogue on Counsel, and finally applied it to his interpretation of the significance of its author's life.

---

[70] Cf. R. D. F. Pring-Mill, «Escalígero y Herrera: Citas y plagios de los *Poetices Libri Septem* en las *Anotaciones*», *Actas del Segundo Congreso Internacional de Hispanistas* (Nimega, 1967), pp. 489-499.

[71] Lester K. Born, introduction to Erasmus, *The Education of a Christian Prince* (New York, 1936).

CHAPTER FIVE

CONCLUSIONS: THE MEANING OF HERRERA'S HISTORICAL WORK

The disappearance of Herrera's *Istoria general* leaves us in a difficult position, among other reasons, because it deprives us of the work which its author seems to have thought of as the culmination of all his efforts as an historian. He offered the *Relacion* in 1572 with apologies for its modest scope: «este mi trabajo es tan pequeño que tiene antes nombre de una no extendida relacion, como lo es, que de historia entera.»[1] Then, as if alluding to the exhortations of his friends, such as Cristóbal Mosquera de Figueroa and Francisco de Medina, his first two prologuists, who had urged him to continue work on a full-blown history, Herrera modestly pleads inadequacy: «porque yo no me profiero á tanta grandeza ni mis fuerzas son poderosas para sufrir el cuidado que se requiere para ella.»[2] In the *Anotaciones,* historical comments are offered under the guise of digressions, «pues se à ofrecido ocasion».[3] Finally in *Tomas Moro,* Herrera once again feels obliged to qualify his title and make clear his purpose: he does not intend to recount all of his hero's life. Rather he has undertaken an evaluation of this one man's life, a kind of meditation on history, the «consideracion de las cosas pasadas» which he turns over in his memory.[4]

Thus what has come down to us of Herrera's historical prose

---

[1] Herrera, *Relacion de la guerra de Cipre,* in *C.D.I.,* XXI (Madrid, 1852), 248-249.
[2] *Ibid.,* p. 249.
[3] *Obras de Garci Lasso de la Vega con Anotaciones de Fernando de Herrera* (Seville, 1580), p. 611; ed. Gallego Morell (Granada, 1966), p. 536.
[4] Herrera, *Tomas Moro,* in López Estrada, «Edición y estudio», *Archivo Hispalense,* XII (1950), 34.

are seemingly offshoots of the central thrust of his activity as an historian. We can see the branches, but the tree itself is lost. Herrera did, however, have very definite ideas about the purpose of his historical efforts in each of these brief pieces. The battle of Lepanto urgently required the dispassionate labors of an historian to sort out the truth about the events relating to it from a maze of conflicting exaggerations.[5] The remarks about history in the *Anotaciones,* evidently composed at a time when the *Istoria general* was in progress, respond to Pacheco's description of the latter work: namely, a defense of Spain's honor against the disservice done to her reputation by the Italians. Herrera has chosen to comment on Spanish history, he says, «por que no sè que animos se puedan hallar tan pacientes, que toleren los oprobrios i denuestos, conque vituperan a los Españoles los escritores de Italia».[6] The *Istoria general* would doubtless have resembled in some ways Gonzalo Jiménez de Quesada's *Antijovio* and his subsequent endeavors to discredit Paolo Giovio's attacks on Spanish imperial policy. Herrera already had in mind Giovio's critical commentaries on Spanish history when he composed the *Relacion.* After the battle of Lepanto, he notes that Spanish valor displayed there should suffice to silence Giovio's sharp tongue and to counteract his derisory remarks about Prevesa.[7] As well as a defense of Spanish integrity, the *Istoria general* would probably have offered an apology for her imperialist foreign policy, which Guicciardini, Bembo, Machiavelli and the hated Giovio, casting Italy in the shape of ancient Rome, had called the invasion of the «barbarian» enemy. While in all previous works Herrera had focused on Spain's manifest destiny and on setting the facts straight, in the *Tomas Moro* he chose to reflect on a subject which did not relate at all to Spanish history of national aspirations. Furthermore, the subject did not require any revision of the information at hand. Herrera supposes the details of the schism of the English Church to be common knowledge to his readers, thanks to the efforts of Rivadeneira, and for a more educated public, those of Nicholas Sander. In the *Tomas Moro,* Herrera sought to make explicit,

---

[5] Herrera, *Relacion,* pp. 247-249.
[6] Herrera, *Anotaciones,* p. 611; ed. Gallego, p. 536. Cf. Francisco de Quevedo, *España defendida,* in *Obras completas* (Madrid, 1961), I, 517; and Raimundo Lida, *Letras hispánicas* (Mexico-Buenos Aires, 1958); and above p. 106.
[7] Herrera, *Relacion,* p. 351.

in a brief account, the nature of More's exemplarity: in other words, he was spelling out the lessons of history.

One thread of method appears to bind these several efforts together. This is Herrera's concern with removing history from the realm of petty, individual bias. Thus, he sees himself in his Dedication to the *Relacion* as the disinterested examiner of first-hand sources.[8] His position as a distant observer of Lepanto allows him the equanimity to sort out the necessarily impassioned reports of eyewitnesses. Reality and truth must result from a wider perspective than that afforded to a single individual. Although we tend to be skeptical about Herrera's own lack of bias in leaping to Spain's defense in the *Anotaciones* and presumably the *Istoria general,* the author was evidently convinced that he was remedying historical injustices inflicted by the narrow passions of individual Italian writers, whose nationality led them to abandon reason in their evaluation of history.[9] If we may use Jiménez de Quesada's work as a kind of analogy, we must say in all fairness that if he has a national bias, it does not lead him to deprive Italians of any glories, but rather to require them to share the honors with their sometime Spanish allies. We cannot, of course, speculate as to Herrera's own disinterestedness.

Finally, the *Tomas Moro* avoids the fantastic exaggerations which it might have borrowed from Sander. Herrera discreetly disclaims a responsibility to delve into the polemics over Henry VIII's divorce, as well as other materials about More: «no me parece acertado traer prolixamente todas aquellas cosas, que fueron maravillosas, i como tales an sido tratadas de onbres doctos.»[10] The «marvelous» things, including perhaps miracles surrounding More's martyrdom, he prefers to leave to others. R. O. Jones's study justly cites Herrera's singular lack of passion (compared to that of Rivadeneira) in recording the events of Henry's reign.[11] Herrera is not interested so much in decrying that monarch's excesses as he is in erecting a model of virtue in Thomas More. He follows his own precept in the *Anotaciones,* and that of Erasmus in the *Institvtio,* of leaving history's

[8] *Ibid.,* p. 248.
[9] Herrera, *Anotaciones,* p. 611 ff.; ed. Gallego, p. 536 ff.
[10] Herrera, *Tomas Moro,* p. 38.
[11] R. O. Jones, «El *Tomas Moro* de Fernando de Herrera», *B.R.A.E.,* XXX (1950), 423-438.

bad examples in the shadows. Likewise he concerns himself, as More himself did, more with speaking of how government should be than with exploring the sordid details of monarchy as it should not be.

In addition to his consistently avowed purpose of removing history from the clutches of passion, we hope to have made clear by now another aspect of the unity of Herrera's historical prose. That is, the unchanging nature, over a period of twenty years, of his conception of heroic virtue, and the identity of the diction used to describe this mode of life in his prose writings.[12] Thus Herrera recalls in the *Relacion* the valor of the crusading princes who defended Christ's honor:

> desanparando su tierra, su casa y sus propios contentos, y en regiones muy apartadas de las suyas, entre el rigor del frio y del calor, sufriendo mucha hambre y trabajos, con las armas en las manos peleando con infieles gentes y bárbaras,[13]

and the perseverance of others like Philip II, Don Juan de Austria and Astor Baglione at Famagusta against the greatest odds. In the *Anotaciones,* the mode remains unaltered. Hernán Cortés carries on a glorious combat for Christ in the New World, «quitando a los Españoles la esperança de todo refugio umano, fuera de la que podian tener en la fortaleza de sus braços».[14] The hapless Don García does not «faint» (Herrera, we recall, used the same word to describe Philip II's persistence and that of Baglione in the *Relacion*) in the face of certain disaster, but gains strength from peril.[15] Finally, Thomas More joins the ranks of those whose «animos ... estavan llenos de vigor, i deseavan mostrar su fortaleza en los casos dificiles».[16] As Herrera says:

> nunca el se mostrò mas ecelso, i de animo mas generoso i sin temor, que en aquella tenpestad; porque no solo no lo quebrantò, pero ni aun lo movio la furia de aquella violencia espantosa. Antes lleno de vigor, i encendido en aquel amor hermosisimo de

---

[12] Cf. above p. 121 ff.
[13] Herrera, *Relacion,* p. 291.
[14] Herrera, *Anotaciones,* p. 615; ed. Gallego, p. 539.
[15] *Ibid.,* p. 594; ed. Gallego, p. 524.
[16] Herrera, *Tomas Moro,* p. 34.

la virtud, se opuso a ella con tanta grandeza de coraçon, i con tanta firmeza i seguridad de conciencia. [17]

Just as Don Juan's men proved that «aun no estaba acabado aquel antiguo valor de los cristianos», [18] at a time when all of Europe seemed to have fallen into apostasy from its Christian duty, as Herrera himself comes to the rescue of Spanish deeds and letters which Spain's writers have failed to protect, so Thomas More earns the crown of true virtue «en la miseria de nuestra edad». [19] Thus even Herrera's seemingly surprising return to the notion of a Golden Age of virtue has been foreshadowed in earlier works. Despite his emphasis on this theme, Herrera asserts to the end that the true desire for virtue will always triumph. Thomas More's life «descubrio claramente que ninguna demasia i ninguna insolencia de la malicia puede derribar la virtud». [20] Time is always ripe for virtue.

If the national prejudice of Herrera's earlier historical works has been eclipsed, his concept of the Christian ruler has not. The first Henry VIII is a defender of the faith with his pen just as Charles V and Philip II were with their armies. Following Henry's tragic metamorphosis, the «fuerça i tirania de aquel endurecido i ostinado Rei» [21] place him on a level with other enemies of the Christian faith, like the «ostinada dureza de corazon» of Don Juan's Turkish enemies. [22] The highest aim of virtue is the defense of the cause of Christ. In the *Relacion*, Herrera asks:

> ¿Y cual podia ser mas glorioso título y honra mas estimada, que poniendo aparte las pasiones proprias, seguir la causa de Cristo, y por su defensa oponer las armas a los que lo perseguian? [23]

In its evident cooling toward «la grandeza del sujeto militar» [24] the *Tomas Moro* requires the same service of virtue for religion:

> Y si es gloriosa muerte, la que se recibe en servicio de los reyes, i en defensa de la patria, cuanto serà mas gloriosa i mas biena-

---

[17] *Ibid.*, p. 38.
[18] Herrera, *Relacion*, p. 311.
[19] Herrera, *Tomas Moro*, p. 35.
[20] *Ibid.*, p. 52.
[21] *Ibid.*, p. 38.
[22] Herrera, *Relacion*, p. 359.
[23] *Ibid.*, p. 291.
[24] *Ibid.*, p. 247.

venturada la que padece el onbre, por no assentir cosa agena i contraria de la religion? [25]

The same similarities can be shown for Herrera's concept of fame and immortality. In all of his historical works, the author, declares that virtue will win for man an afterlife of «glory», in which term are blended the connotations of enduring fame among men and the «Gloria» of eternal union with God. This immortality, in both of its senses, is the fundamental instrument for meting out punishment and reward to history's heroes and villains. Herrera's poetry, as María Rosa Lida de Malkiel has suggested in comparing it with that of Juan de Mena, [26] affirms the existence of another kind of immortality and fame which the poet-lover will achieve by enshrining his beloved and his love in verse. Although nourished by different classical sources, these several concepts of fame tend to fuse in Herrera's diction. There appears to be no discontinuity in any case between worldly glory and a divine immortality.

For Herrera, then, history is essentially the history of virtue and of virtue's battle against passion and vice in all forms. The references to Spanish deeds in the *Anotaciones* indicate that Herrera views history as a continuous line of heroism, his heroes succeeding each other in ardent emulation from past to present, and in the present as it becomes future. Like many works in the tradition of the House of Fame, Herrera's interest in history is often atemporal. [27] The Numantians, Ruy Díaz, Fernán González, Hernán Cortés, Don García, Don Juan de Austria and Thomas More continue to swell the ranks of immortal fame. They are all clearly cut from the same cloth in spirit, even if the circumstances in which they display their courage have changed. The *Tomas Moro*, in its universal character, comes almost as the logical final extension of this ethical view of history. The English Chancellor's virtue is bound by nothing material; it is wholly unarmed. The conflict he faces is not national. Of course, neither was Lepanto, in the sense that its combatants considered themselves to be defending the religion of Christ. But Sir

[25] Herrera, *Tomas Moro*, p. 51.
[26] María Rosa Lida, *Juan de Mena, poeta del prerrenacimiento español* (Mexico, 1950), pp. 366-367.
[27] *Ibid.*, p. 280 ff.

Thomas More himself actually seeks to step off the historical stage, to engage in a cosmic battle with weakness and vice.

If the historical prose of Herrera enjoys such unity, as I am convinced it does, why have critics consistently claimed that the *Tomas Moro* has little in common with works like the *Relacion,* and that the «objective» quality of style in the early work gives way in the second? [28] Undoubtedly there are differences in style and perspective between the two works, which should not be minimized unduly. Yet there is the evident fact of a persistent character of diction and conception that is found throughout the course of Herrera's known historical works. I should like to suggest that the stylistic difference is one of proportion rather than substance. Herrera has certainly not abandoned factual objectivity in the *Tomas Moro.* He simply finds that it is not necessary in this case to detail the events in question for the reader. He either feels that the facts have been adequately set out by Rivadeneira and he need not repeat them, or he —in the positive interest of objectivity— prefers not to raise the dust of scandal again. What he evidently thought was missing in the saga of Thomas More was the proper «loor y vituperio», the full drawing out of the lessons of history as he read them according to his theory of heroic virtue. In the *Relacion* he sought to remedy the absence of a balanced report of details concerning Lepanto. The «loor y vituperio» is not neglected, but it must take second place to the establishment of fact. In the *Tomas Moro,* on the other hand, meditation seems to overshadow narrative, but in reality the two elements of historical reporting are probably in a more nearly equal balance there in Herrera's conception.

A paradigm resembling the one commonly used to explain the affinities of picaresque novel and sermon would serve us well in distinguishing between the two modes of Herrera's historical prose as exemplified by the *Relacion* and *Tomas Moro.* [29] We have already contrasted Herrera's work with the treatises on the Christian prince of Mariana and Rivadeneira. We put these two types of works at the opposite ends of an imaginary scale. On the one hand, we have history totally subordinated and broken

---

[28] López Estrada, «Edición y estudio», pp. 11-12.
[29] M. Herrero García, «Nueva interpretación de la novela picaresca», *RFE,* XXIV (1937), 343-362.

down to provide «examples» for a work of doctrine. On this side belong Mariana and Rivadeneira. At the other end of the spectrum, that occupied by works like the *Relacion,* we have history prevailing absolutely over lesson. History retains its chronological integrity and on occasion inspires its narrator to comment on its significance, to elicit the lesson from the flow of information. The *Tomas Moro,* in my view, can be situated near the halfway mark of this road. History and lesson here go hand in hand, the one never losing its integrity nor in turn distorting the other. Herrera's meditations in the *Tomas Moro* do not destroy the chronological unity of the events of More's life. They merely add to these events that judgment —the «loor y vituperio»— which Cicero demanded and which Herrera as historian could not fail to supply.

A SELECTED BIBLIOGRAPHY

Acuña, Hernando de. *Varias poesías,* ed. Elena Catena de Vindel. Madrid, 1954.
Adams, Robert P. *The Better Part of Valor: More, Erasmus, Colet and Vives on Humanism, War and Peace 1496-1535.* University of Washington, 1962.
— «Erasmus' Ideas of his Role as a Social Critic», *Renaissance News,* XI, i (1958), 11-16.
Alonso Cortés, Narciso. «Acervo biográfico. Fernando de Herrera», *B.R.A.E.,* XXX (1950), 13-22, 197-209.
Antonio, Nicolás. *Censura de las historias fabulosas,* ed. G. Mayans y Siscar. Valencia, 1742.
Aristotle. *Introduction to Aristotle,* ed. Richard McKeon. New York, 1947.
— *Rhetorica,* ed. John Henry Freese. London, 1926.
Augustinus Aurelius, Saint. *De civitate Dei,* ed. J. E. C. Welldon, Vol. II. London, 1924.
Austria, Don Juan de. «Cartas de Don Juan de Austria, hijo de Carlos V, y otros a varias personas escritas desde 1570 hasta 1576», *C.D.I.,* XXVIII.
Avalle-Arce, Juan Bautista. *La novela pastoril española.* Madrid, 1959.
Baron, Hans. *The Crisis of the Early Italian Renaissance.* Princeton, 1966.
Baschet, Armand. *La Diplomatie Vénitienne.* Paris, 1862.
Bassano, Luigi. *Costumi et i modi particolari della vita de' Turchi.* Monaco di Baviera, 1963. (Facsimile of Rome 1545 edition.)
Bataillon, Marcel. *Erasmo y España.* Mexico, 1966.
— «Sur l'humanisme du Docteur Laguna», *Romance Philology,* XVII (1963-1964), 207-234.
Beach, Robert Mills. *Was Fernando de Herrera a Greek Scholar?* Philadelphia, 1908.
Beladiez, Emilio. *España y el Sacro Imperio Romano Germánico,* prol. Marqués de Lozoya. Madrid, 1968.
Bell, Aubrey F. G. *Francisco Sánchez, el Brocense.* London, 1925.
Bembo, Pietro. *Elegantissima Bembi epistola, De imitatione.* Wittemberg, 1540.
Blecua, José Manuel. «Las obras de Garcilaso con anotaciones de Fernan-

do de Herrera», *Estudios hispánicos: homenaje a Archer M. Huntington* (Wellesley, 1952), pp. 55-58.

Blunt, Wilfred, ed. *Pietro's Pilgrimage.* London, 1953.

Bodin, Jean. *Method for the easy comprehension of history,* trans. Beatrice Reynolds. New York, 1945.

— *Les six livres de la République.* Paris, 1577.

Boscán, Juan, trans. *Los quatro libros del Cortesano.* Barcelona, 1942.

Brown, Horatio F. *Venetian Studies.* London, 1887.

Bullock, W. L. «The precept of Plagiarism in the Cinquecento». *Modern Philology,* XXV (1928).

Bury, J. B. *The Idea of Progress.* New York, 1955.

Busbecq, Ogier Ghislain de. *Travels into Turkey.* London, 1744.

Cabrera de Córdoba, Luis. *Filipe Segundo, Rey de España.* Madrid, 1876.

Calderón de la Barca, Pedro. *La vida es sueño,* in *Obras completas.* Madrid, 1966-1967.

Castiglione, Baldassare. *Il libro del Cortegiano,* ed. Vittorio Cian. Florence, 1947.

Castor, Grahame. *Pléiade Poetics.* Cambridge, 1964.

Castro, Adolfo de. «La epístola moral a Fabio no es de Rioja». Cádiz, 1875.

Castro, Américo. *Aspectos del vivir hispánico.* Santiago, Chile, 1949.

— *De la edad conflictiva.* Madrid, 1963.

— *Hacia Cervantes.* Madrid, 1960.

— *La realidad histórica de España.* 2nd ed. Mexico, 1962.

Cervantes Saavedra, Miguel de. *Don Quijote de la Mancha,* ed. Martín de Riquer. Barcelona, 1958.

— *Novelas ejemplares,* ed. F. Rodríguez Marín. 2 vols. Madrid, 1914-1917.

— *Comedia del çerco de Numançia,* in *Comedias y entremeses,* ed. Schevill and Bonilla, Vol. 5 (Madrid, 1920).

— «Poesías sueltas», *Obras completas,* ed. Cayetano Rosell, Vol. VIII. Madrid, 1864.

— *Primera parte de la Galatea,* ed. J. B. Avalle-Arce. 2 vols. Madrid, 1961.

Ceveda, José. «Historia crítica de los falsos cronicones», *Boletín de la Real Academia de la Historia,* I, 33-48.

Chuboda, Bohdan. *Spain and the Empire 1519-1643.* Chicago, 1952.

Cicero, Marcus Tullius. *Brutus. Orator,* Latin ed. and trans. H. M. Hubbell. Cambridge, Massachusetts, 1930.

— *De Oratore.* New York, 1847.

Cirot, Georges. *Les Histoires générales d'Espagne entre Alphonse X et Philippe II.* Paris, 1904.

— *Mariana historien.* Bordeaux, 1905.

— «La Guerra de Granada et L'Austriada», *Bulletin Hispanique,* XXII (1920), 149-159.

Clements, Robert John. *Critical Theory and Practice of the Pléiade.* Cambridge, Massachusetts, 1942.

Collard, Andrée. *Nueva poesía.* Madrid, 1967.

Collingwood, R. G. *The Idea of History.* New York, 1956.

A SELECTED BIBLIOGRAPHY

Corral Castanedo, Alfonso. *España y Venecia, 1604-1607.* Valladolid, 1955.
Correspondencia privada de Felipe II con su secretario Mateo Vázquez, 1567-1591, ed. Carlos Riba García, Vol. I. Madrid, 1959.
Coster, Adolphe. *Fernando de Herrera.* Paris, 1908.
— «Poésies inédites», *Revue Hispanique,* XII (1918), 557-563.
Croce, Benedetto. *La Spagna nella vita italiana durante la Rinascenza.* 4th ed. Bari, 1949.
Daru, P. *Histoire de la République de Venise,* Vol. IV. Paris, 1821.
Díaz Rengifo, Juan. *Arte poética española.* Barcelona, 1727.
Donà, Leonardo. *Corrispondenza da Madrid di Leonardo Donà, 1570-1573,* ed. Mario Brunetti and Eligio Vitale, intro. Fernand Brandel. Venice-Rome, 1963.
Dowling, John C. *El pensamiento político-filosófico de Saavedra Fajardo.* Murcia, 1957.
Du Bellay, Joachim. *Oeuvres françoises,* ed. Ch. Marty-Lavreaux. 2 vols. Paris, 1866-1867.
Eguigaray Bohigas, Francisco. *Los intelectuales españoles de Carlos V.* Madrid, 1965.
Erasmus, Desiderius. *Dulce Bellum inexpertis,* ed. Yvonne Rémy and René Dunel-Marquebrencq. Collection Latonus, Vol. 8. Brussels, 1953.
— *The Education of a Christian Prince,* ed. Lester K. Born. New York, 1936.
— *Enchiridion militis Christiani.* Argentorati, 1523.
— *El Enquiridión o Manual del caballero cristiano,* ed. D. Alonso, prol. M. Bataillon. Madrid, 1932.
— *Institvtio principis Christiani saluberrimis referta praeceptis.* Basel, 1518.
— *Querela pacis vndique gentium ejectae, profligataeque.* Lugduni Batavorum, 1641.
Fernández Álvarez, Manuel. *Política mundial de Carlos V y Felipe II.* Madrid, 1966.
Fernández y Fernández de Retama, P. Luis. *España en tiempo de Felipe II,* Vol. II, in *Historia de España,* ed. Ramón Menéndez Pidal, Vol. XIX. Madrid, 1958.
Fitzgerald, Augustine. *Peace and War in Antiquity.* London, 1931.
Fougasses, Thomas de. *The Generall Historie of the Magnificent State of Venice... Englished by W. Shvte, Gent.* London, 1612.
Foulché Delbosc. «L'authenticité de la Guerra de Granada», *Revue Hispanique,* XXXV (1915), 476-538.
Frankl, Victor. *El Antijovio de Gonzalo Jiménez de Quesada y las concepciones de realidad y verdad en la época de la Contrarreforma y del manierismo.* Madrid, 1963.
Fucilla, J. G. «Notes on anti-Petrarchism in Spain», *Romanic Review,* XX (1929), 345-351.
Gachard, Louis Prosper. *Relations des ambassadeurs vénitiens sur Charles-Quint et Philippe II.* Brussels, 1856.
Gambier, Henri. *Histoire de la République de Venise.* Paris, 1955.

Gallego Morell, Antonio. «Una lanza por Pacheco, editor de Fernando de Herrera», *R.F.E.* XXXV (1951), 133-138.
— ed. *Garcilaso de la Vega y sus comentaristas.* Granada, 1966.
García-Pelayo, Manuel. *Mitos y símbolos políticos.* Madrid, 1964.
Garcilaso de la Vega. *Obras,* ed. T. Navarro Tomás. Madrid, 1963.
— *Obras completas,* ed. Elias Rivers. Madrid, 1968.
Garcilaso de la Vega y sus comentaristas, ed. A. Gallego Morell. Granada, 1966.
Garnier, François, ed. *Journal de la bataille de Lépante.* Paris, 1956.
Gilbert, Felix. *Machiavelli and Guicciardini: Politics and History in Sixteenth-Century Florence.* Princeton, 1965.
Gilmore, Myron P. *Humanists and Jurists.* Cambridge, Massachusetts, 1963.
— *The World of Humanism 1453-1517.* New York, 1952.
Góngora y Argote, Luis de. *Obras completas,* ed. Millé y Giménez. Madrid, 1961.
Green, Otis H. *Spain and the Western Tradition.* 4 vols. Madison, 1963-1966.
Guillén, Jorge. «The Poetical Life of Herrera», *The Boston Public Library Quarterly,* III, ii (March, 1951), 91-108.
Hamilton, Bernice. *Political Thought in Sixteenth-Century Spain. A Study of the political ideas of Vitoria, De Soto, Suárez and Molina.* Oxford, 1963.
Hauser, Henri. *La prépondérance espagnole 1559-1660.* Paris, 1948.
Herrera, Fernando de. *Algunas obras,* ed. A. Coster. Paris, 1908.
— *Controversia sobre sus Anotaciones a las obras de Garcilaso de la Vega.* Seville, 1870.
— *Obras de Garci Lasso de la Vega con Anotaciones de Fernando de Herrera.* Seville, 1580. And ed. Gallego Morell, *Garcilaso de la Vega y sus comentaristas.* Granada, 1966.
— *Poesías,* ed. Vicente García de Diego. Madrid, 1914.
— *Relacion de la guerra de Cipre y suceso de la batalla naval de Lepanto,* C.D.I., XXI (Madrid, 1852).
— *Rimas,* ed. Ramón Fernández. Madrid, 1786.
— *Rimas inéditas,* ed. José Manuel Blecua. Madrid, 1948.
— *Tomas Moro,* in Francisco López Estrada, «Edición y estudio...,» *Archivo Hispalense,* XII (1950), 9-56.
— *Versos,* ed. A. Coster. Strasbourg, 1916.
— *Versos emendados i divididos por el en tres libros,* ed. Pacheco. Seville, 1619.
Herrero García, M. *Ideas de los españoles del siglo XVII.* 2nd ed. Madrid, 1966.
— «Nueva interpretación de la novela picaresca», *R.F.E.* XXIV (1937), 343-362.
Herrick, Marvin T. *The Fusion of Horatian and Aristotelian Literary Criticism 1531-1555.* Urbana, 1946.
Hexter, J. H. *More's «Utopia»: The Biography of an Idea.* New York, 1965.

A SELECTED BIBLIOGRAPHY

Horatius Flaccus, Quintus. *Satires and Epistles,* ed. Edward P. Morris. Norman, 1968.
Huarte de San Juan, Juan. *Examen de ingenios para las ciencias,* ed. Rodrigo Sanz. Madrid, 1930.
Hurtado de Mendoza, Diego. *Comentario de la Guerra de Granada,* ed. Gómez Moreno. Madrid, 1948.
Ibarra y Rodríguez, Eduardo. *España bajo los Austrias.* Barcelona, 1955.
Imaz, Eugenio. *Utopías del Renacimiento.* Mexico, 1941.
Jiménez de Quesada, Gonzalo. *El Antijovio,* ed. Rafael Torres Quintero, intro. Manuel Ballesteros Gaibrois. Bogotá, 1952.
Jones, Royston O. «Some Notes on More's *Utopia* in Spain», *M.L.R.,* XLV (1950), 478-482.
— «El *Tomás Moro* de Fernando de Herrera», *B.R.A.E.,* XXX (1950), 423-438.
Kossoff, A. David. *Vocabulario de la obra poética de Herrera.* Madrid, 1966.
Kristeller, Paul Oscar. *Renaissance Thought.* New York, 1961.
— *Renaissance Thought II.* New York, 1965.
Laguna, Andrés. *Viaje de Turquía,* attributed to Cristóbal de Villalón in *Autobiografías y memorias,* ed. M. Serrano y Sanz, *N. B. A. E.,* Vol. II. Madrid, 1905.
Lasso de la Vega y Argüelles, Ángel. *Historia y juicio crítico de la escuela poética sevillana de los siglos XVI y XVII.* Madrid, 1871.
Lebrija, Elio Antonio. *Gramática de la lengua castellana,* ed. Ignacio González Llubera. Oxford, 1926.
Lida de Malkiel, María Rosa. *La idea de la fama en la Edad Media castellana.* Mexico, 1952.
— *Juan de Mena, poeta del prerrenacimiento español.* Mexico, 1950.
Lida, Raimundo. *Letras hispánicas.* Mexico-Buenos Aires, 1958.
— «Quevedo y su España antigua», *Romance Philology,* XVII, ii (November 1963), 253-271.
— «Sobre Quevedo y su voluntad de leyenda», *Filología* (Buenos Aires), VIII, iii (1962), 273-306.
López Estrada, Francisco. «Edición y estudio del *Tomas Moro* de Fernando de Herrera», *Archivo Hispalense,* XII (1950), 9-56.
— «Las fuentes históricas del *Tomas Moro* de Fernando de Herrera», *Revista bibliográfica y documental,* III (1949), 237-243.
— «Noticias de la muerte de Santo Tomás Moro en España», *Homenaje a don Emilio Alarcos,* Valladolid, 1965.
— «La primera versión española de la *Utopía* de Moro», *Collected Studies in honour of Américo Castro's 80th Year,* ed. M. P. Hornik. Oxford, 1965.
— «Quevedo y la *Utopía* de Tomás Moro», *Actas del Segundo Congreso Internacional de Hispanistas.* Nimega, 1967.
— «Santo Tomás Moro en España y en la América hispana», *Moreana,* V (1965), 27-40.
López de Toro, José. *Los poetas de Lepanto.* Madrid, 1950.

Lucian of Samosata. *The Works of Lucian,* trans. H. W. and F. G. Fowler. 4 vols. Oxford, 1905.

Lynch, John. *Spain under the Hapsburgs. Vol. One: Empire and Absolutism, 1516-1598.* New York, 1964.

Machiavelli, Niccolo. *Discorsi sopra la Prima Deca de Tito Livio,* in *Tutte le opere storiche e letterarie,* ed. Guido Mazzoni and Mario Casella. Florence, 1929.

— *Il Principe,* in *Tutte le opere...*

Macrí, Oreste. *Fernando de Herrera.* Madrid, 1959.

Mal Lara, Juan de. *El libro quinto de la «Psyche»,* ed. Mario Gasparini. Salamanca, 1947.

— *La Philosophia Vulgar.* Seville, 1568.

— *La Philosophia Vulgar,* ed. A. Vilanova. 4 vols. Barcelona, 1958.

— *Recebimiento que hizo la ciudad de Sevilla al Rey D. Phelipe II.* Seville, 1878. (Photographic reproduction of Seville 1570 edition.)

Marañón, Gregorio. «Luis Vives: su patria y su universo», *Españoles fuera de España.* Buenos Aires, 1947.

Maravall, José Antonio. *Los factores de la idea del progreso en el renacimiento español.* Madrid, 1963.

— *El humanismo de las armas en Don Quijote.* Madrid, 1948.

Mariana, Juan de. *Obras del Padre...,* B.A.E., Vols. XXX-XXXI. Madrid, 1854.

Márquez, Juan. *El governador christiano.* Anvers, 1664.

Márquez Villanueva, Francisco. *Don Luis Zapata o el sentido de una fuente cervantina.* Badajoz, 1966.

Mattingly, Garrett. *The Defeat of the Spanish Armada.* New York, 1965.

— *Renaissance Diplomacy.* Boston, 1955.

Menéndez y Pelayo, Marcelino. *Historia de las ideas estéticas en España.* 5 vols. Madrid, 1946-1947.

Merriman, Roger Bigelow. *The Rise of the Spanish Empire.* 4 vols. New York, 1934.

Mesnard, Pierre. *Jean Bodin en la historia del pensamiento,* intro. José Antonio Maravall. Madrid, 1962.

Mexía, Pedro. *Historia del Emperador Carlos V,* ed. Juan de Mata Carriazo. Madrid, 1945.

Moncada, Francisco de. *Expedición de los catalanes y aragoneses contra turcos y griegos,* ed. Samuel Gili Gaya. Madrid, 1924.

Montero Díaz, S. «La doctrina de la historia en los tratadistas españoles del Siglo de Oro», *Hispania* (Madrid), I, iv (1941), 3-39.

Montoliú, M. de. «Fernando de Herrera, poeta imperial», *El alma de España y sus reflejos en la literatura del Siglo de Oro.* Barcelona, 1942.

Morales, Ambrosio de. *La corónica general de España.* 2 vols. Alcalá, 1574-1577.

More, Thomas. *Selections from his English Works,* ed. P. S. and H. M. Allen. Oxford, 1924.

— *Utopia,* ed. Edward Surtz, S. J. New Haven, 1964.

— *The Utopia,* ed. J. H. Lupton. Oxford, 1895. (In Latin from the edition of March 1518 and in English from the first edition of Ralph Robynson's translation in 1551.)

Morel-Fatio, A. *Historiographie de Charles-Quint.* Paris, 1913.

Morley, Henry, ed. *Ideal Commonwealths.* London, 1893.

Mosquera de Figueroa, Cristóbal. *Obras.* Vol. I, *Poesías inéditas,* ed. G. Díaz-Plaja. Madrid, 1955.

Osterc, Ludovik. *El pensamiento social y político de Don Quijote.* Mexico, 1963.

Pacheco, Francisco. *Libro de descripción de verdaderos retratos de illustres y memorables varones.* Seville, 1881-1885. (Reproduction of Seville 1599 edition.)

Palma, Bachiller. *Divina retribución sobre la caída de España en tiempo del noble Rey Don Juan el Primero.* Madrid, 1879.

Papell, Antonio. «La poesía épica culta de los siglos XVI y XVII», in *H.G.L.H.,* ed. G. Díaz-Plaja, Vol. II. Barcelona, 1949.

Paruta, Paolo. *Historia vinetiana. Parte Seconda. / Nella quale in libri tre / Si contiene la guerra fatta dalla Lega de' Prencipi Christiani / contra Selino Ottomano, / Per occasione del Regno di Cipro,* Venice, 1605.

Pereña Vicente, Luciano. *Teoría de la guerra en Francisco Suárez.* 2 vols. Madrid, 1954.

Pérez-Rioja, J. A. «Numancia en la poesía», *Celtiberia* (Soria), IV (1954), 69-103.

Picatoste, Felipe. *Los españoles en Italia.* 3 vols. Madrid, 1887.

Plato. *Great Dialogues,* trans. W. H. D. Rouse, ed. Eric H. Warrington and Philip G. Rouse. New York, 1956.

— *The Republic,* ed. Francis MacDonald Cornford. New York, 1957.

Ponce de la Fuente, Constantino. *Suma de doctrina cristiana,* ed. Luis de Usoz. Madrid, 1863.

Porreño, Baltasar. *Historia de D. Juan de Austria,* ed. Antonio Rodríguez Villa. Madrid, 1899.

Pring-Mill, R. D. F. «Escalígero y Herrera: Citas y plagios de los *Poetices Libri Septem* en las *Anotaciones*», *Actas del Segundo Congreso Internacional de Hispanistas* (Nimega, 1967), 489-499.

Quevedo Villegas, Francisco de. *Obras completas. Prosa.* Madrid, 1961.

«Relación de la batalla naval de Lepanto», ed. Martín Fernández de Navarrete, *C.D.I.,* III (Madrid, 1843), 239-270.

Rivadeneira, Pedro de. *Obras escogidas,* ed. Vicente de la Fuente, *B.A.E.,* Vol. LX. Madrid, 1868.

Rodríguez Marín, F. *El divino Herrera y la condesa de Gelves.* Madrid, 1911.

«Romances de Lepanto», *Romancero general,* ed. Agustín Durán, *B.A.E.,* Vol. XVI. Madrid, 1921.

Ronsard, Pierre de. *Oeuvres complètes,* ed. Gustave Cohen. Paris, 1958.

Roper, William. *The Life of Sir Thomas More,* in *Two Early Tudor Lives,* ed. Richard S. Sylvester and Davis P. Harding. New Haven, 1962.

Rosales, Luis, ed. *Poesía heroica del Imperio.* 2 vols. Madrid, 1941-1943.

Rouillard, Clarence D. *The Turk in French History, Thought and Literature 1520-1660.* Paris, 1938.

Roussel, Michel. *L'Antimariana ou réfutation des propositions de Mariana.* Paris, 1610.

Rubio, Julián María. *Los grandes ideales de la España imperial.* Valladolid, 1937.

Rufo, Juan. *La Austriada, Poemas épicos,* ed. Cayetano Rosell, Vol. II; *B.A.E.,* Vol. XXIX. Madrid, 1851.

San Gerónimo, Fray Juan de. *Memorias de...,* C.D.I., VII (Madrid, 1845).

Sánchez Alonso, B. «El concepto de la historiografía española», *Hispania* (Madrid), III (1943), 179-194.

— *Historia de la historiografía española.* 3 vols., Madrid, 1947.

— «La literatura histórica en el siglo XVI», *H.G.L.H.,* ed. G. Díaz-Plaja. Barcelona, 1949.

— «La literatura histórica en el siglo XVII», *H.G.L.H.*

Sánchez Escribano, F. «Algunos aspectos de la elaboración de la *Philosophia Vulgar*», *R.F.E.,* XXII (1935), 274-284.

— «Los *Adagia* de Erasmo en la *Philosophia Vulgar* de Juan de Mal Lara», New York, 1944.

— *Juan de Mal Lara, su vida y sus obras.* New York, 1941.

Sandoval, Prudencio de. *Historia de la vida y hechos del Emperador Carlos V.* Anvers, 1681.

Santa Cruz, Alonso de. *Crónica del Emperador Carlos V,* ed. Ricardo Beltrán y Rózpide and Antonio Blázquez y Delgado-Aguilera. 5 vols. Madrid, 1920.

Scaliger, Julius Caesar. *Poetices libri septem.* Stuttgart, 1964. (Facsimile of 1516 edition.)

Schuster, Edward J. «Pedro de Mexía and Spanish Golden Age Historiography», *Renaissance News,* XIII (1960), i, 3-6.

Serrano, Luciano. *Correspondencia diplomática entre España y la Santa Sede durante el Pontificado de San Pío V,* Vols. III and IV. Madrid, 1914.

— *La Liga de Lepanto.* 2 vols. Madrid, 1918-1919.

Serviá, Miguel. «Relación de los sucesos de la armada de la Santa Liga, y entre ellos el de la Batalla de Lepanto», *C.D.I.,* VII (1845), 359-454.

Shepard, Sanford. *El Pinciano y las teorías literarias del siglo de oro.* Madrid, 1962.

Sherley, Sir Thomas. *Discours of the Turkes,* ed. E. Denison Ross. London, 1936.

Smith, L. G. «Fernando de Herrera and Argote de Molina», *Bulletin of Hispanic Studies,* XXXIII (1956), 63-77.

Spivakovsky, E. «Lo de la Goleta y Túnez. A Work of Diego Hurtado de Mendoza», *Hispania* (Madrid), XXIII (1963), 366-379.

Stapleton, Thomas. *The Life and Illustrious Martyrdom of Sir Thomas More,* trans. Philip E. Hallett, ed. E. E. Reynolds. New York, 1966.

A SELECTED BIBLIOGRAPHY

Stirling-Maxwell, Sir William. *Don John of Austria.* 2 vols. London, 1883.

Suárez, Francisco. «Disputatio XIII de Bello», ed. Luciano Pereña Vicente, *Teoría de la guerra en Francisco Suárez. II. Texto crítico.* Madrid, 1954.

Tasso, Torquato. *Discorsi della poema heroico.* Naples, 1594.

Tate, Robert B. «An Apology for Monarchy», *Romance Philology,* XV (1961), 111-123.

— «A Humanistic Biography of John II of Aragon», *Bulletin of Hispanic Studies,* XXXIX (1962), 1-15.

— «Four Notes on Gonzalo García de Santa María», *Romance Philology,* XXVII (1963), 362-372.

— «Italian Humanism and Spanish Historiography», *Bulletin of the John Rylands Library,* XXXIV (September, 1951).

— «Mythology in Spanish Historiography of the Middle Ages and the Renaissance», *Hispanic Review,* XXII (1954), 1-18.

— «Nebrija the Historian», *Bulletin of Hispanic Studies,* XXXIV (1957), 125-146.

Terry, Arthur. «The continuity of Renaissance criticism: poetic theory between 1535 and 1650», *Bulletin of Hispanic Studies,* XXXI (1954), 27-36.

Thiriet, Freddy. *Histoire de Venise.* Paris, 1952.

Thomas Aquinas, Saint. *Summa Theologica,* Vol. 35. New York, 1964.

Thompson, C. R. *The Translations of Lucian by Erasmus and St. Thomas More.* Ithaca, 1940.

Thucydides. *The Peloponnesian War,* trans. Rex Warner. New York, 1959.

Uscatescu, George. *Utopía y plenitud histórica.* Madrid, 1963.

Valbuena Prat, Ángel. *Historia de la literatura española.* 3 vols. Barcelona, 1963-1964.

Valderrama, Carlos. «Jiménez de Quesada y el humanismo contrarreformista», *Thesaurus,* XX (1965), 213-240.

Valdés, Alfonso de. *Diálogo de las cosas ocurridas en Roma,* ed. José F. Montesinos. Madrid, 1956.

Valdés, Juan de. *Diálogo de doctrina cristiana,* ed. Domingo Ricart. Mexico, 1964.

— *Diálogo de la lengua,* ed. José F. Montesinos. Madrid, 1964.

Vega Carpio, Lope Félix de. «Arte nuevo para hacer comedias en este tiempo», *Obras escogidas,* ed. Federico Sainz de Robles. Madrid, 1964.

— *Crónicas y leyendas dramáticas de España,* in *Obras,* ed. M. Menéndez y Pelayo, Vol. XII. Madrid, 1901.

— *Novelas a Marcia Leonarda,* in *Obras escogidas.*

Vilanova, Antonio. «Fernando de Herrera», in *H.G.L.H.,* ed. G. Díaz-Plaja, Vol. III. Barcelona, 1951.

— «Preceptistas españoles de los siglos XVI y XVII», *H.G.L.H.,* Vol. III.

Virués, Cristóbal. *El Monserrate,* in *Poemas épicos,* Vol. I, ed. Cayetano Rosell, *B.A.E.,* Vol. XVII. Madrid, 1851.

Vitoria, Francisco de. *De Indiis et De Ivre Belli Relectiones,* ed. Ernest Nys. Washington, 1917.

Vives, Juan Luis. «De subuentione pauperum», *Opera, in dvos distincta tomos,* Vol. II. Basel, 1555.
Zanta, Léontine. *La Renaissance du Stoïcisme au XVIe siècle.* Paris, 1914.
Zavala, Silvio. *Sir Thomas More in New Spain: A Utopian Adventure of the Renaissance.* London, 1955.
— *La «Utopía» de Tomás Moro en la Nueva España, y otros estudios.* Mexico, 1937.

COLECCION TAMESIS

SERIE A - MONOGRAFIAS

Edward M. Wilson and Jack Sage: *Poesías líricas en las obras dramáticas de Calderón*, pp. xix + 165.

Philip Silver: *'Et in Arcadia ego': A Study of the Poetry of Luis Cernuda*, pp. xv + 211.

Keith Whinnom: *A Glossary of Spanish Bird-Names*, pp. 157.

Brian Dutton: *La 'Vida de San Millán de la Cogolla' de Gonzalo de Berceo. Estudio y edición crítica*. El tomo I.º de las *Obras completas* de Gonzalo de Berceo, pp. xiv + 248.

A. D. Deyermond: *Epic Poetry and the Clergy: Studies on the 'Mocedades de Rodrigo'*, pp. xix + 312, with two maps.

Abdón M. Salazar: *El escudo de armas de Juan Luis Vives*, pp. viii + 136.

P. Gallagher: *The Life and Works of Garci Sánchez de Badajoz*, pp. x + 296.

Carlos P. Otero: *Letras, I*, pp. xviii + 202.

Emma Susana Speratti-Piñero: *De 'Sonata de otoño' al esperpento (Aspectos del arte de Valle-Inclán)*, pp. viii + 341.

'Libro de buen amor' Studies. Edited by G. B. Gybbon-Monypenny, pp. xiii + 256.

Galdós Studies. Edited by J. E. Varey, pp. xii + 204.

Dorothy Sherman Severin: *Memory in «La Celestina»*, pp. x + 73.

Ralph J. Penny: *El habla pasiega: Ensayo de dialectología montañesa*, pp. 478, con láminas y mapas.

Francisco Carrasquer: *«Imán» y la novela histórica de Sender*, con prólogo de Ramón J. Sender, pp. xiii + 302.

Mary Gaylord Randel: *The Historical Prose of Fernando de Herrera*, pp. xii + 205.

SERIE B - TEXTOS

Lope de Vega: *Triunfo de la fee en los reynos del Japón*. Edited by J. S. Cummins, pp. xlix + 116, with seven illustrations and one map.

Fernán Pérez de Guzmán: *Generaciones y semblanzas*. Edición crítica con prólogo, apéndices y notas de R. B. Tate, pp. xxvii + 112.

El sufrimiento premiado. Comedia famosa, atribuida en esta edición, por primera vez, a Lope de Vega Carpio. Introducción y notas de V. F. Dixon, pp. xxvii + 177.

José de Cadalso: *Cartas marruecas*. Prólogo, edición y notas de Lucien Dupuis y Nigel Glendinning, pp. lxiii + 211. (Segunda impresión.)

Virgilio Malvezzi: *Historia de los primeros años del reinado de Felipe IV*. Edición y estudio preliminar por D. L. Shaw, pp. liv + 206, with 3 illustrations and 3 maps.

La comedia Thebaida. Edited by G. D. Trotter and Keith Whinnom, pp. lxi + 270.

Juan Vélez de Guevara: *Los celos hacen estrellas*. Editada por J. E. Varey y N. D. Shergold, con una edición de la música por Jack Sage, pp. cxvii + 277, with 24 illustrations (5 coloured and 19 black-and-white).

Francisco Bances Candamo: *Theatro de los theatros de los passados y presentes siglos*. Prólogo, edición y notas de Duncan W. Moir, pp. cii + 191.

Pedro Calderón de la Barca: *La hija del aire*. Edición crítica, con introducción y notas de Gwynne Edwards, pp. lxxxviii + 298.

SERIE D - REPRODUCCIONES EN FACSIMIL

Cayetano Alberto de la Barrera y Leirado: *Catálogo bibliográfico y biográfico del teatro antiguo español, desde sus orígenes hasta mediados del siglo XVIII (Madrid, 1860)*, pp. xi + 727.